THE UNIVERSITY OF EXETER
History of Exeter Research Group
MONOGRAPH NO. X

NONCONFORMITY IN EXETER

1650–1875

THE REVEREND MICAIJAH TOWGOOD, 1700–92. MINISTER AT
JAMES' AND GEORGE'S MEETINGS, EXETER, 1750–82

From a painting by James Opie, R.A.
Engraved and published by E. A. Ezekiel, Fore Street,
Exeter, 1794

NONCONFORMITY
IN EXETER

1650–1875

by

ALLAN BROCKETT

Published on behalf of
THE UNIVERSITY OF EXETER
by

MANCHESTER UNIVERSITY PRESS

LWI8
E964
B681

Made and Printed in Great Britain by Butler & Tanner Ltd., Frome and London

PREFACE

Brought up in the Nonconformist tradition, and always keenly interested in history, it is not surprising that I should have undertaken this book. This account of the Exeter Nonconformists should be regarded as a memorial to my father, who was for more than 40 years a Congregationalist Minister.

My thanks are due to a multitude of people who have helped me to acquire the material used in the following pages. My greatest obligation is to the Trustees of George's Chapel in South St., and to the Trustees of the Exeter Assembly for allowing me to have their records on loan for a period of almost four years. Both deserve commendation for having preserved so well sets of records which have enabled me to reconstruct in detail the story of the Exeter Presbyterians. I am also most grateful to the officers of the following churches for allowing me to use for shorter periods their surviving church records: Southernhay and Heavitree Congregational churches; South St., and St. Thomas (Cowick St.) Baptist churches (the latter being the successor of the old Bartholomew St. church); and the Free Church of England, Grosvenor Place. When dealing with the Methodists I received help from Mr. Brian Le Mesurier of the Mint, and for the Society of Friends I am indebted to the researches of the late Mr. W. J. M. Thomasson.

Many of my librarian and archivist colleagues have smoothed my pathway. Amongst them is Mr. G. J. Paley of Exeter City Library who, if he cannot always supply what he is asked for, invariably produces something of equal interest; Mrs. Margery Rowe who gave invaluable assistance in translating the Sessions Records relating to Nonconformity; Miss Joan Sinar and Mr. Michael Cook, of the County Record Office, and Mrs. Audrey Erskine, Cathedral Library archivist, who have continually made helpful suggestions and put me in touch with material I might otherwise have overlooked; Rev. Roger Thomas, of Dr. Williams's Library, has also been a source of continual encouragement.

Personal thanks are due in large measure also to Mr. Stanley Griffin of Plymouth, who has for many years made a habit of collecting material on Devon Nonconformity; and to Mr. W. D. Handcock,

v

who has read my script and criticized it helpfully as I delivered each section to him.

Finally I wish to thank the Publications Committee of the University of Exeter, whose generous support has made this publication possible.

A. B.

CONTENTS

FRONTISPIECE

The Reverend Micaijah Towgood, 1700–92. *Reproduced by kind permission of the Trustees of George's Meeting, Exeter*

SKETCH MAP

Exeter, 1790–1800: To show distribution of Nonconformist Churches and other places mentioned in text. The streets are according to Charles Tozer's map of 1792   *end of book*

CHAPTER I

BEFORE THE RESTORATION

AFTER clinging to the old Catholic faith rather longer than many other counties, its conservatism in religion lending considerable strength to the Western Rebellion of 1549, Devon had become strongly Protestant by the end of the sixteenth century.[1] This was particularly the case in the seaports of Plymouth, Dartmouth, Bideford and Barnstaple, and in the manufacturing towns of Exeter, Tiverton and East Devon. Names of important county families are noticeable in the ranks of ministers ejected from their livings in 1660–2—Ford, Stucley, Polwhele, Yeo, Woolcombe, Prideaux—and it is unlikely that this Puritan colour was wholly of such late origin. A trace of Puritan clergy is evident in 1606 when a group united to publish a defence of themselves entitled 'A Removal of Certain Imputations, etc., etc.' [2]

Little information is available on religious affairs within the City of Exeter from the Reformation until 1640. The monastic properties within the walls were confiscated by the Crown between 1536 and 1539 and by the end of Edward VI's reign portions of these had reached the hands of leading citizens of Exeter. More was later acquired either by the Chamber or by individuals and this gave the Corporation material reasons for standing by their Protestant faith.[3]

At the same time the power of the Bishop had been seriously reduced, both in status and revenue. Under Bishop Veysey the income of the See decreased by two-thirds, from £1500 to £500, and in consequence instead of being one of the richest Sees Exeter became one of the poorest. The Cathedral Chapter was also reduced numerically by the abolition of the Chantry Priests and the reduction of the number of Canons Residentiary to nine.[4]

The short episcopate of Miles Coverdale, Protestant translator of the Bible, from 1550 to 1553, cannot have had a great effect on the situation. When the news of Mary Tudor's accession reached Exeter, Coverdale was preaching in the Cathedral, and all but a 'few godly men' left

[1] Worth, R. N., 'Puritanism in Devon & the Exeter Assembly', (*Trans., Devon. Assoc.,* 1877, Vol. 9, pp. 250–70).
[2] Neal, D., *History of the Puritans*, 1794 edn., Vol. 2, p. 66.
[3] Youings, J., 'The City of Exeter and the property of the Dissolved Monasteries' (*Trans., Devon Assoc.*, 1952, Vol. 84, pp. 122–41).
[4] Boggis, R. J. E., *History of the Diocese of Exeter*, 1922, p. 347.

the service.[1] They would have become Protestants again quickly enough when Mary died five years later. William Herne, rector of St. Petrock's from 1528 to 1566, found no difficulty in conforming to all the changes of religious fashion.

The 1561 Visitation of the Clergy of the Diocese shows that Exeter churches were not served by a learned clergy, and in some cases they had no incumbents at all. Six parishes were vacant, and none of the eleven priests in the others had a degree. Neither were any of them in the habit of preaching.[2] The situation must have become worse by 1601, when the City Chamber went so far as to put forward a Draft Act of Parliament which would have joined six of the smaller parishes into one, with a new church to hold 2000 people. It was not passed.[3]

Such a situation would have been extremely distressing to the sincere Puritan. The presence of many such may be inferred from the agitation beginning about 1587 for the establishment of a lectureship to supplement the meagre preaching of the regular clergy. The man appointed in 1599, Edmund Snape, D.D., was paid £50 a year and expected to preach every Sunday at the Cathedral, and in the larger parish churches at regular intervals.[4] About 1613 it became possible to appoint a second lecturer, and in 1616 a third, when a legacy was received from Canon Lawrence Bodley of the Cathedral. These appointments were made without the Bishop's approval, and they serve to indicate the presence in Exeter of an influential group of Puritan merchants by the reign of James I.

Further evidence of Puritanism in Exeter came in 1615 when the Chamber passed orders for Sabbath Observance. Prohibitions included the sale of food, and all manual labour. Ominously enough for the future, informers were promised half of any fine imposed, a precedent which was followed in the 1670 Conventicle Act from which so many Puritans of a later generation were to suffer.[5]

Individual instances can be given of Puritanism in Exeter and its neighbourhood in the first half of the seventeenth century. John Reynolds, born at Pinhoe about 1549, was the leading Puritan spokesman at the Hampton Court Conference of 1604, and was later one of the translators of the Authorized Version of the Bible. Ignatius Jour-

---

[1] MacCaffrey, W. T., *Exeter, 1540–1640*, Harvard U.P., 1958, p. 189.
[2] Visitation Return Photostat in Exeter City Library.
[3] MacCaffrey, op. cit., p. 196.
[4] Historical Manuscripts Commission: Report on the Records of the City of Exeter, 1916, p. 40.
[5] Act Books of the City Chamber, VIII, pp. 161 and 171.

dain, that uncompromising figure in early Stuart Exeter, dated his conversion to 1576, and by the turn of the century was taking a leading part in municipal affairs, being Bailiff in 1599, Sheriff in 1611, Mayor in 1617. His courageous stand in 1624 when plague was abroad in the City did nothing to prejudice the Puritan cause. The Mayor, Thomas Walker, left the town, but Jourdain almost unaided set about organizing relief. That he had the affections of the voters of the City was evident next year when he was elected Member of Parliament, and again in 1628. In the House of Commons he was mainly concerned with religious affairs, supporting amongst other measures the imposition of the death penalty for the crime of adultery. Jourdain in his old age conducted an energetic personal campaign against vice in his City, directing his main effort against excessive drinking. He achieved a temporary success. His final political demonstration took place in 1638 when the King ordered his proclamation denouncing the religious revolt in Scotland to be read in all parish churches. Ignatius Jourdain, in company with the Mayor and one of the other Councillors, protested by remaining seated in church with his hat still on. The three were summoned to appear before Star Chamber in London. The other two went to London and submitted, but Jourdain refused. On account of his advanced age the affair was not pursued further. He died on 18th June, 1640, and was buried in St. Mary Arches Church.[1]

The Rector of Mary Arches was another outstanding Puritan of the pre-Commonwealth period. Ferdinando Nicholl (b. 1598) obtained the living of St. Mary Arches in 1631. He was a strict Puritan and became closely associated with Jourdain for the remainder of the latter's life. Later he became the only Exeter incumbent to remain in undisturbed possession of his living through the Civil Wars, the Commonwealth, and the Restoration, although he was ejected after St. Bartholomew's Day, 1662. He died on 14th December of that same year.[2]

Simon Snow was elected as one of the two Members of Parliament at the beginning of 1640: as his brother was ejected from his living in 1662 and came to reside with him in Exeter it is probable that the rest of the family was tending towards Puritanism.[3] In higher circles, Bishop Joseph Hall (1627–42) was early noted for his Calvinist beliefs and Puritan leanings, and during his episcopacy exercised a moderating influence within the Diocese. Other indications of the general feeling

[1] Nicholl, F., *Life and death of Mr. Ignatius Jourdain*, 1654.
[2] Rose-Troup, F. 'An Exeter worthy' (*Trans. Devon. Assoc.*, 1897, Vol. 29.)
[3] Calamy, E., *Account of the Ministers ejected . . .*, rev. by A. G. Matthews, 1934.

in Exeter were the difficulty in collecting Ship Money there, and the refusal of the City Chamber in 1640 to allow the Earl of Bath to garrison the Castle for the King. In January, 1642, before the Civil War had actually begun, the Chamber petitioned Parliament in the sense that true Protestantism should be preserved, and votes taken away from Bishops and Popish Lords.[1]

None of the parish incumbents in the City retained their livings right through the Civil Wars and Commonwealth, and after St. Bartholomew's Day, 1662. Apart from Ferdinando Nicholl already mentioned, John Bartlett was Vicar of St. Thomas', just outside the City, from about 1628 until 1657, when he was given the church of St. Mary Major from which he was ejected in 1662. Mark Down was Curate of St. Petrock's from 1637, but did not become its Rector until 1657, and was deprived in 1662. His brother Thomas Down did not become Rector of St. Paul's until 1648, and of the combined livings of St. Edmund's and St. Mary Steps until 1657: he was also ejected in 1662. Henry Painter was Rector of St. Petrock's from 1635 to 1643, was then invited to be one of the Exeter representatives on the Westminster Assembly (which advised the House of Commons on religious matters), and remained out of the City during its occupation by the Royalists. He returned to Exeter in 1646, being one of the Bodley lecturers at St. Mary Arches in that year. Exactly when he left Exeter again is not known.[2] All these men were definitely Presbyterians by conviction, and as they were freely at work in Exeter from the 1630s onward, the extent of their influence by the year 1662 must have been considerable.

At no time before 1662, however, could the term Nonconformist be attached to the Presbyterians. They never wished to go outside the National Church, and resented being forced out of it after the Restoration. Neither can the term be applied to Congregationalists and Baptists under the Commonwealth, when both were tolerated and even encouraged in certain districts. The only Nonconformists under Cromwell were Anglicans, Papists, and Quakers, a strange combination indeed.

Here it is necessary to pause to define the terms relating to denominational nomenclature used in the remainder of this study.

UNIFORMITY was the aim of the Anglican Archbishops and of the Crown. They wished to set up a broad-based national church to which

---

[1] Cotton, W. and Woollcombe, H., *Gleanings from the Municipal . . . records . . . of . . . Exeter*, 1877, p. 83.
[2] Cresswell, B., *Exeter Churches*, 1908.

all must belong. The Presbyterians during the Interregnum had the same purpose: their power, however, was limited by the presence of Independents and Baptists in Cromwell's Army.

NONCONFORMITY is therefore the opposite of Uniformity, a refusal on the part of some members of the nation to accept the idea of being compelled to attend services and accept religious rites with which they were not in agreement. In an age when all believed in the after-life, and that those not so enlightened as themselves were irretrievably damned, attempts to compel uniformity aroused hard and bitter feelings. This is a term which should embrace Roman Catholics as well as Protestant Nonconformists, but it has not normally been so used. It is more correct to use the name Dissenters for those Protestants who refuse to conform to the usages of the Church of England.

The PURITANS were that portion of the nation which desired to carry the English Reformation further, and establish a national church of an extreme Protestant type. A few of them seceded from the Church of England (most of this group emigrated, notably to New England) but the vast majority remained loyal members of that church, hoping that eventually the changes they desired in ritual and government would take place.

Most of these were PRESBYTERIANS. They wished to return to what they conceived to be the primitive organization of the Church, and their essential feature was their theory of the Ministry, which may be divided into three parts:

1. The equality of preaching Pastors and Presbyters. Bishops and Presbyters are of the same order, and should have no higher order over them.
2. Church government and administration should be in the hands of a council of Pastors and Elders of the Churches.
3. Unity would come through the association of individual churches by means of Synods or Councils of Elders. Each parish should be governed by a Church Session, each group of parishes combined into a Classis, and above this would come County Assemblies, the whole being crowned by a National Assembly. In England the laity were in the minority in such synods and assemblies as were eventually set up.

A smaller and more extreme group of Puritans were the INDE-PENDENTS. Like the Presbyterians they were Calvinist in doctrine, but they emphasized the idea of the 'Gathered Church'; that each group of

Christians could constitute an independent church, spiritually self-sufficient and capable of managing its own affairs without interference from other quarters. Decisions went by the majority vote of members, although in some cases after election the officers then held complete control for the period of their office. In the early period CONGREGA-TIONALISM may be used as a synonymous term with INDEPENDENCY, although there arose a distinction later. The chief difference between Independents and Presbyterians was in the respective positions of their Ministers. Presbyterian ministers were ordained to the ministry at large, while the Independents considered that the ministerial office derived essentially from a call by a particular church, and no young candidate would be ordained by them until he had received such a call to a pastorate.

The BAPTISTS were very similar to the Independents in organization, but differed on two important points.

1. They considered that the ancient method of showing that a man is converted to the Christian faith is by Baptism, by total immersion. Infant Baptism is of no avail.
2. They believed that the essential quality for any leader or pastor was that he should have received the Holy Spirit. Hence at times arose some prejudice against and neglect of learning by their ministers.

Baptists believed in closer association of individual churches than did the Independents, and they soon formed local and national associations. Yet divisions also arose early amongst them. The GENERAL BAPTISTS, whilst accepting the general beliefs mentioned above, rejected strict Calvinism in favour of Arminianism. That is, they taught Salvation for Everyone, and not just for the Elect, those set apart by God. The PARTICULAR BAPTISTS, on the other hand, held fast to the Calvinist doctrine of Particular Redemption. In addition there were the SABBATARIAN BAPTISTS, who were Particular Baptists who held the Seventh Day of the week as their holy day instead of Sunday.

The QUAKERS, or members of the SOCIETY OF FRIENDS, pursued the Reformation to its logical end, by ignoring all forms and ceremonies whatever. Their beliefs were very simple. They believed in the Inner Light, the voice of God within Everyman, and the possibility of direct communion with God in this way. This involved living in a spirit of love one with another, and the exercising of a loving care and watchfulness over all other members of their communion. They believed that all existing churches had become corrupt in doctrine, discipline and life. They were given the name of Quakers because in their meetings they sat in silence until the Inner Light impelled one of them to speak, and this often involved an ecstatic outburst, accompanied by physical trembling and shaking.

UNITARIANISM did not make any considerable impact in England until after the beginning of the eighteenth century. Its holders rejected the miraculous in religion, and came to regard Christ as entirely human, although inspired. They believed, logically enough, that the One God was the only proper object of worship. The Toleration Act of 1689 expressly omitted Unitarians from its benefits.

From the 4th of September, 1643, until 13th April, 1646, Exeter was in the hands of the Royalists, under the governorship of Sir John Berkeley. At the outbreak of the Civil War the Earl of Bedford had successfully brought the City on to the Parliamentary side, and preparations were made to defend it. The Earl was invited, in company with John Bond (Presbyterian lecturer at St. Sidwell's, 1641–3), Edmund Prideaux (Recorder, 1642–3, and again in 1646), Bishop Ralph Brownrig, Henry Painter of St. Petrock's, and Thomas Ford, to attend the Westminster Assembly when it was summoned. But Bedford went over to the King in August, 1643, and Exeter came into Royalist occupation very quickly afterwards.

Under the Royalist régime there was a cessation of Puritan activity in the City. The situation was quite otherwise when in 1646 Exeter was garrisoned by three Parliamentary regiments under a Colonel Hammond. The articles of capitulation had stated that the Cathedral and the other churches should not be defaced, and that loyal citizens would not be penalized.[1] Thomas Fuller bore witness to the due carrying out of these terms. The amount of defacement and destruction of ecclesiastical property at this time has also been grossly exaggerated. A detailed inquiry into this matter as far as the Cathedral was concerned has revealed without question that many of the charges levelled against the Parliamentarians at the time of the Civil War should really have been made against the reformers of Edward VI's reign.[2] Even the Presbyterians could not approve the execution of the King on 30th January, 1649. Richard Crossing refused the Mayoralty in 1649 'because the kingly government was then by armed violence obstructed'. And in

[1] Freeman, E. A., *Exeter*, 1901, pp. 121–6.
[2] Morris, P., 'The Cathedral during the Reformation and the Interregnum', Part 2 (typed Thesis in Cathedral Library, Exeter).

1650 the commandant of the Castle, Major Blackmore, was warned to keep a sharp watch on two preachers named Ford and Nichols, who had been criticizing the government strongly in their preaching. These would be Thomas Ford, who preached in the Cathedral, and Ferdinando Nicholl of St. Mary Arches. Thomas Ford had been made a Freeman of Exeter on 23rd February, 1647, and probably became Rector of St. Lawrence's about the same time.[1]

Meanwhile, on the national scene, on 13th March, 1645, Parliament after prolonged debate passed the Presbyterian 'Directory for the Publique Worship of God' and issued an ordinance suppressing the Prayer Book. This was followed late in 1646 by an Act abolishing the dignities and titles of Archbishops and Bishops and appropriating their lands. The City Chamber from this time took over the control of the Cathedral and the parish churches. On 29th August, 1648, Parliament issued 'The Form of Church Government to be used in the Church of England and Ireland'. Each county was to set up a Presbyterian organization of its own, and send representatives to a National Assembly. A later ordinance had the title 'For the speedy dividing and settling the several counties of the kingdom into distinct classical Presbyteries and congregational Elderships'.[2] The intention was to have a system of provincial assemblies meeting half-yearly to take the place of the now abolished episcopal government of the Church of England. Under a true Presbyterian system each congregation would send a minister and a layman to represent it in the monthly district assemblies, known as Classes, and these in turn would send delegates to County Assemblies. Only in London and Lancashire did the full scheme become established, but Devon also proved congenial soil for Presbyterian seed. The County was divided into seven Classes, and ministers of the First Division are on record as performing ordinations in 1654, and may have done so before.[3] The County Assembly came into being in October, 1655, when George Hughes (St. Andrew's, Plymouth) with Thomas Ford, called a meeting at Exeter of ministers from all over the County. This cannot, however, be termed a definitely Presbyterian organization. First, its members were Ministers only. Secondly, no election occurred: all the ministers of the County were entitled to attend, subject to certain guarantees of conduct and sub-

---

[1] Freeman, op. cit., pp. 127–8.

[2] Drysdale, A. H., *History of the Presbyterians in England*, 1889.

[3] Shaw, W. A., *History of the English Church during the Civil Wars and under the Commonwealth, 1640–1660*, 1900, Vol. 2, pp. 374, 447.

scription clearly laid down in the rules drawn up at this first meeting, attended by 24 ministers of Devon.

These Articles of Association showed that this was a voluntary association of ministers only, and emphasized the Presbyterian outlook of the first members, seeking uniformity of doctrine, worship and discipline, with the substitution of the Directory in place of the Book of Common Prayer. Another was directed against the more violent sectaries like the Fifth Monarchists, and the Quakers, whose presence was felt for the first time this year in the West of England. Presbyterians were quite as hostile to such people as the Anglicans would have been. Provision was made for differences of opinion amongst the membership: no dictation was envisaged. Ordinations were not to be carried out by order of the County Assembly, but by the Divisions of the County. Similar Associations in neighbouring counties were referred to, for which independent evidence also exists.

Article 3 declared that all members of the Association should sign their names in the minute book.[1] They did this according to the Divisions of the county, and the lists of names show how these were arranged. Division One may be called the Teign Valley group, covering the district around Newton, Moreton, and Christow. Division Two covered Totnes, Paignton, Dartmouth; Division Three, Plymouth, Lifton, Okehampton; Division Four the whole of North Devon; Division Five, the district around Shobrooke, Cheriton, Morchard Bishop, Nymet Tracy; Division Six, the coastal districts of East Devon from Axmouth to Topsham; and Division Seven the remainder of East Devon, including Tiverton, Honiton and Cullompton. Nowhere in these seven divisions can be found the names of the Exeter ministers. They appear in the first list of all, which is also misleadingly headed 'Division the 1st', and immediately follows the Articles of Association laid down at the Assembly's first meeting. This list has been taken[2] to be the names of those actually attending the inaugural Assembly, but this fact is nowhere stated in the minute book, and it seems more likely that the Exeter ministers formed yet another Division, a Presbyterian 'Deanery of Christianity'. If this were really a list of those coming to the first Assembly one would have expected to find the name of George Hughes in it, supposedly one of the conveners of the gathering.

[1] Minute Book of the Commonwealth Exeter Assembly, MSS. owned by present-day Trustees of Exeter Assembly, normally kept at National Provincial Bank, Exeter.

[2] Hoskins, W. G., and Finberg, H. P. R., *Devonshire Studies*, 1952, p. 371, note 2.

B

Thomas Ford signed in his place as an Exeter minister, but Hughes signed in Division Three.

At the second meeting of the Assembly, 22nd May, 1656, the Articles of Association were signed with slight reservations by the two leading Independents of the County, Lewis Stucley and Thomas Mall, who were jointly in charge of the Independent meeting begun in the Cathedral about 1650 by Stucley. The Articles referring to the Westminster Confession and the use of the Directory for Worship, would have effectually kept outside all sincere Anglicans, of the few who had escaped sequestration. The names of those signing the minute book are almost all Presbyterian, although several of them conformed at the Restoration.

The remaining activities of this first Exeter Assembly may be summarized here. At the May, 1656, meeting Stucley and Mall submitted a paper pleading for mutual toleration. The Assembly did not accept all the points made, but decided to associate with their Independent brethren, 'leaving all further differences to a brotherly and amicable debate'. They concluded by drawing up a 'Humble Petition' to Cromwell, requesting his favour upon their work in Devonshire. On 27th May, 1657, the Assembly was concerned with admission to the Lord's Supper, and with the withdrawal of 'church priviledges' from any members guilty of scandal. The next entry related to a meeting of delegates of the Divisions in March, 1658, to select questions of importance for debate at the forthcoming full Assembly. One recommendation was that 'some expedient may be resolved on for the continuance of Classical meetings'. Apparently the Presbyterian system was not working as well as formerly apart from the County Assembly. Two subjects dominated the deliberations of the May meeting. First, the ministers had a paper on the subject of incestuous marriages, which was recommended to the Justices for comment. Secondly, the ministers debated 'Whether the Parochial Congregations in England be true visible Churches of Christ'. In 1659 the members only reconsidered their decisions of 1657 on the subject of the Lord's Supper, and made some minor alterations. Those refusing to take the Sacrament after due warning and pleading from the Minister would be publicly named, and other members of the Congregation recommended to 'have no Company with him'.

This proved to be the last meeting of the Commonwealth Exeter Assembly, for by the time of the 1660 meeting the Restoration was taking place, and ecclesiastical affairs were thrown into the melting pot once again. It was considered wiser not to attract attention by meeting formally in the County capital.

Meanwhile the new order had been stamped more firmly on the country at large. On 20th March, 1654, came a Parliamentary Ordinance setting up mixed commissions of laymen and ministers for each county, to judge whether candidates for the ministry or for a lecturership were fit for their appointments. These were known as the 'Triers'. On 28th August followed a supplementary ordinance providing for the ejection of 'scandalous ignorant and insufficient ministers and schoolmasters', and commissioners were appointed for every county to execute this order. Anyone not a strict Puritan or supporter of the Protectorate could be ejected from his living. Finally, on 2nd September, 1654, came a third ordinance consolidating the existing legislation, empowering trustees of the Fund for the Better Maintenance of the Ministers to augment the incomes of poor livings and to unite several parishes into one for this purpose. Three of the Exeter ministers were nominated assistants to the Devon Triers: the Presbyterians Thomas Ford and John Bartlett, and the Independent Lewis Stucley.

Two years later, in 1656, taking advantage of the legislation enabling parishes to be amalgamated, the City Chamber procured an Act for uniting the seventeen City parishes into four, keeping the churches of St. Mary Arches, St. Mary Major, St. Petrock's, and St. Edmund's. On 11th August, 1657, the Chamber decided on the following presentations to these churches after the reorganization:

Mary Arches: Ferdinando Nicholl. (No change.)
Mary Major: John Bartlett. (Formerly Vicar of St. Thomas', but may possibly have had Mary Major as well since the ejection of the former Royalist Rector Thomas Baker at an unknown date, but probably soon after the Parliamentary forces entered the City in 1646.)
St. Edmund's: Thomas Down. (Previously Rector of St. Paul's.)
St. Petrock's: Mark Down (Formerly Curate only).[1]

In addition to these four large parish churches, the Cathedral was throughout this period in use as a preaching centre. Thomas Ford had been appointed for the Presbyterians as early as 1648, and Lewis Stucley arrived in Exeter and began to gather an Independent Church in the western half of the Cathedral as early as 1650. In 1653 a Samuel Stoneham was appointed as his assistant, but nothing further is heard

[1] Act Books of City Chamber, 11th August, 1657.

of him.[1] As another Independent, Thomas Mall, became co-pastor with Stucley by May, 1656, Stoneham's residence in the City was of short duration.[2] The use of the Cathedral by two distinct congregations, one Presbyterian and the other Independent, had obvious disadvantages, and by December, 1656, the City Chamber decided, at the instance of Stucley, to divide the great church physically into two parts by building a wall between the Nave and the Choir. Ford was against this division, but there would seem to have been no alternative if the already established custom of allowing two different types of worship to be held there at the same time was allowed to go on. The Presbyterians used the Choir, or East Peter's, while the Independents used the Nave, or West Peter's. At their meeting on 11th August, 1657, the City Chamber appointed Robert Atkins as assistant to Ford in East Peter's, at the same time allowing Ford to take a Wednesday lecture in 'West Peter's (one wonders what Stucley thought of that) and to assist others 'as he finds strength and opportunity'. Finally completing the complement of City ministers, in November, 1657, John Tickel was appointed, but without a preaching place. On 3rd November £10 was granted towards his removal expenses and a salary of £100 a year voted.[3]

That the dividing wall in the Cathedral was not begun by mid-1657 is shown by an Order of the Chamber on 11th August directing that this should now be made, at a total cost of £800. It had presumably been completed by 4th November, when the Act Book of the Chamber notes a bond given for the repayment of money borrowed to meet the cost of the partition. The names of those concerned form definite evidence of a substantial body of Puritan laymen in the City.

Thomas Ford . . .	£100	
Nicholas Brooking . .	50	
Simon Snow . . .	100	
James Gould . . .	25	
Thomas Bampfield . .	100	
Ralph Newman . .	30	
James Pearse . . .	25	
James Marshall . .	30	To be repaid with
Bernard Bartlett . .	25	interest on
Thos. Lethbridge . .	30	4th November, 1658.
Henry Gandy . . .	25	
Walter Scoble . . .	25	
John Pym . . .	25	
John Arland . . .	25	

[1] Harte, W. J., Presidential address, in *Trans. Devon. Assoc.*, 1937, Vol. 69, p. 67.
[2] Calamy Revised: Section on Mall, Thomas.
[3] Act Books of City Chamber, 3rd November, 1657.

Walter Golditch . . . 25
Malachy Pyne 25
Humfry Solomon of London . 35
Dr. Vilvaine 100

£800

Several of these men appear in later records as Nonconformists in the days of persecution after 1662. Thomas Ford was the Presbyterian minister. Simon Snow was a previous Mayor of Exeter, brother of Robert Snow, ejected Vicar of Morchard Bishop in 1662. Thomas Bampfield was the 8th son of John Bampfield of Poltimore, was Recorder of Exeter from 1654 to 1660, and M.P. in 1654, 1656, 1658, and 1660, becoming Speaker of the House of Commons in Richard Cromwell's Parliament. He survived to take a part in the emergence of the Presbyterians into the open when James II's Declaration of Indulgence ended the period of persecution.[1] John Pym was fined many times for nonconformity, and in particular at the April Sessions, 15 Car. II (1663) he was fined £100 for uttering scandalous words concerning the Civil Magistrates, and against Thomas Bere, Rector of St. Petrock's, in that church at the time of prayer. The names of Nicholas Brooking and James Pearse also appear in Sessions records, although this may refer to a later generation in the 1670s. Dr. Vilvaine's place in affairs under the Commonwealth is ambiguous, for he appears to have been mainly concerned with preserving the old parish churches, and but for his purchase of several of them when they were up for sale after the amalgamation of parishes in 1656, they might have been demolished completely. He also deserves our gratitude for his part in preserving the invaluable Cathedral Library. However, a Grace Vilvayne was the wife of Thomas Snow, the father by her of Simon and Robert Snow, and he may be assigned with some reservations to the Puritan party. The Bond for repayment of the money lent in the previous year was brought in to Mr. Snow in the Chamber on 2nd November, 1658, and it was decided that the money should be repaid from the proceeds of the sale of the redundant parish churches when the work was finished. This suggests that the job had not been completed to their satisfaction even then.

The unsatisfactory nature of the division of the Cathedral was emphasized in 1657 when a public dispute broke out between Stucley and Ford. Stucley had excommunicated two women members, Mary Allein and Susanna Parr, for attending Presbyterian services, and there

[1] *Dictionary of National Biography*, Bampfield, Thomas.

were at the same time differences of opinion over singing. Next year, on 22nd March, was published in London Thomas Mall's 'True Account of what was done by a Church of Christ in Exon.', which gave the Congregationalist view of the incident. A third Congregationalist minister, Thomas Powell, was on 22nd September, 1658, admitted as Curate of St. Sidwell's. He had formerly been Rector of Truro with St. Clement's, in Cornwall.

A sign of what might have been, if the rule of Cromwell had been prolonged, came in October, 1658, with one of the few real Declarations in favour of liberty in religious expression in these stormy years. On the 12th of that month was issued 'A Declaration of the faith and order owned and practiced in the Congregational churches in England: agreed upon and consented unto by their elders and messengers in their meeting at the Savoy.' This Savoy Conference in London, although an admirable statement of principles, came too late. With the passing of Oliver Cromwell the power of the Independents was already at an end, and the temper of the other sects was far from favouring toleration in any form.

The passing of Oliver Cromwell, which automatically raised the hopes of Royalists and Episcopalians everywhere, did not lead to any immediate changes in Exeter. To the contrary, there were in September, 1658, loyal demonstrations in the city on the proclamation of Richard Cromwell as the new Lord Protector.[1]

So matters stood as far as the official religious organization of the city was concerned, on the eve of the Restoration. To complete the picture, however, two other bodies of worshippers should be considered. These were the Baptists and the followers of George Fox.

The Baptist interest in Exeter and neighbourhood dates from the coming of Cromwell's armies to Devon in April, 1646, in which month the Parliamentary forces took Exeter. It is known that Captain Paul Hobson, one of the signatories to the Baptist Confession of 1644, was in Exeter in June of the same year, and that he was active in encouraging new Baptist causes in Devon. Hobson later adopted Fifth Monarchy ideas, and possibly the early Baptist society in Exeter was influenced by these extreme sectaries. They were men whom unaccustomed freedom and a surfeit of Bible reading had made into republicans in politics. Not content to wait for the Second Coming of Christ they wished to bring in Christ's kingdom by force immediately. At first meeting either in the open air, or in private houses, the Baptists in Exeter secured at some

[1] Davies, G., *The Restoration of Charles II, 1658–1660*, 1955, pp. 6–7.

time between 1649 and 1654 a place of worship in the Deanery Hall. In 1649 the City Chamber purchased the Deanery and it soon after passed into the hands of John Carew, one of the Regicide judges, and a West-countryman. He had the dining-hall fitted up as a Baptist meeting house, while the rest of the building was made into dwellings for working-class people whose homes had been destroyed during the siege of the city. In 1660 when Dean Peterson was able to return to Exeter after the Restoration he found 'his house spoild and full of Weavers and worsted combers', which was the occupation of many Baptists. The society may have moved to St. Paul's Church after 1656, for when the Chamber in March of that year obtained an Act of Parliament for combining many of the old parishes, it was ordered that the best parish church left should be given to the Baptists. The main body of the church was violently seized by the Anabaptists, who held their assemblies there. This Church also, unlike the rest of the redundant places of worship, remained unsold until after Cromwell's death.

In 1655 Henry Jessey, a leading Baptist minister in London, visited the West to combat the growth of heretical opinions there. In 1656 the west-country Baptist churches met in Assembly at Bristol and published a Declaration of Faith, a further attempt to regulate member churches and prevent deviations from orthodoxy. The Exeter Baptists were represented at this assembly, and date their foundation as a separate church from this year. With the coming of the Restoration the Exeter Baptists were immediately dispossessed of the Deanery and of St. Paul's Church, and entered upon a period of harsh persecution.[1]

The first extension of Quaker activity to Devon came in 1654, when six men set out from Swarthmore on a mission to the south of England. Two of these 'First Publishers of Truth' were John Audland and Thomas Ayrey. Ayrey was a man of middle age, beginning to lose courage, for after getting to Plymouth he does not appear on such enterprises again. Audland, a young man of 24, combined a pleasant appearance with intelligence and Scriptural learning, much the more effective evangelizer. In this year, however, neither had much time to stay in any one place, and soon after leaving Plymouth Audland met his remaining missionary colleagues in London, where plans for a more systematic visitation were laid. In 1655 there came two other Quaker pioneers, Miles Halhead and Thomas Salthouse, both Northerners. Then late in 1655 came George Fox himself, accompanied by Edward Pyott. He did not visit Exeter at first, and on reaching Launceston, he

[1] Gabb, Arthur, History of South St. Baptist Church, Exeter, 1956.

was imprisoned, not to be released until 9th September, 1656. He then came to Exeter 'on a Saturday evening in the middle of September'. On the 14th he held a meeting in the prison, where some twenty Friends were receiving hospitality, including the well-known James Nayler. The names of these Quaker prisoners do not include any Exeter residents.[1]

Four months later the first General Meeting of Quakers in Devon and Cornwall was held at the Seven Stars Inn near Exe Bridge, and Fox journeyed to Exeter to attend it. He successfully evaded an attempt to imprison him while in the City, which he never visited again. While in Exeter he stayed with John Gannicliff, a cordwainer of St. Thomas Parish, the leader of the society in Exeter until his death in 1701, aged about 80.

The Society of Friends has always been zealous in recording the deeds and endurance of its members, and such works as Joseph Besse's 'A Collection of the Sufferings of the people called Quakers' (published in 1753) contain many incidents of the persecution in the West at this time.

Quakers were most usually charged under the Blasphemy Act of 1650, under which a Justice could for the first offence commit to prison for between six months and one year. A second offence meant prison until the Assizes, and, if there convicted, banishment under pain of death. George Fox was imprisoned for a year at Derby, 1650–1, under the first part of the Act, on a charge of 'affirming himself or any other mere creature to be a very God or to be infinite or almighty or equal with God, or that the true God or the eternal Majesty dwells in the creature and nowhere else'.

There were very few Quakers in Exeter itself until after 1680, except those actually imprisoned in the gaols. Probably this was because the County Town was too much in the public eye, and it would have been easy enough for the Justices to suppress them at a time when public opinion was violently aroused against them. Nearby at Topsham, however, was the most flourishing of the early Quaker communities in the county, continuing so until 1692, when the Exeter Meeting-house was built, and thereafter took its natural place as the county centre for the Society of Friends.[2]

The degree to which Puritanism took hold of Exeter citizens during

---

[1] 'The West Answering to the North', 1657, (Anon.), p. 107.
[2] Thomasson, W. J. M., 'The Friends of East Devon and their Meetings, 1654–1928', (in typescript: copies in Exeter City and University Libraries).

the Commonwealth must remain uncertain. The mass of the population surely remained indifferent or followed the example of its leaders, as it has always done. That there was a substantial group of Puritan merchants among the controlling oligarchy, perhaps a majority, is likely. Yet their motives were never unmixed. The removal of Bishop, Dean and Chapter, and the passing of church property into their control, was greatly to the advantage of the civic authorities. Throughout the history of the city the Chamber had carried on periodic warfare with the ecclesiastical establishment, and at last under the Commonwealth this rival had disappeared. A Presbyterian monarchy was most likely the choice of the majority of the leading citizens in 1660, when the Commonwealth broke down under the threat of renewed Civil War between sections of the Army. The adroit political manœuvres of the Anglican representatives in the discussions between both parties which took place in 1660 and 1661 resulted, however, in a return to the religious order of Charles I's reign, and all except those who were ardent in their faith decided to swim with the tide. Yet the large number of those prosecuted for Nonconformity during the following 25 years is evidence that many Exonians did feel strongly enough to refuse to follow their material interests against the urging of their conscience.

CHAPTER II

RESTORATION AND EJECTION: THE FIRST PERIOD OF PERSECUTION, 1660–1672

ALTHOUGH too great an emphasis can be laid upon religion as a cause of the English Civil Wars, it was undoubtedly one of the major factors involved in the struggle between Crown and Parliament and Army. The Anglican extremism of Laud had brought about an extreme Presbyterian reaction under the rule of Parliament, and a counter-persecution of the Episcopalians. This reaction itself provoked a counter-reaction which ensured the King's return. The greater part of the country did not wish the continuation of the Presbyterian experiment. The rule of the Saints had proved more unpalatable than the reign of the 'Man of Blood, Charles Stuart'. The Restoration of the Monarchy involved the restoration of the Anglican Establishment, substantially as in 1642. The only debate necessary was whether reforms could be adopted which would enable large numbers of clergy and people of convinced Presbyterian views to remain in communion with the national church. Independents and Baptists could not be included without changing the whole nature of the Church of England, and this was never contemplated. The Presbyterians, however, believed in a National Church, and were prepared to accept a modified form of Episcopacy such as had been proposed by Archbishop Ussher in 1641, and was the basis of Charles II's Worcester House Declaration in October, 1660. The King in this favoured limitations of the power of the Bishops by subjecting them to the advice of elected bodies of Presbyters (parish priests) and by increasing the number of Suffragan Bishops. The Prayer Book was to be revised and a national Synod would decide upon ceremonies in dispute.[1] This was in line with a letter sent by certain London Presbyterian Divines (Calamy the Elder, Ashe, and Manton) to Scottish ministers on 10th August, 1660, in which the following passage appeared:

'. . . therefore no course seemeth likely to us to secure religion . . . but by making presbytery a part of the public establishment; which will not be effected but by moderating and reducing episcopacy to the form of synodical government.'[2]

[1] *English Historical Documents*, 1953, Vol. 8 (1660–1714), p. 365.
[2] Wodrow, R., *History of the Sufferings of the Church of Scotland*, 1828, Vol. 1, p. 54.

That the King would have been willing enough to accord both this modified episcopacy and an accompanying toleration for minority sects is shown by his further pronouncement in favour of Toleration dated 26th December, 1662, after the Act of Uniformity had actually been passed.[1]

The Cavalier Parliament would have none of this, however, its view of 'allowable differences' being far removed from that of the leading Presbyterians. The Four Acts known as the Clarendon Code, designed to enforce conformity to one national Church of England, excluded a large and influential section of the population from that Church. The Presbyterians were now to be counted with the Independents, Baptists and Quakers, as Nonconformists. The story of what happened in Exeter will be followed in detail, with continual reference to national events.

The return of the King was followed by that of the loyal clergy. The survivors evicted from their livings during the Interregnum demanded their immediate restoration. Their action was restrained by a Proclamation of 29th May, 1660, and the whole position defined on 13th September by 'An Act for Confirming and Restoring of Ministers'. The sequestered clergy were restored, as were also those presented to livings by accredited patrons during the Commonwealth but refused admission by the 'Triers', and also those presented by patrons who were members of the House of Lords. With minor exceptions no other changes took place, and all other incumbents were confirmed in their livings. It was understood by all, however, that this was only a temporary measure.

Meetings of Exeter Cathedral Chapter were resumed on 30th August, 1660, when Dean William Peterson and Treasurer Robert Hall were the only members present.[2] On 2nd December, the new Bishop, John Gauden, who favoured comprehension for the Presbyterians, was consecrated in Westminster. The Cathedral and Parish Churches were handed back to the Church authorities after 25th August, 1660. As early as 26th October the King 'required the immediate removal of a wall put up to separate the choir from the body of the church'[3] and the Cathedral was restored to its former condition between November, 1660, and March, 1661.[4] The ejected

---

[1] *English Historical Documents*, Vol. 8, p. 371.

[2] Chapter Act Books, 1660.

[3] Calendar of State Papers, Domestic Series, 1660, p. 215.

[4] Entries in Extraordinary Solutions Book, 1660/1, M.S. D. & C. No. 3787, in Cathedral Archives. Also Chapter Act Book for 8th November, 1660.

Presbyterians and Independents vainly petitioned that they should still be allowed to use part of the Cathedral.[1]

Meanwhile in London, as a prelude to the enactment of a new measure of Uniformity, and in order to carry out the promise made by the King at his Restoration, the Savoy Conference took place, beginning on 15th April, 1661. This was limited to Anglicans and Presbyterians. The latter were now struggling for a limited episcopacy only, realizing that a true Presbyterian order was no longer possible. The Anglicans, however, demanded:

1. Re-ordination of all clergy not episcopally ordained.
2. Unfeigned 'assent and consent' to all the Book of Common Prayer.
3. An oath of obedience to ecclesiastical superiors (i.e. Bishops).
4. Adjuration of the Solemn League and Covenant.
5. An oath of non-resistance to the King.

Few Presbyterians could agree to these demands, and the Conference failed as many of the Anglicans had intended from the first.[2]

The new 'Bill for the Uniformity of Public Prayer and Administration of the Sacraments' first went before the House of Commons on 29th June, 1661. It received the royal assent on 19th May, 1662. The long time spent in carrying the Bill through was due to the work involved in revising the Prayer Book of 1604. The revision was carried out with an anti-Puritan bias. By this 1662 Act of Uniformity none but episcopal ordination was considered valid; all clergy were required to declare their unfeigned assent to the revised Prayer Book; all clergymen had to sign a declaration of non-resistance to the Crown; the Solemn League and Covenant had to be renounced in very strong terms; and a promise given to conform to the Liturgy of the Church of England. All the points made by the Anglican representatives at the Savoy Conference, therefore, were included. The Act had to be complied with by St. Bartholomew's Day, 24th August, 1662, or else ejection would take place. Ministers preaching in their former parishes thereafter would be liable to three months' imprisonment.[3]

There were two ejections of Nonconforming clergy after the Restoration. The first occurred in 1660 with the return of the surviving

[1] Pope, W., *Life of . . . Seth, Lord Bishop of Salisbury* . . . 1697, pp. 55–6.
[2] Gee, H., and Hardy, W. J., *Documents illustrative of English Church History*, 1896, pp. 588–94.
[3] English Historical Documents, Vol. 8, pp. 377–82.

episcopally ordained clergy; the second on St. Bartholomew's Day, 1662. In Devon 40 ministers lost their livings or were silenced in 1660: and 73 were ejected in 1662, while in the case of 8 of them no date can be firmly fixed. The total of Nonconforming clergy in the county was therefore 121, a figure higher than that for any other county.[1]

In Exeter the picture is confused by the reorganization of all the parishes in 1656. The clergy active in the City in the period 1656–60 were, however:

Ferdinando Nicholl:	St. Mary Arches.	
John Bartlett:	St. Mary Major.	
Thomas Down:	St. Edmund's.	
Mark Down:	St. Petrock's.	All these were
Thomas Ford:	East Peter's.	Presbyterians.
Robert Atkins:	East Peter's.	
John Tickel:	No specified place	
Lewis Stucley:	West Peter's.	
Thomas Mall:	West Peter's.	Independents.
Thomas Powell:	St. Sidwell's (Curate).	

The first four were episcopally ordained, and as previous incumbents of St. Mary Major, St. Petrock's and St. Edmund's had died since being evicted, these men were left undisturbed until 1662, when they all refused to conform. All the ministers at the Cathedral had to leave in 1660. Ford remained in the City, without charge. Atkins was instituted as Rector of St. John's, on 31st January, 1660/1; but he refused to conform in 1662. Tickel was silenced at this time, and he later conformed, becoming curate at Barnstaple in 1669, and of Widecombe in 1674, the only one of the Exeter Puritan clergy who did eventually conform. Lewis Stucley and Thomas Mall had to leave the Cathedral in 1660. Powell retained his appointment until 1662, when he, also, was ejected. To these ten should be added Alexander Hodge, Vicar of St. Thomas' from 1657.

All these men remained in the City until the Five Mile Act of 1665, quietly enough for the most part, and public opinion was sympathetic towards them, judging by a letter from Bishop Seth Ward to Archbishop Sheldon, of 19th December, 1663:

That I myself have met with more then ordinary difficulty . . . yr Grace will easily conceive, when yu shall be informed that the onely persons in this

---

[1] Calamy Revised by A. G. Matthews, 1934. Figures are summarized in the Introduction. Calamy has been drawn upon extensively for data relating to all the ejected ministers associated with Exeter.

city, who have had the heart and courage to endeavour an obedience to the
laws, have been checked and discouraged for their labour, and some putt
out of employment, as being too pragmaticall and forward to draw the
people to obedience, and when yr G. shall know that there are in this County
of Devon . . . at least 14 Justices of the Peace, who are accounted arrant
Presbyterians . . . .[1]

That one of the Presbyterian clergy had been popular in Exeter is
clear from the records of the April, 1663, Quarter Sessions in the city,
when there was a Grand Jury presentment of 14 named persons (including John Tickell and Thomas Crispyn, the latter of whom appears
more frequently than anyone else in Sessions records for offences
against the Clarendon Code) and 100 other unknown persons, 'for preventing the Rector of St. Mary Arches from burying the body of
Ferdinand Nicholls, formerly Rector, according to the rites of the
Church of England'. Nicholls had died on 14th December, 1662. The
plea entered was not guilty, but some demonstration had definitely
taken place to show that the parishioners did not approve of burying a
man according to a Prayer Book which he had refused to accept.[2]

Further correspondence between Seth Ward and his Archbishop
took place throughout this period. The following passage comes in a
letter of 4th January, 1664:

'Yr Grace is pleased to aske who in this city have been discouraged
for doeing their duty. Indeed . . . I cannot name many such, for this
place hath never afforded many friends to the Church.' The Bishop
continued to say that he tried all the new City Chamber for support and

could find none . . . besides Mr. John Butler (who is now Mayor) and such
as he persuaded to assist him . . . he caused the Rioters to be endited, he
watched the conventicles and meetings of those persons, he discovered their
designes, and correspondencies, and was the chief and almost onely person
that I could relie upon to effect any thing for the publique interest. His
reward was to be traduced and cried downe . . . He was baffled in the
enditemt., by tricks & traverses . . . he hath abated his Activity to the great
prejudice . . . of affairs here. One or 2 more there are who assisted him and
their spirit is fallen with his.

[1] Devon and Cornwall Notes and Queries, Vols. 21–22, 1940–3. The whole series of
letters from Bishops of Exeter quoted in this section and the next are printed in the Documents Sections of these two volumes.
[2] Exeter City Sessions Records. (a) Quarter Sessions Rolls, 1662–87. (b) Records of
Fines imposed under the Conventicle Acts, 1673–87. Preserved at the Muniment Room,
City Library, Exeter.

It was possible during the short interval between the Restoration and the passing of the 1662 Act for clergymen of Presbyterian opinions both to be presented to new livings, and to be ordained without subscribing to the Prayer Book, or even giving a promise of obedience to the Anglican Establishment. Local instances are the presentation of Rev. Robert Atkins to the living of St. John's in Exeter at the beginning of 1661, and the ordination as both Deacon and Priest on 13th January, 1661, of John Gidley (of an Exeter family) and John Hopping (of whom we shall hear again). It is doubtful, however, whether such incidents were common, and would certainly have ceased as soon as Seth Ward became Bishop of Exeter.

The sources of information for the period between 1662 and 1687 are not adequate to decide the relative strength of Anglican and Nonconformist groups in the city. But they do indicate that Nonconformist influence was considerable, and that the attempts of the authorities to suppress Nonconformity were consistently hampered by local sympathies with those persecuted. The main sources are: a series of letters from the Bishops of Exeter to the Archbishop of Canterbury; Episcopal Returns when requested for detailed reports on the extent of Nonconformity in the Diocese in 1665, 1669 and 1675; records of prosecutions for offences against the Penal Laws; and licenses issued under the 1672–3 Declaration of Indulgence.

After Bartholomew's Day, 1662, there was an influx of dispossessed ministers into the city. Not only previous incumbents of City parishes are found here, but many from country livings nearby, and one or two from further afield who may have had family connections in Exeter. Bishop Ward wrote to Archbishop Sheldon on 16th January, 1664:

There have been constantly (since Bartholom: 62) in this city above twenty ministers some of them the chief of the whole party they have nothing els to doe but to lie gnaweing at the root of Governmt & religion, and to that purpose have many secret meetings & conventicles. Those who are the Sage and the Wise amongst our friends, winke at them and thinke it by no meanes fit to discourage them. . . .

Enclosed with this letter was a list of 22 ejected ministers living in Exeter:

Mr. Thomas Ford in Bedford house.
Mr. John Bartlett in part of ye said house.
Mr. Marke Downe in Northgate street.
Mr. Thomas Downe on stripcott hill.

Mr. Thomas Trescott (of shobbrooke) without Northgate.
Mr. Robert Atkins in part of st. Nicholas Priory.
Mr. John Tickel in part of the said Priory.
Mr. Robert Snow at his house in Highstreete.
Mr. John Gidley liveing with Mr. Clare neare Key gate.
Mr. Alexander Hodge living in st. Thomas Parish.
Mr. (Robert) Gillard (formerly of Ede) living with his father.
Mr.   Taunton in Southgate street.
Mr. Lewis Stewkley in mr. Gandyes lane.
Mr. Thomas Mall in the same lane.
Mr. (Thomas) Powell living in st. Sidwells.
Mr. Robert Oland living about Westgate.
Mr. Robert Carle (Carel) living with his father in southgate streete.
Mr. Mathew Pemberton with Mr. Thomson in Highstreete.
Mr. John Mauditt with his father in Highstreete.
Mr. Samuel Tapper with his mother in Highstreete.
Mr. (John) Hill formerly of Newton fferris.
Mr. (Leonard) Hyne formerly of Loddiswell.

Most of these men have been mentioned before. Robert Oland is something of a mystery: he was Rector of All Hallows on the Wall from
1636 to 1639, of All Hallows, Goldsmith St. from 1636 until 1645, and
is said to have been Rector of St. Paul's from December, 1635, apparently until 1662. As Thomas Down was definitely Rector of St. Paul's
in 1648, when the Devon ministers met together and signed a 'Testimony' of their faith, this record cannot be correct. Perhaps a clue is
given in a declaration as late as 1704 by an old parishioner of St. Paul's,
Mr. Thomas Pennington, that 'Mr. Robert Olden was before the
breaking out of the war rector of this church, that he was a person
extremely vicious and ignorant and that he rifled the church . . . and
fled to the Parliamentary army'. His misconduct and absence from the
city may have led to sequestration, and the giving of the church of
St. Paul to a worthier man. In 1660, when the old parish churches were
restored to those who had held them before the Civil Wars, he would
have returned, only to be ejected again in 1662.[1] Robert Carel was
Rector of Uplowman before his ejection, Matthew Pemberton of Clay-
hidon, John Mauduit from Penshurst in Kent, and Samuel Tapper from
St. Merryn in Cornwall. 'Mr. Taunton' is not mentioned in any other
list of ejected ministers.

That Bishop Seth Ward was not antagonistic towards these ministers
on personal grounds is shown by his treatment of Samuel Tapper, who

[1] Harte, W. J. Presidential Address, 1937, *Trans. Devon. Assoc.*, 1937, p. 62.

became his friend, and on occasions dined at the Palace. At the instance of the Cathedral Treasurer, Baldwin Ackland, the Bishop even allowed Tapper to preach in his private Chapel without interference until some of the more extreme of his supporters clamoured against this.

1662–1665 was a period during which both sides weighed each other up, not quite certain how things would develop. The Presbyterians in Exeter did not flout the established church by openly holding conventicles, although they preached privately to their closest adherents. Despite the uncompromising Act of Uniformity there may have remained a hope of obtaining a form of comprehension which would enable them to return to the national church. The attitude of the ejected ministers was most likely that of John Quick, formerly of Brixton, reported on by Seth Ward in a letter of 19th December, 1663:

He saith that after his removeall, he staid some moneths, to se whether any other would supply his place, but at length finding that no man was putt in his stead, and that the people went off, some to Atheisme and debauchery others to Sectarisme . . . He resolved to adventure to gather his flock againe.

Quick's reward was to be arrested and brought prisoner to the Castle in Exeter to stand trial. The incident spotlights the greatest difficulty facing the Church of England after 1662. The ejected ministers could not be replaced by men of equal standing immediately: it took considerable time to find fully qualified successors. With the greatest desire possible to avoid giving offence the former ministers could hardly stand by and watch their flocks breaking up through lack of a shepherd, while they were both willing and able to continue their former work.

That no relief could be expected from the Cavalier Parliament was made clear by the passing of the First Conventicle Act of 1664. This made it illegal to hold an assembly of five persons or more, in addition to those of the household, for religious purposes other than those of the Church of England. Penalties for the first offence were £5 or 3 months' imprisonment. The second conviction meant a fine of £10 or 6 months, and the third £100 or 7 years' transportation. Magistrates were themselves liable to a fine of £100 if they neglected their duty in suppressing conventicles. But the Act afforded loopholes where a sympathetic judge tried the cases. A letter of 30th September, 1664, from one H.P. to John Knowles[1] reads:

There is great hope, from a report of Judge Hale, that the proceedings on

[1] Calendar of State Papers, Domestic Series, 1664/5, p. 20.

C

the Conventicle Act will stop, for at Exeter the Quakers were by his means found not guilty, because no sedition appeared, and the Act is not against religious meetings but seditious conventicles. The statute would do little hurt, if put in execution by impartial judges.

That Seth Ward was capable of exaggeration at times appears from his letter to the Archbishop of April 24th, 1665.[1]

'Finds Exeter as well conditioned as may be, with 40 revolted ministers nestling there, and no power to remove them.'

This can only be taken as referring to a larger area than the city of Exeter, for the Bishop's official return later in the year gives a total of only 16 ejected ministers residing there.

It was in 1665 that Archbishop Sheldon first formally demanded from his Bishops detailed information about the number of conventicles in their dioceses, and the conduct, livelihood, and political opinions of ejected ministers. Most of the diocesan returns have been lost, but by good fortune those for Exeter survived complete at Lambeth Palace Library.[2] Sixteen ministers were living in Exeter. Two former incumbents of Exeter parishes, Ferdinando Nicholl and Thomas Down, had passed from the scene through death. The remainder were still in the City: Robert Atkins, John Bartlett, Thomas Ford, Mark Down, and John Tickell, of the Presbyterians; and Lewis Stucley, Thomas Mall and Thomas Powell, of the Congregationalists. Of those reported privately by Bishop Ward in 1663 we find the Presbyterians Robert Carel, Robert Snow, Thomas Trescott, Samuel Tapper and John Hill. Three additional names appear, those of Henry Hallett (ejected from Brampford Speke), John Jordan (from Stoke Canon), and Alexander Robinson (from Porlock). The Bishop reported that all the Presbyterians kept the peace and were not known to hold conventicles, but that the three Congregational ministers did hold meetings regularly.

The Archbishop had a double purpose in ordering this survey at this time. First, it would supply information on the effect of the First Conventicle Act passed the year before. More important, however, it would prepare the ground for the enforcing of another more stringent Act of Parliament which was being made ready. This was 'An Act for Restraining Nonconformists from Inhabiting in Corporations', passed while Parliament met at Oxford to avoid the Great Plague of London.[3]

[1] Calendar of State Papers, Domestic Series, 1664/5, p. 329.
[2] Turner, G. L. Original records of early Nonconformity, 1911–13, 3 vols. These contain the Episcopal Returns of 1665, 1669 and 1675; and the Licenses issued in 1672.
[3] English Historical Documents, Vol. 8, pp. 382–4.

This came to be known either as the Oxford Act (from its place of enactment) or as the Five Mile Act, from its prohibition upon all Ministers of the Church who had neither subscribed the declaration of the Act of Uniformity, nor taken the oath of non-resistance to the Crown, from coming within five miles of any corporate town or place where they had formerly worked. At the January Assizes of 1666 the ejected ministers were expected to comply with the requirements of this Act, and we fortunately have a graphic account of what happened in Exeter in the correspondence between Seth Ward and Archbishop Sheldon. On 8th January, 1666, he wrote:

This day being the first day of the Sessions here, 4 Presbyterian minrs . . . came to me to tell me that themselves & divers of their brethren were ready to take the Oath, but forseing . . . that they shld suffer some reproach, they desired that I would send to the Mayor & Justices to take care that they might be civilly treated. This I willingly did, and now I am informed that Eight have taken the Oath, but that some others have petitioned (to no purpose) that they may be forborne untill the 24 of March. . . .

I understand that there have been frequent meetings & great agitations amongst them, that diverse who had promised to subscribe have been by some interposition kept off from it. . . . But they tell me they are convinced of the wickedness of rebellious principles & for their justification they have printed an half-sheet . . . to shew the obligation wch lies on them from the Scriptures to take every parcel of the Oath.

The Bishop evidently considered it important to keep his superior closely informed of developments, for on 14th January he wrote again:

. . . I lately sent yr G. an acct of what passed the first day of the Sessions for this City, viz: that 8 tooke the Oath and prepared themselves to justify it by those 2 printed papers wch I sent to yr Grace. The rest of those who were then present in the city & residents thereof subscribed this frivolous paper wch I have here enclosed by this yr Grace wil perceive what a sweet concurrence there is betwixt the Presbyterians & Independents in the principles of rebellion. No greater enemies in the world than Mr. Ford and Mr. Stewkly, they preached they wrote bookes one against another, but now they unite, however though hand joyne in hand I cannot believe that they wil goe unpunished.

Of the Country-ministers I am informed that 18 have taken it, and because it was suggested that some were aged, others sick, others ignorant of the law, it was desired of the justices (and granted) that they would meet againe upon the 15 of February to se if other would take it . . . I perceive that the breach is very great betwixt the takers & refusers.

A week later, on 27th January, he wrote again:

I am apt to think that I am not to expect in my Diocese many more subscribers than those who did appeare at first. . . . This morning one of the
Subscribers was with me & he tells me that all commerce is cutt off betwixt
them and the Refusers, he saith that he himself hath recd. very unkind
messages from them. And from the Independents & Anabaptists hath lately
recd. such threats, that he feares there is some designe of creating suddein
trouble; the truth is they are very angry and very bold in their language,
especially such of the Anabaptists as are in prison.

His final report came on 24th February, 1666.

Of the City & County of Exon: no man came in, & so the Justices have
proceeded so farr with the recusants (who are 12) as to take bond for their
behaviour till the 24 of March, at wch time they are to remove. . . .
So that 30 persons have subscribed at Exeter 6 of the City & 24 of the
Country. . . .

This total of 30 for the County, compared with the 121 ejected in
1660–2, is high. It would have been composed of those who had
expected some measure of toleration to be passed by Parliament under
the influence of the King, of those conservative Presbyterians who had
never had any desire to be in a position of rebellion against authority,
who thoroughly disliked association with Independents (even less with
Baptists), and of a few elderly men who wished to put an end to
schism and to die at peace with the Church.

Although Bishop Ward did not give the names of those who conformed in Exeter at this time, the Bodleian Library has preserved an
undated copy of a petition from 13 Presbyterian ministers living in
Exeter to the Mayor, Recorder, and Justices of the City. This is
undoubtedly the 'frivolous paper' mentioned in the Bishop's letter of
14th January. It was an honest enough petition, offered, as the closing
words indicate, by men 'not as desiring or expecting thereby to escape
the penaltyes of the Act afforesd; But that we may not upon the account
of forbearing ye. Oath at present be reputed or represented as persons
disloyall or disaffected to his Majesties person or Government'.

Of those mentioned in the Episcopal Return of 1665, the signatories
include Robert Atkins, Mark Down, Thomas Ford, Lewis Stucley,
Thomas Mall, Thomas Powell, Thomas Trescott, Henry Hallett and
John Jordan. The remainder were John Taylor, who lost his living at
Combe Raleigh in 1660 when the previous incumbent was restored,
Robert Gaylard (Gillard) of Ide, who had been named in Bishop

Ward's letter of 1663, John Hopping, and William Crompton (ejected from Cullompton).[1]

Seven of the men who were resident in Exeter at the time of the 1665 Return did not sign this petition, and the six who took the Oxford Oath at the beginning of 1666 according to Bishop Ward must therefore be found among them. The seven were John Tickell, Samuel Tapper, Robert Snow, John Bartlett, Robert Carel, John Hill, and Alexander Robinson. Tickel is known to have conformed; and was ordained curate at Barnstaple on 20th June, 1669. Tapper, being a friend of the Bishop and a mild man, is correctly included, and may have been the minister who visited Seth Ward on 27th January, 1666. Edmund Calamy claimed that Robert Snow took the Oxford Oath, though this is not recorded elsewhere. Hill, Bartlett, Carel, and Robinson, although they did not sign this Petition, did later take out licenses as Presbyterian teachers in 1672, and so, if any three of them conformed at this time they did not really change their opinions.

The value of the Five Mile Act to the Anglicans was not that it forced a large number of the more timid Nonconformists again into the arms of the Church of England, but that it removed the most able and vigorous of their ministers from the centres where they had previously worked and still had great influence. Thomas Ford withdrew to Exmouth. Alexander Hodge, formerly Vicar of St. Thomas', went to Holland, and became minister of the English church at Delft by 1668, later moving to Amsterdam. By 1669, when the next Episcopal Return was made to Archbishop Sheldon, Robert Atkins was reported preaching at Chard in Somerset, Thomas Mall at Cruwys Morchard and Crediton, and Thomas Powell had moved to London, described as 'A very factious Man'. At that time also Lewis Stucley was active at Netherexe, Cruwys Morchard and Crediton, and possibly also at Bideford, where his family had great influence. By 1672 John Jordan had moved to Newton Abbot where he received a licence under the Declaration of Indulgence, and Thomas Mall was similarly licensed then for South Molton. Certain other ejected ministers were removed by death in these years. Robert Snow was buried in St. Mary Arches Church on 21st June, 1668, five months after his brother Simon. Henry Hallett was buried on 19th July, 1670, and Thomas Mall's will was proved on 16th September, 1673.

To reinforce the depleted ranks of Nonconformist teachers in Exeter now came a somewhat belligerent figure, George Trosse, a

[1] Bodleian MS. 28186, fol. 212.

member of an Exeter family, who after a wild youth had undergone a violent conversion. After this he had passed to Pembroke College, Oxford, in 1657, to study Divinity. In 1666 he returned to Exeter, underwent Presbyterian ordination in secret, and devoted himself to the task of rallying the Nonconformist cause there.[1] He was soon joined by the man who was to be his chief colleague throughout the period of persecution, Joseph Hallett I, born at Bridport, and ejected from the living of Chiselborough in 1662. Hallett most likely came to Exeter in 1670, on the death of Henry Hallett. A connection by birth between the two men is not proved, but both came from Dorset, Henry having been Vicar of Powerstock in that county from 1649 to 1654, when he moved to Brampford Speke.

The Five Mile Act did not altogether keep out the former unrepentant Exeter ministers. This is shown by a Grand Jury presentment at Exeter Assizes in July, 1669, of Robert Atkyns and Robert Gillard, with over 100 unknown persons for 'Assembling illegally at Thomas Crispyn's house'. The case was sent for trial but no verdict noted. The Exeter magistrates appear to have been unusually active in enforcing the laws against Nonconformists in 1669, for in addition to the case just mentioned, at the January Sessions 'Thomas Crispen of Exeter fuller, Robert Atkyns of Exeter clerk' were brought up with 17 other people on a charge of assembling illegally. This case was dismissed. At the July Sessions 'Nicholas Savery of St. Petrock linendraper, William Packer of St. Thomas the Apostle Woolcomber', with 6 other named and 30 unknown persons, were sent for trial on the same charge. At the same time a second charge was laid against Crispyn for assembling illegally at his own house with more than 200 other persons. The verdicts of these latter cases were not recorded in the Sessions Rolls.

If ever it was possible for the Anglicans to enforce conformity to their version of a national church this period between February, 1666, and March, 1672, was the most favourable. Here the story is resumed in letters from the Bishop of Exeter to Archbishop Sheldon. Anthony Sparrow had been consecrated Bishop of Exeter on 3rd November, 1667, and was less sympathetic to Dissent than his predecessor. A letter of 29th July, 1668, says:

May it please your Grace when you see chief Justice Vaughan to take notice of the great service he hath done at Exeter. Before his comeing the Justices were spirit faln, & no man allmost durst appeare against the Factions who had even overrun us, speaking big of the kgs. favour to them, and

---

[1] Trosse, George, *Life*, 1714.

reporting that this Judge had instructions from his Matie. to favour them, which being told him, he fully declared the laws against them & freely & heartily declared the bad consequences of permitting their Conventicles . . . I have in several churches set up Catechiseing my self, and all the Clergy in the City joyne with me, and they persuade me it will have good successe, divers of the moderate Presbyterians seem well satisfied, and the Loial party more.

The First Conventicle Act had expired in 1667, and the royalist party in Parliament had ever since been agitating for its renewal. The Second Conventicle Act of 1670 was the result. Although the penalties under this measure were lighter than had previously been the case, they hit the leading Nonconformists much harder. Its chief provisions were three:

i. Both the Preacher at the meeting, and the owner of the house where the meeting was held could be fined £20.
ii. The fines on any poor people present (5s. for the first offence, doubled for a second time) could be levied on any well-to-do person who was also present up a maximum of £10.
iii. The fines collected under the Act were to be divided into three portions, one third going to the Poor Fund, as before, while another third went to the Treasury. The last part was to go to the informer(s) who had brought the offence to the notice of the magistrates. It was this last provision which hurt the Dissenters, and ensured that the Act would be enforced.

The Exeter Dissenters did not wait long before feeling its effect. At the November Sessions, 1670, Andrew Jeffery of St. Mary Major, fuller, and 20 other named people, including Thomas Crispyn, were judged guilty of assembling illegally at Jeffery's house. Jeffrey was fined £20 and the rest 5s. each, but Crispyn had to pay the fines of 7 of these as they were so poor. As Jeffery and Crispyn were the only men mentioned as being present, either this was one of the earliest recorded instances of that typical Nonconformist institution, a Women's Meeting; or else the women had decided to stay while their menfolk escaped, in the hope that the magistrates would treat them more leniently. This may have been the occasion recorded in George Trosse's 'Life':

For a long time together I preach'd in the very Heart of the City, every Wednesday about Two or Three of the Clock in the Afternoons, to a very considerable Society, which fill'd two Chambers. This could not but be observ'd by the Church Party; but for a considerable while we continu'd without Disturbance; till at length a Magistrate came upon us, and found us assembl'd. But, by God's good Providence, I escap'd tho' very narrowly. For I got into another Chamber, where I was hid; and tho' I was diligently sought for, and every Coffer open'd, yet could they not find me.[1]

Jeffery and Crispyn were the type of Dissenters at whom the 1670 Act was directed. Crispyn's wealth is shown in the Exeter Tax Assessments. In the Poll Tax of 1660 he and his wife were assessed in the parish of St. Kerrian at 40s. 6d., while under the Hearth Tax of 1671 he paid tax on 10 hearths. Both these figures were very much above the average. Jeffery was assessed on 7 hearths in St. Mary Major Parish in 1671.[2]

Whilst the chief figures in Nonconformist circles were being harried by the law, the clergy began an all-out attempt to win over the Dissenting congregations. Archbishop Sheldon sent a letter on these lines to his clergy dated 7th May, 1670,[3] to which Bishop Sparrow's response was;

I am assured from divers of the most factious places, that the churches fil apace & the Conventicles are shrunk into almost nothing. A little more time, if this method be continued, will I hope settle us very quiet if we have some new Justices in some parts, as I hope we shall ere long.

Later, on 19th June, he continued;

I cannot forbear to tell your Grace how active our Justices have bene last week at their Sessions. Many Conventiclers appeald to them, & omitted no arts nor spared cost to prevail, but all in vain, for they were cast & fined in City & County, every one of them.

The Bishop was well satisfied with the trend of affairs in the fall of 1671, after his return from a Visitation of the Diocese. On 24th October he wrote;

Our City this week ordered their whole Corporation. . . . to come constantly in their formalityes to our Quire on Sundayes, resolving by all the waies they can to expresse their Conformity to the Ch. & to countenance the Service. This hath not bene done since the kgs returne. I could give your Grace many more instances of this kinde, to shew that the Churches interest daily increases in these parts . . .

---

[1] Trosse, p. 91.
[2] Devon and Cornwall Record Society, N.S., Vol. 2. *Exeter in the 17th century: Tax and Rate Assessments, 1602–1699*, ed. W. G. Hoskins, 1957.
[3] Wilkins, D., *Concilia, 1736–7*, Vol. 4, pp. 589–90.

The position of the Dissenters in Exeter at the beginning of the year 1672 was cheerless. Their legal disabilities had been reinforced by the Second Conventicle Act in a way which hit their leaders where it hurt them most—in the pocket—and these restrictions were being enforced more consistently than had previously been the case. The Bishop was steadily encouraging his clergy to greater activity in their pastoral work, to be more regular in their services, and he had been introducing a better qualified type of man into livings as they fell vacant. Yet by the Sessions records we know that Conventicles continued to be held despite the penalties attached, attended by more than 200 persons at one time. It seems likely, however, that had the pressure on the Dissenters been kept up indefinitely, without allowing them any interval for reorganization, with no prospect of eventual relief, then the majority of them would have conformed by slow stages, leaving only a small number of extremists, mainly Baptists, Quakers and Independents, who could have had little influence on the life of the City.

Such a temporary relief for the Dissenters was at hand, however, and in the brief interval between the issue of Charles II's Declaration of Indulgence on 15th March, 1672, and the passing of the Test Act in March, 1673, it is possible to assess the position of the Nonconformist interest in Devonshire, and in Exeter in particular. The motives behind the King's action were diverse. He had little reason to love the Nonconformists, whose predecessors had deprived his father of both his throne and his life, even though his own return in 1660 was largely through the aid of the Presbyterians. Charles II was received into the Roman Catholic communion at his death, and he was throughout his reign well disposed towards that church. Yet Charles' father was revered as a Martyr of the Church of England, and he knew well enough that he could not hold his throne if he permanently antagonized the Anglican party in the state. Charles may well have considered this Indulgence an experiment worth trying. By gauging the extent of the reaction to it he would have a good idea of the reception he might expect for other religious measures. Had toleration for the Protestant Dissenters been accepted calmly, full permission to the Catholics to build Churches and worship openly in them would have been granted soon after. More important still, had Charles been able to dispense with the law in religious affairs, the way would have been clear for him to use similar methods in political matters, and at last set up the absolutist monarchy which all the Stuart kings of England desired. The King also took the commonsense view that these awkward people who had refused to conform despite persecution for the past 12 years had better be recognized and allowed to worship in the open. This is mentioned in the preamble to the Declaration:

'. . . we hope . . . for preventing for the future the danger that might otherwise arise from private meetings and seditious conventicles.' [1]

Under the Declaration all penal laws 'in matters ecclesiastical' were suspended, for Protestants and Catholics alike. Public places of worship were allowed only to the Protestant Dissenters, who had to register both the place and the minister officiating there.

It is from the licences to meet and preach that information is obtained on the numbers and position of Dissenters in the year 1672/3. The largest numbers of licences were granted for London, Lancashire, the Midland counties, and the South West. In the counties of Cornwall, Devon, Dorset and Somerset 263 licences to Nonconformists are recorded. The Presbyterians had 192 of these, compared with only 169 in London itself. The Independents were relatively weak in the South West, having 37 licences. In Devon there were 83 licences granted to Presbyterians, 19 to Independents, and 3 to Baptists. The last named seldom bothered to apply for licences, which explains why so few were given to them.[2] The Quakers refused to acknowledge the royal supremacy in religious affairs, in any case, and the Declaration made no difference to them. They did benefit from the amnesty granted to those previously imprisoned under the Acts against Nonconformists.

The first reaction in Devon was a series of addresses of thanks to the King for the relief granted. On 22nd March 72 Devon ministers signed such a petition, the names including many of those known to have been active in Exeter. This was presented to the King on the 6th April by John Hickes and T. Martin, both of Plymouth. Hickes took an active part in obtaining licences for West Country ministers, taking up residence in London during part of the year 1672 for this purpose.

One of the first men to petition for a licence to preach was Lewis Stucley, granted on 2nd April, 1672.[3] Amongst the licence documents preserved in the Public Record Office is one from his followers in Exeter. It is a fair sample of the multitude of similar addresses being presented by Dissenters all over the nation:

To the Kings most Excellent Matie: the Cordiall acknowledgmt. & humble Petition of a Church of Christ in Exeter.

---

[1] *English Historical Documents*, Vol. 8, pp. 387–8.
[2] Calendar of State Papers, Domestic Series, 1673. Survey of the Licence Documents.
[3] Turner, G. L. Original records, etc. Licence documents are given in full in Vols. 2–3.

Humbly Sheweth, That yor. Maties. late declaracon for the suspencon of the execucon of the Penall Statutes against Non-Conformity & for indulging us in or. publike Worship and Devotion in places you. Matie, shall aprove of, Hath abundantly refreshed or. weary spiritts, hath given us great inducemt. to blesse God in yor. Maties. behalf; And hath layed on us the deepest obligacons to serve yor. Matie. with our Lives and Fortunes. Wee cannot but looke on yor. Matie. as the breath of or. Nostrills, as a Repairer of or. breaches, & a Restorer of Paths to dwell in: May it please yor. Matie. soe far to condiscend to yor. Maties. faithful and Loyall subjects and to give yor. Royal Grant & favr. that Mr. Lewes Stucley be allowed by yor. Matie. to be or. Teacher in an howse belonging to Mr. Nicholas Savery in the said Citty of Exeter. And the said Mr. Stucley and yor. Peticonrs. shall ever Pray for yor. Maties. longe Prosperous and Peaceable Raigne, and that God will be pleased to requite yor. Maties. remembring of us in or. Low Condicon.

There were 38 names attached to this address. This is first-hand evidence of a Congregational church in Exeter in this year. Nicholas Savery, whose house was the place of meeting, was referred to in Sessions records as a linendraper in the parish of St. Petrock. He was assessed on 7 hearths in the 1671 Hearth Tax, and his brother Thomas on 6 hearths. Whether the house in which the church met was also in this parish is not apparent: the place of meeting after 1689 was in Castle Lane. Nicholas Savery, and certain others of the signatories (William Packer, Thomas Dare, and the wife of Peter Menteir or Manheare) were summoned before the magistrates in July, 1669, for assembling illegally with some 30 unknown persons. Some of the names of those prosecuted at that time are different from those on the Stucley Petition of 1672, and as this latter petition was not signed by a single woman, it can be confidently asserted that between 100 and 150 people were members of the Independent Church in Exeter at this time. These would be those who had accepted the teaching of Stucley, Mall and Powell in the 1650s, and their descendants. Powell, although licensed as an Independent teacher in Exon., had spent several years in London, and probably went back there soon afterwards, for his wife was buried at St. Mary Aldermanbury in 1679. Mall had left the City after the passing of the Five Mile Act.

The Presbyterians are more difficult to sum up. These were the Ministers and houses licensed in Exeter:

1. Robert Atkins. 2nd April. For his own house and at John Palmer's.
2. John Bartlett. 2nd April. For his own house and Anthony Smith's. Also given a general licence to preach at any licensed place.

3. Benjamin Berry. 11th April. For his own house and Thomas Sheers'. He was the ejected curate of Trull. St. Mary Magdalene, Taunton, and later settled at Topsham.

4. William Crompton. 13th April. For any allowed place. He had been ejected from the living of Cullompton.

5. Mark Down. 30th April. A general licence, and for his own house and for Nowel Pearse's house.

6. Thomas Ford. 30th April. For his own house, and for Thomas Crispyn's. Said only to be able to preach twice afterwards because of ill-health.

7. Robert Gaylard or Gillard. 11th April. General licence.

8. John Gidley. 20th April. General licence. A modest man, who remained always in the background.

9. Joseph Hallett I. 22nd May. Licensed for the house of Mr. Pym. One report states that it was at this time that he came to Exeter.

10. John Hill. 30th April. A general licence.

11. Edward Hunt. 11th April. General licence. He was the ejected Rector of Dunchideock, and had been living peaceably in St. Thomas' parish since 1665. By 1690 he had moved to South Molton.

12. John Mortimer. 11th April. General licence. Had been ejected from Sowton.

13. Thomas Trescott. 11th April. Licence for his own house and for John Boyland's.

14. George Trosse. 30th April. A general licence.

15. Alexander Robinson. 11th April. General licence. Had been ejected from Porlock, and had a nephew, David Robinson, a grocer in Exeter. Not known how long he remained in the City, but his will was made in Barnstaple on 18th August, 1687.

Besides these 15 cases, there were two houses licensed without the preachers being named.

On 25th May, 1672, Edward Hutchinson prayed for a licence to teach Congregationalists at the house of Adam and Samuel Pearse in Exon., and for his own house at Bishop's Clyst. As Adam Pearse's house had already been licensed on 10th May as an Anabaptist Meeting, we may assign Hutchinson to the Baptist meeting, which still struggled on despite small numbers and lack of help from the other Nonconformist sects. The authorities at this stage did not always distinguish clearly between Congregationalist and Baptist: the form of church government being the same in both cases.

One other licence was granted in Exeter, to a certain Robert Heins, at an unspecified date, and of an unspecified denomination.

Ministers previously recorded as active in Exeter, but not there in 1672, were:

1. John Hopping. Licensed as Presbyterian on 9th May at Christow.
2. Francis Bampfield. 29th June. General licence. He had previously been released from prison, and had baptized himself in the river at Salisbury. He was a Baptist by this time, although he had begun his religious pilgrimage as a Prebendary of Exeter Cathedral in 1641.
3. Robert Carel. No date given. Presbyterian, at house of Mary Kendall at Cofton.
4. Richard Herring. General licence, as Presbyterian, near Exon. This would be either at Perridge, Kenn, or at Ide, though he is said to have preached sometimes in the city at the house of Mr. John Mayne. He had been ejected from Drewsteignton.
5. John Jordan. 11th April. Presbyterian. Near Newton.

The total for the city of Exeter was 15 Presbyterians, 2 Congregationalists, and 1 Baptist, granted licences to preach under the Declaration of Indulgence of 1672, together with one of unspecified allegiance, In addition there were 5 Presbyterians and 1 Congregationalist near at hand who had all had previous associations with Exeter, one of whom, John Hopping, later returned to the city to work. The names of those whose houses were used as meeting-places were those like Thomas Crispyn and Nicholas Savery whom we know were the lay leaders of the Nonconformists from the frequency with which their names appear in Sessions records. It is difficult to estimate what proportion of the population followed these men. It is unlikely that all the ministers had the following of Stucley. From the prominence of George Trosse and Joseph Hallett I later on it may be assumed that they were at this time the most active of the Presbyterians. Robert Atkins and Thomas Trescot were the two next most active. John Bartlett (d. 1677), Mark Down (d. 1680), Thomas Ford (d. 1676), and John Hill (d. 1682) were now old men, probably very willing to allow younger colleagues to take the lead.

Taking into account that the Presbyterians were generally accepted to outnumber the Independents by at least 4 to 1, and that at the end of the period of persecution Exeter Dissenters exercised considerable weight in municipal elections, the figure of 1000 persons as being of the Presbyterian persuasion in 1672 in unlikely to be too high. With the addition of about 200 Congregationalists and Baptists, this becomes 1200. The Poll Tax figures for 1660 suggest that the population of Exeter in that year was about 13,500 people. By this reckoning, at the time of Charles II's Declaration of Indulgence one person in every twelve in the city of Exeter was a Nonconformist.

The picture of Church affairs in Exeter in the period of the Declaration of Indulgence is completed by Bishop Anthony Sparrow. Writing to his superior on 2nd September, 1672, he said:

May it please your Grace,
. . . the account I can give at present is this, that in divers places the Churches are not so well fild as lately they were, the seducers are many and busy, more heerabouts than in any other parts that I can hear of. Yet the govermt. of this City stands as firme as ever, & the best & most of the Gentry, and now the Judges have given such good directions, and appeard so earnest in the behalf of the church & the laws, that I hope it will give a check to the insolence of our enemies. . . .

CHAPTER III

THE SECOND PERIOD OF PERSECUTION, 1673–1687

THE royal experiment of granting toleration to religious opinions differing from those of the Established Church, by means of the Dispensing Powers traditionally invested in the Crown, proved unacceptable to Parliament. Not only was the withdrawal of the Declaration of Indulgence demanded in March, 1673, but Parliament immediately proceeded to pass 'An Act for Preventing Dangers which may happen from Popish Recusants' (25 Car. II, cap. 2), the First Test Act. This excluded both Catholics and Nonconformists from offices under the Crown, and was followed in 1678 by a Second Test Act which prevented Catholics from sitting in either House of Parliament. Further, if Parliament had been allowed a free hand it would have excluded the King's brother from the succession to the throne, as an avowed Catholic. Charles' handling of the Popish Plot crisis prevented this and he was able to bequeath his crown to James under favourable conditions, with royal power and popularity at a height never exceeded since before the Civil Wars.

Reactions to the withdrawal of the Declaration of Indulgence varied. Nonconformist historians have differed in their accounts of this period. A study of the orders of Exeter City Sessions fining persons for assembling in Conventicles reveals conclusively that here the withdrawal of the Indulgence was quickly followed by a severe renewal of persecution. There are 30 of these orders preserved in the City Archives for the period 1673–87, and a further 14 entries in the Sessions Rolls referring to summonses issued in connection with Nonconformist activities. When arranged according to dates the figures are:

1673—8 cases		1681—3 cases	
1674—4 „		1682—4 „	
1675—2 „		1683—3 „	
1676—2 „		1684—1 case	
1677—1 case		1685—5 cases (2 refer to same)	
1678—0 cases		1686—4 „	
1679—2 „		1687—1 case	
1680—4 „			

The eight orders for 1673 all concern the period from 14th May to 11th August. The parchments bear examination in some detail.

The first is an order fining persons for assembling in a conventicle at the house of John Palmer, merchant, in the Cathedral Close, on Wednesday, 14th May, 1673. Proceedings were under the 1670 Conventicle Act, for the householder, Palmer, and the preacher, Joseph Hallett I, were both fined the statutory £20 each, while the remainder were fined 5s. each. Two of those named, Anthony Mapowder and Isaac Burch (both brewers) had the fines of 30 people transferred to them, and paid £4 each.

The second order refers to another conventicle held at the house of John Palmer on 4th June, and again he was fined £20, and the preacher, George Trosse, the same, 5 others are named and 50 others, too poor to pay, were said to have been present, their fines being imposed on three of the 5 named, Richard Crossinge, Esq., John Mayne, merchant, and John Starr, merchant.

The magistrates made two orders on the 23rd of June, the first relating to a conventicle held at the house of Humphrey Bawdon in Holy Trinity parish on Sunday the 15th of June. Again the householder, and the preacher, Mark Downe, were fined £20 each. There were 29 other named persons in the list, and 60 more unnamed were present, of whom 20 were said to be insolvent and their fines added to those of people better able to pay. The other order concerned a conventicle at the house of John Boyland, fuller, on Sunday 22nd June. Boyland and George Trosse were each fined £20, 36 others were named, and 40 more unnamed said to have been present. In this document Trosse is stated to have been unable to pay (it was the second fine of £20 imposed on him within a month) and his fine was divided amongst 6 of the others, Christopher Payne, butcher, Hugh Abell, grocer, Benjamin Arundell, merchant, Daniel Skibbowe, fuller, John Starr, merchant, and Andrew Jeffery, fuller. The fines of 20 of those unnamed were added to those of others most able to pay.

A most comprehensive haul was made by the magistrates at the house of John Palmer on Wednesday, 25th of June, Palmer and Hallett were again each fined £20, and in the list of 43 other persons named in the order appear John Bartlett, John Hopping, George Trosse (all Presbyterian ministers), Lewis Stucley and Thomas Powell (Congregationalist ministers). Hallett was unable to pay, and his fine was divided among John Pym, merchant, Edmund Starr, grocer, Abraham Trowte, merchant, John Boyland, fuller, Christopher Payne, butcher,

George Masters, butcher, William Lobb, fuller, and Richard Crossinge, merchant. Eleven people had their fines doubled because it was their second offence.

The unfortunate John Palmer suffered for another conventicle held at his house on Wednesday, 2nd July, when the preacher was John Hixe (more usually spelt Hicks). Thirty-nine more were named and fined, this time 18 for the second offence. The minister's fine was shared by John Pym, merchant, Thomas Crispyn, fuller, John Boyland, fuller, Elizabeth Gibbs, widow, Anthony Mapowder, brewer, John Cheares, fuller, John Barnes, innkeeper, Joseph Pince, fuller, and Abraham Trowte, merchant.

George Trosse was fined £20 for the third time for preaching at a conventicle held on 6th July at the house of Nowel Pearse, fuller. 14 others were mentioned by name, and 50 others said to have been present. The fine of 20 of these unnamed people were added to those paid by persons cited.

Nowel Pearse suffered for another conventicle held at his house on Monday, 11th August, but this time no minister was summoned by the magistrates. 30 others are named, 40 unnamed, of whom the fines of 15 were added to those cited.

This is evidence enough that the Exeter magistrates, encouraged no doubt by Bishop Anthony Sparrow, used the powers of the 1670 Conventicle Act to the full in this 25th year of the reign of Charles II. It would seem also that they profited by the very information provided by the Dissenters themselves, in the licenses taken out under the Declaration of Indulgence. The preachers and householders fined the maximum penalty under these orders were:

Joseph Hallett l	(Twice)
George Trosse	(Three times).
Mark Downe	
John Hicks	
John Palmer	(Four times)
Humphrey Bawdon	
John Boyland	
Nowell Pearse	(Twice).

Hallett, Trosse, and Downe have already appeared. John Hicks was not an Exeter man, but was well known in South Devon, having been evicted in 1662 from a curacy at Saltash, and he had published anonymously and without licence in 1671 a 'Narrative' of the sufferings of local Nonconformists. He had been licensed as a Presbyterian preacher at Kingsbridge in 1672. Later he removed to Portsmouth, and was

D

executed in 1685 for taking part in the Monmouth Rebellion. His part in the negotiations with the King for Indulgence licences has already been noted. He was definitely the type of man that Anglican magistrates throughout the country were delighted to be able to sentence in their courts.

The houses of John Palmer, John Boyland, and Nowell Pearse were all licensed as meeting places in 1672, and all were men of some wealth. In the Exeter Hearth Tax records of 1671, Palmer's house in the Close was assessed on 9 hearths, Boyland's in St. John's parish on 6 hearths, and Pearse's in the parish of All-Hallows-on-the-Walls on 5 hearths. Not licensed in 1672 in Exeter, Humphrey Bawdon was assessed on 10 hearths in Holy Trinity Parish. At this time more than half the households in the city had 2 hearths or less, and so it is clear that these men, although not of the inner circle of very rich merchants who governed the city, were comparatively well-to-do, and exercised some influence in the community through the men in their employ. It was at this type of citizen, those who were the financial backbone of the Nonconformist causes, that the Conventicle Act of 1670 was aimed, and it was effectively used in Exeter in this year.

It is an interesting fact that these prosecutions were all aimed at known Presbyterians. Stucley and Powell, Congregationalists, had each been fined for attending the conventicle at Palmer's house on 25th June, 1673, but this was the small sum of 5s. each, of little significance to them. Stucley evidently went to his relations at Bideford, whence he wrote in September, that he was afraid to return to Exeter, lest a warrant under the Five Mile Act 'should confine me as it hath lately Mr. Hallet'.[1] He was confusing two pieces of legislation, for Hallett's conviction was under the Conventicle Act. It was not until 1674 that Congregationalists were fined heavily. Then Nicholas Eveleigh, whose house had been licensed in 1672, was fined £20 for a conventicle held at his home on 18th January. The hardest blow came on 8th November, in connection with another conventicle held in Eveleigh's house. He and Stucley were then each fined £20. 16 others were named, and 40 others said to have been present.

That the attack on the Presbyterians had not been relaxed is shown by an order dated 11th November, 1674, dealing with a conventicle held at Nowel Pearse's house on 8th November, a Sunday. Both Pearse and John Hopping were fined £20. 23 people were named in this order, and 80 others said to have been present.

[1] Calamy Revised, by A. G. Matthews; Stucley.

The conclusions to be drawn from these cases in 1673–4 are that in Exeter after the withdrawal of the Declaration of Indulgence the Penal Laws against Dissenters were immediately enforced with more than usual zeal; that the informers and magistrates made use of their knowledge of licences taken out by the Dissenters while the Declaration was in force; and that they selected their victims with care, choosing to strike first at those they knew to be the leaders.

Meanwhile, Bishop Sparrow had been trying to put his own house in order. In a letter to the Archbishop, dated 30th September, 1674, he claimed:

I have made a strict inquiry into the behaviour of the clergy, and . . . there is no ground for the loud complaint of a scandalous Clergy . . . I have found but four in the whole Diocese that deserve that censure & those poor men in scandalous livings.'

The Bishop ended on a well satisfied note when he added:

The Corporations in Cornwall are generally very conformable to the church, and few Conventicles in the country. The Villages in Devon as quiet & orderly as in Cornwal, but some Corporations there I finde more factious, & yet I doubt not, but that in a little time, we shal finde a reformation, if that they finde not too much incouragement elsewhere.

The appointment of Thomas Lamplugh, a moderate man, as Bishop of the Diocese in the autumn of 1676, suggested that a relaxation of the pressure on Dissenters might follow. Lamplugh had taken the Covenant under the Commonwealth, thereby retaining his Fellowship of Queen's College, Oxford, throughout the Interregnum. At the same time he secretly did all he could to help the royal cause, with which his real sympathies lay. As Bishop he at times pursued the same policy, in the opposite direction, retaining his office throughout the reign of James II, and then making his peace with William III, becoming Archbishop of York from December 1688 until his death on 5th May, 1691.[1] Lamplugh's treatment of John Hopping is illustrative of his character. The Bishop,

. . . being desirous to gain him to the Church sent for him to his Palace in Exon; and . . . promis'd him safe Ingress and Egress. When he came, his good Lordship . . . bade him read Hooker's Ecclesiastical Polity. Mr. Hoppin replied, That from a position in that Book, it appear'd that Hooker himself, were he now alive, must be a Nonconformist. The Bishop took down the

[1] Devon & Cornwall Notes and Queries, Vol. 22, p. 76 (1942).

Book and asked him, Where it was? But tho' he had not read it in many Years before, it yet happen'd that he dipp'd upon the very Place, which his Lordship read, and clapping fast the Book again, said no more, but with his usual Passion, said, Go your way: I promis'd you indeed safe Conduct out and home, but afterwards look to yourself. And not long afterwards he was apprehended, and cast into the South-Gate Prison . . . where he was detain'd six months . . . and thereby got such a Rheumatism, as rendered him a perfect Cripple to the Day of his Death: So that he was carried to the Pulpit constantly in a Chair, and liv'd many Years in Misery.[1]

From this we may surmise that the Bishop's desire to effect a reconciliation did not amount to more than a hope of avoiding personal unpleasantness. At all events, even at the time when, in other parts of the country, the excitement of the Popish Plot had diverted attention away from the Dissenters, they were not so neglected in Exeter. On the 17th October, 1675, both Thomas Crispyn and Richard White were fined £20 for conventicles held at their houses on that date. Crispyn and White both appear on the Hearth Tax Lists in 1671 as being resident in the parish of St. Kerrian, together with some other men believed to have been Presbyterians. This would appear to have been one of the centres of Nonconformity in the city in the seventeenth century, and, as will be shown later, one of the three Presbyterian Meetings set up after 1687 was in this parish. In May, 1676, John Pym, merchant, was again fined £20 for a conventicle at his house, and he incurred a further fine of £3 5s. in the following September in connection with a meeting surprised at Crispyn's house. Crispyn was then fined £20, Robert Tristram £4 10s., Joan Goddard, widow, £2 5s., and Thomas Dowdall, clothier, £1 5s. For another meeting at Crispyn's house on Sunday, 30th September, 1677, fines were levied on one hundred and eleven persons.

A different kind of petty persecution of Nonconformists took place in 1678 and 1679. In 1678 Nowell Pearse, whom we know was one of the Presbyterian laymen prominent from 1672 onwards, was elected one of the Stewards of the City. He refused to accept the office, probably fearing prosecution under the Corporation Act of 1661. He was fined for refusing to execute his duties as a citizen. In 1679 came similar cases. These men were unwilling to resort to the expedient of Occasional Conformity—taking the Sacrament according to the Anglican rite in order to qualify for election to municipal office. That this was not always the case is easily shown. In 1674 Simon Trobridge

---

[1] Calamy Revised; John Hopping.

was elected Bailiff and did not refuse. Again in 1677 his example was followed by John Boyland.[1]

Continuing the catalogue of penalties imposed, Robert Atkins was fined £9 15s. in connection with a conventicle at his house on the 28th April, 1676.[2] Two well-attended meetings on consecutive Sundays, 23rd and 30th of November, 1679, both at the house owned by Roger Light in the parish of St. George, were dealt with severely. Light, a weaver, was fined £20 on each occasion. Joseph Hallett I, the preacher concerned, was fined £40 for the first meeting, this being recorded as his 'second' offence. These two meetings were referred to by Bishop Lamplugh, writing to Archbishop Sancroft on the 24th of April, 1680:

The Meeting house lately erected was presented this Sessions and is now put down. One Hallet a very pernicious fellow, who used to preach there, doth abscond, they searched his house for him last Wednesday, but could not find him.'

This letter is important because it seems to refer to a definite building being erected for a Meeting-house, as distinct from a meeting held in a private house belonging to one of the Nonconformist leaders. The phrase 'now put down' suggests that the meeting-house was literally wrecked by the authorities, not just that the congregation was dispersed. As will be seen, it was in the parish of St. George that the second largest of the Presbyterian chapels was built after 1687: this may have been a forerunner. No less than 183 persons attended a conventicle at the house of Robert Atkins on Sunday, 25th April, 1680.

The magistrates were very active in this year 1680. In June a small conventicle was discovered at the house of John Pope, in St. Petrock's parish, which cost that merchant £20. In July Robert Atkins suffered once more, in the company of 23 others. An order of the 23rd of December dealt with the only case of Quakers meeting in the city which came before the magistrates. 44 people were cited, but only 6 of these were Exeter residents, including William Gravett, in whose house in St. Sidwell's parish the meeting had been held on the 30th September previously.

The pattern changed little from this year until the end of the persecution in 1687. Of the cases dealt with under the 1670 Conventicle Act

[1] Izacke, R., *Remarkable Antiquities of the City of Exeter*, 2nd edn., by S. Izacke, 1724, pp. 178 and 181.
[2] Calamy Revised; Robert Atkins.

there were meetings involving 90 persons at Thomas Boyland's house on 3rd July, 1681; 17 people at the house of Joshua Branscombe, locksmith, on 24th July, 1681; 63 at Robert Atkins' house again on 9th July, 1682; 39 at the house of Elianor Starr, All-Hallows-on-the-Walls, on 29th October, 1682; 22 at the house of Arthur (Anthony?) Downe, on 5th October, 1685; 157 at the house of John Hopping on 6th February, 1686; and 144 at the house of John Guswell on 6th March, 1687.

The conventicle broken up at Anthony Downe's house in October, 1685, was described by George Trosse himself, one of the three ministers who were arrested on that occasion.[1]

We were discover'd by a malignant Neighbour, who went and inform'd against us to the Magistrates, who were then at Feast with the Mayor of the City. Hereupon no less than Three Magistrates, with Constables, and some of the baser and ruder Sort, came to find us out and seize us. After they had search'd an house or two, at length they discover'd our little Meeting, and found about Twenty People, of whom Three were Aged Ministers, and I the Youngest of them. They gave us hard language, and treated us as if we had been the worst of Malefactors. The Ministers were committed to the Care of the Constables, to be by them sentenc'd to be sent to Goal, unless we would take the Oath . . . [the Oxford Oath] . . . We refus'd that Oath . . . Then, they reply'd, 'You must go to prison'. I pleaded, That the Act did not extend to me, because the Law expressly says: 'That he must either be a Non-conformist turn'd out for Nonconformity, or one convicted of keeping Conventicles'. Now I was obnoxious upon neither of these Accounts: for I never had a Benefice to be turn'd out of, neither was ever legally convicted of keeping Conventicles. But . . . yet they committed me to Prison, without any Law to warrant what they did.

Trosse must have emphasized the phrase 'legally convicted' in his own mind when writing this passage, for as we have seen, he was thrice fined sums of £20 in the year 1673. The eldest of these three ministers, Anthony Down (ejected from Northam in 1662) did later agree to take the Oath, but Trosse and Robert Gillard went to Prison, where they found three other ministers already incarcerated for non-payment of fines: John Searle of Plympton, Joseph Hallett I, and John Hopping.

Conditions in the South Gate Prison, although unpleasant, were not unendurable for prisoners with friends outside. Trosse related:

We were not confin'd strictly to our Apartments, but were allow'd the

[1] Trosse, G., *Life*, 1714, p. 93.

Liberty of walking in the common-Hall and in the Garden. Our Victuals were brought to the Prison to us. Fourteen wealthy Friends by turns sent us a Dinner every day. In the Night Season, having a Bed to myself, I found my Meditation upon God in Christ more pleasing and delightful than ever I had done before, at least for Frequency.

The Monmouth Rebellion in 1685 affected the Exeter Dissenters very little. This is surprising, as the Dissenters in the towns in the immediate path of Monmouth's army, in Lyme, Axminster, Chard, Taunton, and Bridgwater, eagerly joined him. The Independents of Axminster supported the rebellion wholeheartedly, the son of one of their former ministers, John Ashwood, only narrowly escaping with his life. When the dreaded visit of Judge Jeffreys to Exeter took place, on the 14th September, 1685, only 14 men were sentenced to death, and two of these were afterwards pardoned. Of these 12 who were hanged, only 2 suffered this penalty in Exeter itself, and can therefore be assumed to have been Exeter men. Their names were Thomas Broughton and John Foweracres. There is no evidence that either of them were Dissenters. In addition to the men hanged, there were 8 rebels sentenced at Exeter to transportation to the colonies, and another 12 were found guilty of uttering seditious words and were given varying sentences of fines, imprisonment or whipping. Only one of those sentenced to transportation may have been an Exeter Dissenter. This is John Follett, who was assigned with 5 others to Jerome Nipho, the Queen's secretary, acting as agent for the colonists. A John Follett, a woolcomber, had been fined 5s. for attending a conventicle at the house of Thomas Crispyn, on Sunday, 30th of September, 1677.[1]

During these years of persecution more of the older generation of Nonconformist ministers was passing away. Thomas Ford was buried in St. Lawrence's on the 28th December, 1676; John Bartlett at St. Mary Major, his former church, on 15th June, 1680, and on the 7th October of the same year Mark Down was put to rest in St. Petrock's. John Hill, licensed in Exeter in 1672, was buried at Wolborough on 5th September, 1682, and Thomas Trescott died on 26th December, 1684. On 2nd April, 1685, died Robert Atkins, followed in July, 1687, by Lewis Stucley, who had retired to Abbotsham, in North Devon, by that time.

After 25 years of persecution a generation of Dissenters was coming to the fore which had not known anything but Nonconformity, and had not that strong desire for reunion with the Church of England

[1] Muddiman, J. G., ed. The Bloody Assizes, Edinburgh, 1929 (Famous Trials Series).

which had been present in their elders in 1662. The newcomers desired freedom to worship in their own way without interruption and were determined to continue struggling to reach that goal. The persecution under the later Stuarts was hard enough to provide a very real challenge to the existence of Nonconformity as a way of life, yet not hard enough to smother it completely. By responding to the challenge presented to them, the Dissenters not only survived as an organization, but emerged far stronger than before. The aged ministers who had died during this period were replaced by men ordained secretly, like George Trosse and Joseph Hallett II, and later by younger men who had pursued their studies either at the Nonconformist Academies or abroad in the Netherlands. For example, immediately following the 1687 Declaration of Indulgence of James II, on 25th August the ordination took place at Lyme Regis of Bernard Starr (of an Exeter family), Christopher Taylor, Richard Towell of Dulverton, Isaac Gilling (who will appear many times later) Josiah Woodcock, Thomas Hoare, John Goswell (also of Exeter) and John Edwards. The ordaining ministers were Samuel Tapper, Thomas Crane, Matthew Warren (head of the Taunton Academy) and Ames Short, all of whom were Bartholomaeans. Ames Short had been carrying on a small Academy at Lyme Regis, and on 2nd October, 1682, he had been arrested at the house of John Starr in Exeter, and imprisoned for six months. He was stated to have been teaching about this time, and had as pupils the sons of 'Three considerable persons in Exeter', Gregory Brewen, Bernard, son of John Starr, and Benjamin, son of Paul Draper, and had also taken the son of Robert Atkins (Samuel) for training.

To sum up, the period of 1673–87 was one of renewed and extended persecution of the Nonconformists, which seems to have been more severe in Exeter than in some other parts of the country. Yet it was never severe enough to have much prospect of causing a large-scale return to the Church of England. Rather did it confirm the Nonconformists in their determination to resist the laws aimed against them, and the ties formed amongst them by enduring suffering together carried them forward united, once Toleration had come, into the period of their greatest prosperity and influence.

CHAPTER IV

'FREEDOM AFTER EJECTION', 1687-1690

THE fining of John Goswell £20 for a conventicle held in his house in St. Olave's parish on 6th March, 1687, attended by 144 persons, was the last prosecution within the city of Exeter under the Acts against the Nonconformists. On 4th April, James II issued his First Declaration of Indulgence, suspending the operation of all the 'penal laws in matters ecclesiastical', for both Protestant Dissenters and Roman Catholics. It was a more generous measure than that of 1672–3 for, apart from the equal freedom now allowed to Catholics, there was no question of licences having to be obtained before the Nonconformists could practise their religious observances. There is no doubt of the motive of the King in issuing his Declaration. He clearly states, at the beginning of the second paragraph,

'We cannot but heartily wish, as it will easily be believed, that all the people of our dominions were members of the Catholic Church.'

The Declaration was explicitly renewed in the following April, 1688.[1]

The reaction of the Protestant Dissenters was not wholly favourable. It was quite natural that they should welcome the end of official persecution. Yet their hatred of all included under the term 'Popery' was so great that some were willing to continue to suffer themselves rather than exempt Catholics from their disabilities. In fact most of the Dissenters accepted the Declaration, and began to hold their services and other activities openly; some even sent addresses of thanks to the King for his favour.[2] The situation was aptly summed up by George Trosse, of Exeter: when the news of the Declaration reached Exeter he found that:

. . . all the Nonconforming Ministers in the City beside accepted it to preach in the very Time of publick Worship upon the Lord's Day; yet I forbore it, because I was under Apprehensions that the Design of the King was to withdraw the People from the Publick, and so to weaken the Party of the Church of England, whom if he had once brought into Contempt, the Dissenters would have been easily crush'd . . . Wherefore I . . . declin'd preaching on the Lord's Days till the Prelatical Worship in the Afternoons was ended; tho' I sometimes preached on other Days, and administer'd the

---

[1] *English Historical Documents*, Vol. 8, pp. 395–6.   [2] Ibid., p. 397.

Lord's Supper as usual. I was resolv'd, that if the Magistrates should disturb any of the Meetings where I preach'd, and proceed against me as a Conventicler, I would rather have suffer'd than have pleaded the King's Licence, which I thought contrary to the Subjects Liberty establish'd by Law, and as having a direct Tendency to overthrow our Religion.[1]

By so doing he got little credit from either side, as often happens with moderate men. This passage, as compared with the Address of the followers of Stucley in 1672 is an interesting revelation of the degree of trust inspired by the royal brothers. The Dissenters of 1672 were willing to regard Charles II as a friend: in 1687 they were well aware of the true intentions of James II, although prepared in most cases to accept what benefits were going despite the motive behind them.

Before considering the growth of the Dissenting societies in Exeter in detail, it is first desirable to relate their reactions to the far-reaching changes on the national stage in the years 1687–9. While the Exeter Dissenters seem hardly to have noticed the Monmouth Rebellion and its consequences, the crisis of 1688 affected them directly.

Charles II had demanded the surrender of Exeter's municipal charter in 1683, along with those of corporate towns, taking advantage of the royalist reaction at the end of the Popish Plot agitation. The new Charter gave the Crown power to nominate the city officers and councillors. High Church royalists had been nominated for the most part, and one of these, John Snell, had been elected Mayor for 1687–8. By this time, however, James II was committed to his new policy of religious toleration, having issued his first Declaration of Indulgence in April, 1687. Accordingly an order of Privy Council was sent to Exeter on the 28th November, 1687, removing Snell, and the majority of his fellow Alderman and Councillors, from office, and requiring the election of 'Thomas Jefford, Esq; to be Mayor'.

Jefford was not a Nonconformist, but many of the other nominees of the Crown had been among those fined at various times for Nonconformity. These were Edmund Starr and Humphry Bawdon, of the new Aldermen; John Starr, John Pym, John Boyland, Jeremiah (or Jerome) King, Robert Tristram, Tobias Allen (or Allyn), and Hugh Bidwell.[2] There is no record of serious opposition to the King's order in the city, and Jefford and his colleagues continued in office until the fall of James II. One of his last desperate attempts to conciliate his opponents was a Proclamation restoring the ancient charters to cities

[1] Trosse, George, *Life*, 1714, p. 92.
[2] Izacke, R., pp. 183–7.

which had surrendered them, and his nominees in Exeter were then immediately replaced.

It is surprising that a city where over many years persecution of Dissenters by legal process had been continuous and accepted without major disturbance, should have accepted quietly this abrupt change in the situation in 1687. First came Toleration in religious affairs, and then dictation in municipal elections by the King, putting in control of civic affairs the very people who had been persecuted. One can only assume that the citizens of Exeter were rather more concerned with their business affairs than with either politics or religion. The High Church Party and the Presbyterians were evenly matched in Exeter, and the influence of the King, cast on either side, was enough to carry the day.

When James II reissued his Declaration of Indulgence in April, 1688, he made an Order in Council that it should be read in all churches at the time of Divine Service. This was more than many of the Anglican clergy, for all their belief in non-resistance to royal authority, could stand, and seven Bishops, headed by Archbishop Sancroft of Canterbury, refused to obey this order. The Bishop of Exeter, Dr. Lamplugh, was not one of these. A letter by Bishop Trelawny of Bristol, to Sancroft, dated 16th August, 1688, gives a report on what happened at Exeter, though admittedly by a hostile witness.

His Lordship . . . had giv'n order for the publishing the declarations . . . and was at last brought to recall them by the deanes sending him word that if he would betray the church he should not the cathedral, for he would rather be hang'd at the doors of it, than the declaration should be read there or in any part of his jurisdiction . . .[1]

It is difficult to separate religious from political motives at this period. Possibly the gentry and clergy who were vehement against the action of the King were inspired not so much by their dislike of Dissenters, nor even by their hatred of Roman Catholics, both of which feelings were very real, but rather by their fear of the King's assumption of absolute power in the country, and his evident intention to rule in the future in the grand manner, like his cousin in France. But whatever the reason, the result was beneficial to the Protestant Nonconformists. It became clear to the dominant Anglican party that in order to make certain of defeating the King's clear intention of establishing both his own absolute power and the Roman Catholic religion, the alliance of

[1] Devon and Cornwall Notes and Queries, 22, p. 168.

the Nonconformists was very desirable. The latter had always had more faith in Parliamentary than in Royal support, and were willing to make terms. There was therefore no opposition from Dissenters to the invitation to William of Orange in the summer of 1688.

One more attempt by James II to win over Nonconformist support, or at the very least to sow dissension amongst his Protestant opponents, has received little attention. Following the reissue of the Declaration of Indulgence in April, 1688, he issued a commission from the Court of Exchequer 'for inquiring after what moneys or goods have been levyed received or taken of or from any of his maiestys dissenting subjects in the County of . . . for any matter relating to religion since the 29th of September 1677'. The returns to this inquiry for Devon, including the city of Exeter, have been preserved in the Bodleian.[1] The more than 350 returns, some on printed forms, some in the plaintiffs' handwriting, all bear dates in July, August, and September, of 1688. It should be remembered that the birth of 'James III', and the acquittal of the Seven Bishops, both took place in June, 1688; these two events together are usually considered to mark the point at which the 'Glorious Revolution' became inevitable. Yet this Commission was operating through the summer months while preparations were going on, on both sides, for the coming of William and his Dutch army in the autumn. About one third of the entries in the Devonshire returns relate to Exeter people. They add very little to information already derived from Sessions records, but they do fit in very well with this information. The plaintiffs who came before the commissioners seem to have been for the most part humble people who were hopeful of regaining the small sums which had been levied on them in fines. That they in fact had no chance of obtaining anything was well known in some circles. On 19th August Mathias Combe, one of the Constables for Exeter, gave evidence:

The informant maketh oath that he was present in the house of Mr. Parsons, innkeeper at the New Inn . . . in ye beginning of August 1688 where Walter Phillips . . . and his wife came to . . . attend ye Commissioners . . . and this informant further states that Thomas Gibbons, Esq. . . . was then . . . present. Reflecting on the said Commission (he) spake these words to ye said Phillips & his wife saying what would you trouble yourselves not a farthing will come into your pocketts or words to that effect.

Walter Phillips was a Quaker. Mathias Combe considered he had a

[1] Bodleian MSS. Rawlinson D. 372.

grievance against authority. In 1680 he had been himself fined £5 for refusing to distrain on one Wm. Brown for attending a Conventicle, and he hoped now to get his money refunded.

During the slow progress of William's army from Brixham to London, the Exeter Presbyterians had to undergo one further trial, this time from one of their fellow Dissenters. Robert Ferguson (ejected from Godmersham in Kent in 1662) had been chaplain to Monmouth's army in 1685, had escaped, and now returned with William's expedition, but this time only in a subordinate capacity. The following passage tells the story:

At Exeter his chagrin at his subordinate place in the prince's expedition, compared with his dominant influence in Monmouth's counsels, seems to have got the better of his discretion. When Burnet was officiating before the prince in the cathedral, Ferguson asked to preach in the presbyterian church (James' Meeting). The keys were refused him, whereupon he resolved in his own words, to 'take the kingdom of heaven by violence' and, having broken open the door, ascended the pulpit sword in hand, and preached from the sixteenth verse of the 94th Psalm, 'Who will rise up for me against evildoers?' [1]

Ferguson lost any further expectation of reward from William, became a Jacobite, and was involved in several plots.

The reward for their forbearance and support during the crisis of 1688 came to the Nonconformists in 1689, in 'An Act for Exempting Their Majesties' Protestant Subjects Dissenting from the Church of England from the penalties of certain laws' (1 William & Mary, ch. 18.). From this time onwards, subject to certain conditions which were not rigorous, Nonconformists were able to organize their societies as they wished, free from legal penalties and interference. Under the Act, Meeting Places had to be certified to the Bishop of the Diocese, or to the Archdeacon of the Archdeaconry, or to the Justices at Quarter Sessions for the place where the meeting was to be held, and consequently registered in the Bishop's or Archdeacon's Court, or recorded at Quarter Sessions by the Clerk of the Peace. Registers thus made were very unreliable and no distinction was made between temporary and permanent meeting-houses. Statistical analyses of what records have survived would be valueless. To take an example outside Exeter (where the earliest of these records have not survived), in Bideford there were 11 places licensed by Dissenters between 1693 and 1732, but the Great Meeting-House in Bridgeland St. erected in 1696 for the Independents was not registered at all.[2]

[1] *D.N.B.*, Ferguson.   [2] *Trans. Cong. Hist. Soc.* Vol. 6, 1913–15, p. 199.

This Toleration Act, as it came to be called, did not exempt anyone from attending worship on Sundays: no relaxation of the Sunday Observance Act of 1677 was thought of. Yet prosecutions under it would inevitably become practically impossible, for it would be easy to evade Anglican services on the grounds of being a Dissenter, and vice-versa.

The position of the Quakers was further clarified by the 'Act in Relief of Quakers' of 1696 (7 & 8 William III, ch. 34) which explicitly provided for a solemn affirmation and declaration rather than the customary oath, to which the Friends had always objected.

The immediate reaction of the Exeter Presbyterians, the largest group of Dissenters in the city, to the 1687 Declaration of Indulgence, was to build their main Meeting-House. They called it James' Meeting, ironically enough when one considers the religious beliefs of the King. The actual building still stands (1960) converted into dwelling houses in James St., a narrow lane which connects the lower end of South St. with Coombe St. The Accounts Book of James' Meeting from 1687 until it closed down in 1760 has been preserved. The front leaf is headed:

Memorandum about a New Meeting house Built near Southgate in the City of Exon for the use of the Three United Congregations of Presbeterian [sic] Protestant Dissenters, Built 1687. The three Principall Undertakers in it were Mr. John Lavington, Mr. Andrew Jeffery, Mr. Thomas Heath, to whom was assistant Mr. Willm. Pool.

Andrew Jeffery has already been shown to have been one who suffered under persecution. John Lavington about this time became the owner of Larkbeare House, and was engaged in woollen manufactures, as were many of his colleagues. Another member of the family, Jonathan Lavington, was Master of the Company of Weavers, Fullers and Shearmen in 1700, and John's son Andrew was similarly honoured in 1717. Thomas Heath had been assessed on 10 hearths in Trinity parish in 1671. The total cost of the new chapel proved to be £442 14s. 7d. The first £279 of this was subscribed immediately, and the rest paid off from seat rents. Lavington himself gave £50, Andrew Jeffery £20 and Thomas Heath £10. The land was not freehold, for there is a memorandum to say:

. . . the sd. house is held of my Lady Walker paying yearly head rent £2 5s. in two separate leases, viz. the East parte is held by & during the natural lives of John Lavington, Clement Weekes Junr., Richard White,

Peter Chearse. The West Parte is held during the lives of Joseph Hallet, John Lavington, Daniel fforse, Junr., John Prew.

The capacity of this meeting-house can be roughly estimated. In 1715 it was claimed that James' Meeting had 1100 'Hearers'. If this was true, not all would attend at the same time for a service, and the chapel would most likely have been able to hold about 600 at any one time. This would only have been possible within the bounds of the building standing today if every possible inch of space within were fully used. This was, indeed, the practice in this first stage of Nonconformist architecture. Everything was sacrificed to the prime consideration of providing a forum for the preaching of the gospel. No attention what-ever was paid to aesthetic ideas: the object was to allow as many people as possible to hear the minister's sermon. Galleries would have been built around three sides of the building, and the pulpit, with its heavy sounding-board above the preacher's head to throw his words forward to the congregation, would have been on one of the long sides of the oblong-shaped chapel. A good example of this type of meeting-house is the Bowden-Hill Unitarian chapel at Crediton, which has changed little since its building in the first quarter of the eighteenth century.

The James' Meeting Accounts Book opens with a reference to the 'Three United Congregations'. The other two were known as Bow Meeting and the Little Meeting. The former took its name from its proximity to St. John's Bow parish church, from which the Rev. Robert Atkins, traditionally the founder of this society, was ejected in 1662. When the chapel was built, and its exact position, cannot be definitely proved. It has been shown that a conventicle meeting twice at the house of Roger Light in the parish of St. George was dealt with severely in November, 1679, and this may have been the forerunner of the Bow Meeting which emerged into the open after 1687. Answers to the Bishop's Primary Visitation Queries for the years 1744 (Clagett), 1764 (Keppel), and 1779 (Ross) show clearly that Bow Meeting was in the parish of St. George.[1] Taken in conjunction with the statements of Micaijah Towgood[2] and Jerom Murch[3] that it was near St. John's Bow, it must therefore have been at the nearest point of St. George's parish to this church. This would place Bow Meeting at the lower end

[1] Answers to Primary Visitation Queries, Exeter Diocesan Record Office.
[2] Letter of Micaijah Towgood to Josiah Thompson, in Thompson's Survey of Noncon-formity, 1773. MS. in Dr. Williams' Library.
[3] Murch, J., *History of the Presbyterians . . . in the West of England*, 1835.

of Smythen Street or the top of Stepcote Hill, on the eastern side of the roadway.

The Little Meeting can be placed in the same way. A survey of Protestant Dissenters over the whole country made in 1715[1] said that this third Presbyterian meeting was 'near North Gate'. This is supported by the Primary Visitation Returns of Bishop Clagett in 1744, which places Little Meeting in the parish of St. Kerrian. The matter is settled by a further survey of local Nonconformity in manuscript, made in the year 1794, which reveals that Little Meeting was in 'Theatre Lane'.[2] The first Theatre in Exeter was in Waterbeer Street, and while it was in existence the term 'Theatre Lane' was an alternative name for this narrow thoroughfare. The site of Little Meeting was therefore in the parish of St. Kerrian, on the north side of Waterbeer St. It is interesting to note that the Hearth Tax records of 1671 show that Peter Parr, Thomas Crispyn, Richard White, and John Starr, all Presbyterians and well-to-do citizens, were residents of St. Kerrian's parish. Richard White's daughter Susannah married George Trosse, and it is probable that the Little Meeting grew up around this group of Presbyterian families, and one of their own dwellings may have been adapted for a chapel.

These Presbyterian Meetings had four ministers between them. Two (originally Joseph Hallett I and George Trosse) were appointed to James' Meeting, and two others (originally John Hopping and Samuel Atkins) to Bow. The four took it in turn to preach at Little Meeting. The list of ministers at Bow Meeting is open to question, for Edmund Calamy reported that one of the first ministers of this society was Robert Gillard (or Gaylard). He was imprisoned with Trosse in 1685. Yet he does not appear in the Presbyterian records which have survived. It may have been that Gillard was too old by this time to be able to do very much, and that he was regarded as a 'minister emeritus'. He died in 1697. Samuel Atkins was the son of Robert Atkins, and had been baptized in 'East Peter's' on the 12th August, 1660.[3]

In order to co-ordinate matters of common interest, and to raise money for the payment of their Ministers, the Exeter Presbyterians elected a Committee representing all three meeting-houses. The

[1] Evans, John, Survey of Nonconformity in England and Wales, 1715. MS. in Dr. Williams' Library.
[2] Survey of Nonconformity in Devon in 1794, preserved in back of the first Minute Book of the Exeter Assembly. Handwriting resembles that of Rev. James Manning, minister at George's Chapel, 1776–1831.
[3] Calamy Revised, Atkins.

number of persons first chosen was thirteen, and it was invariably known later as the Committee of Thirteen. The earliest surviving Minute Book, which contains the accounts from 1708 and Minutes from 1722, both continued until 1760, bears the title 'The Committee to Administer the Fund for the Presbeterian Ministers in Exon, set up in 1687'. By its title, therefore, its sole function was to handle this Fund. However, it was inevitable that as time went on, being composed of the most influential members of the society, this Committee should obtain control of most of the business which had to be transacted. Vacancies in its membership were filled up not by open election, but by co-option. The first members were all men of good standing and wealth in the City or neighbourhood. First on the list was Thomas Bampfield, now a very old man, who had played a prominent part in the affairs of Exeter and England under the Commonwealth. Thomas Crispyn, Andrew Jeffery, and Joseph Pince, had all been before the magistrates under the Acts against Nonconformists, and each had served as Masters of the Company of Weavers, Fullers and Shearmen.[1] Abraham Trowte and John Pym were both described as Merchants in Sessions Records, and the same name would fit Benjamin Brinley (actually referred to as a Spicer of St. Martin's parish) and Jerome King, a grocer, better known as the father of Peter King, who later became Lord Chancellor. The other members were William Roper, a brewer of St. David's parish, John Munkly, a fuller, William Poole, a yeoman of St. Mary Arches, Benjamin Hawkings and Thomas Turner. Their total personal subscriptions to the Fund were £61 each year, or about one-fifth of the amount raised for ministers' salaries.

Not everyone who attended the Presbyterian meetings would be expected to subscribe regularly to the salaries of the ministers, nor even to the keeping in good repair of the chapel itself. The 'Payers' to the Ministers' Fund were at first those who were fairly well-to-do. The City was divided into Four Quarters, North, East, South and West, and one person was made responsible for the collection in each. The North Quarter included St. David's, and the West, St. Thomas. Later it was found desirable to divide both East and South Wards into two for easier administration, according to whether the people lived within or without the old City walls. The upkeep of the Chapel depended on the payment of Seat Rents, but a section of the building, usually in the Gallery, was set aside for the use of poorer members who

---

[1] (i) Exeter Sessions Records relating to Nonconformity. (ii) Cresswell, B., *Short history of the* ... *Weavers, Fullers and Shearmen of Exeter*, 1930. List of Masters.

E

were unable to pay. This was definitely done at George's Meeting after 1760, and the practice at that time seems to have been longstanding. The only other demand on the purses of members was in connection with the Poor Fund, organized by Quarters of the City in the same manner as the Ministers' Fund. Finances will be dealt with in some detail in a later section.

In addition to the three Presbyterian chapels there were in Exeter by 1691 Congregational, Baptist, Quaker and Huguenot societies. The short career of the Huguenot and Congregational churches may conveniently be dealt with here as a whole, although it takes the story beyond the dates fixed for this section. Lewis Stucley, founder of Exeter Congregationalism, had died in North Devon in July, 1687. His place as minister was taken by John Ashwood, son of Bartholomew Ashwood who had been expelled from the living of Axminster in February, 1661, to make room for the return of the previous Anglican incumbent. John Ashwood had worked at Axminster with his father for some years, and also at Chard. Like many other Axminster Independents he took part in the Monmouth Rebellion, had been captured, and only narrowly escaped execution.[1] He was definitely in Exeter in the year 1691, according to a survey made by the London Common Fund Board in that year. This was the Board set up under the terms of the 'Happy Union' which temporarily united Presbyterians and Congregationalists in the capital.[2] Ashwood stayed as minister of the Exeter Congregationalists, who had their Meeting-house in Castle Lane, until about 1698, when he moved to London, Two years later he was called to a church at Peckham in Surrey, remaining until his death at the age of 49, in 1706. There are no surviving records of the Castle Lane Meeting, and it is only possible to obtain the briefest outline of its fortunes from odd references from outside sources. John Ashwood attended the Exeter Assembly regularly, being its Scribe in October, 1693. There is an entry in the minutes of the London Congregational Fund Board (this separated from the Common Fund in 1693) for the 1st June, 1696, recording the vote of £10 to 'Mr. Ashwood of Exeter'.[3] In September, 1696, he and Stephen Towgood I of Axminster were censured by the Exeter Assembly for ordaining candidates for the ministry at Bridport in Dorset, without the sanction of the Dorset County Association.

[1] (i) *D.N.B.*, Ashwood, J. (ii) Muddiman, J. G., *The Bloody Assizes*.
[2] Gordon, A., *Freedom after Ejection*, 1917.
[3] *Trans., Cong. Hist. Soc.* Vol. 5, 1911–12, p. 134.

Ashwood's last recorded attendance at the Exeter Assembly was in May, 1697. At the September Assembly of 1698 his successor, Deliverance Larkham, formerly of Launceston, acted as Scribe, and it seems likely that Ashwood had by then left Exeter. Larkham was also a regular attender at Exeter Assembly meetings, but without taking a very active part in them. In 1715 the number of Hearers attending Castle Lane Meeting was estimated at 400. Deliverance Larkham died early in 1723, and was succeeded for a short time only by a young man called Peter Jillard. At this time he appears in the attendance lists of the Exeter Assembly under the 'Candidates and Strangers', and he was not ordained until after the September, 1724 Assembly had made the necessary arrangements for the ceremony. This took place at Crediton, and his name appears on the list of ministers there from that time. With Jillard's departure the Castle Lane Meeting called a Rev. George Denbury, who attended the Exeter Assembly of May, 1725, and was accepted formally by it after making the customary declaration of orthodoxy on the doctrine of the Trinity. The minutes of the Assembly do not exist from 1728 to 1733, and when they begin again the pastor of the Castle Lane Meeting is found to be Robert Atkinson, who, it is noted, was ordained on 1st July, 1730. His health broke down, however, for the September, 1733, minutes include the paragraph:

'Agreed that Mr. Atkinson have Two Guineas for present exigency he having been long sick and continuing so still.'

Similar entries occur from time to time, indicating that Atkinson remained in poor health, and that his own congregation was too poor, or too small, to help him sufficiently. The last of such entries came in September, 1744: 'Agreed that Mr. Atkinson instead of forty shillings have four pounds per annum'.

Atkinson must have resigned his pastorate several years before this, however, for the Minutes of the Committee of Thirteen for 23rd January, 1738, referring to a year's interest on a mortgage, reads:

'. . . also £2 to be lodged with Mr. Blake to please Mr. Norden who claims a 5th Pt. for Castle Meeting when there shall be a Minister there officiating'.

With this entry, the story of the first Congregational church in Exeter comes to an end. Its members joined with the Presbyterians.[1]

The French Protestants, or Huguenots, appeared in large numbers in Devon towns following the Revocation of the Edict of Nantes in 1685. Even before this there must have been some Huguenots in

[1] Murch, J., p. 373.

Exeter, for on 7th March, 1681–2, the City Chamber ordered £21 4s. 5d. of the money obtained by fines under the Conventicle Act to be paid to the 'indigent French Protestants'. A considerable section of the Huguenots conformed to the Church of England, and in Exeter they were given the parish church of St. Olave's to use, in 1686. Their most celebrated minister was Jean Courtail, instituted 3rd July, 1708, ordained Presbyter 29th September, 1708.[1] There was, however, another section which would not conform to the Church of England, and organized a Nonconformist society. Its minister up to about 1700 was a Monsieur Viollet, and from then until about 1720 Andrew Majendie, who then moved to Dartmouth. The Exeter Assembly in October, 1693, decided 'That Mons. Violet have 40s. per annum' and in September, 1716, Majendie received £8. As time went on, in both congregations, the young people married and were absorbed by the other churches in the city, and these separate congregations came to an end. In his answer to Bishop Clagett's Visitation Queries in 1744, Jean Courtail reported that there were

'. . . hardly any children in my congregation' and 'several persons who are members of it are married to persons who go to their respective parish churches.'

The same process undoubtedly occurred in the Nonconformist Huguenot congregation, which may be assumed to have become extinct when Majendie moved to Dartmouth in 1720–1.[2] There is no indication of the part of the City in which the Huguenot Nonconformists held their meetings.

With the coming of religious toleration the Baptist society in Exeter likewise began to develop. A William Phipps was Pastor between the years 1685 and 1690, and attended the first general meeting of Baptists in London, in 1689. His last recorded act was to be one of the signatories at the founding of the Bampton Baptist church in 1690. The Exeter Baptists' original church minute book (now lost) began on 9th February, 1682. The numbers were then very small. In 1689, when James II's temporary hold upon Ireland drove many Protestants away in fear of persecution, some Irish Baptists took refuge in Exeter. In these years the Baptists met in 'an Old Chapel in Catharine's Gate'.[3] most likely the chapel of St. Katherine's Almhouses, which was

---

[1] Answers to Primary Visitation Queries of Bishop Clagett, in 1744.
[2] Pickard, R., 'The Huguenots in Exeter' (*Trans. Devon. Assoc.*, Vol. 68, 1936, pp. 261–97).
[3] Micaijah Towgood to Josiah Thompson, op. cit.

destroyed in the Air Raids of May, 1942. The numbers attending must indeed have been small, for the maximum capacity at one time of this building could never have been more than 40, and that would have been far from comfortable. In 1712 the society moved to larger premises in Gandy St., only leaving there for their present site in South St. in 1725. A successor to Phipps was not called until 1692, when a student from Bristol Baptist College, Richard Sampson, became their minister. It was owing to the steady growth of the cause under his guidance that St. Catherine's Chapel became too small in 1712.

The only Baptist layman of importance at this time was Benjamin Heath, fourth son of the Thomas Heath who was the Master of the Tuckers and Weavers' Guild in 1676, and who may have been the same who was one of the principals in the building of James' Meeting in 1687. Benjamin Heath was definitely a member of the Baptists at the age of 25, in 1697, and remained so until his death in May, 1728. He was a fuller and merchant, and made a substantial fortune during his lifetime. He gave the land on which the present South St. chapel was built, and a small endowment to go with it. The gift was made conditional on certain orthodox articles of Faith being maintained. That this was necessary is shown by the fact that Arianism and Unitarianism affected the Baptists in the West of England throughout the period 1715–34, resulting in several of their churches abandoning the orthodox faith.

The Indulgence of 1687 also provided the opportunity for the Society of Friends to secure a place of meeting in the County Capital. All their meetings had been held in private houses up to this time. Gatherings in Exeter right under the eyes of the Justices had always been hazardous. An attempt made on 30th September, 1680, at William Gravett's house in St. Sidwell's parish, had been severely dealt with, 45 people from all over the eastern part of the county being fined and Gravett himself suffering the householder's penalty of £20. But at a Quarterly Meeting held on 6th August, 1687, at Honiton,

It was proposed . . . for a Meeting house to be gotten at Exeter for ye worshipp & service of truth . . . & in order thereunto, John Ganeclife, Robert Ford, Jno. Chapple, Geo. ffea, Jno. Colsworthy, & Joseph Nott . . . are desired, . . . to endevor to gett such a one as may be fitt; and if they do agree for a house, as farr as ten or twelve pounds pr. annum for a yeare or two, this meeting do unanimusly agree for ye sake & service of truth yt. what ye friends of Exeter cannot do of themselves (to defray ye charge of it) ffriends of other Meetings will generally contribute to their Assistance.

After certain false starts the land in Wynard's Lane, where the present Meeting-House stands, was purchased in 1690. The original deed is dated 17th February, 1690, the chief trustee being Walter Phillips. The deed refers to 'all that close of land adjoining the Wynards in the parish of Holy Trinity, and County of the City of Exon, containing 1½ acre, more or less, being heretofore the lands of Robert Phipps, Gent, deceased'. The cost of the land was £77 3s. The various Monthly Meetings were asked to contribute towards the cost of building. Finally on 31st January, 1692, the first Devonshire Quarterly Meeting was held 'at ye Meeting house in Exon', the first permanent building for Worship possessed by the Society in this area. The 'father' of the Society in Exeter at this time was still John Gannicliff, who had received George Fox on his first visit.[1]

This section is fittingly closed by reference to the survey made by the London Common Fund Board in 1691. This Common Fund had been set up by the London Presbyterians and Congregationalists to assist those country ministers who were financially in difficulty, and to encourage the preaching of the gospel in areas where it had been neglected. To this end a survey of the position in the counties was made, the manuscript of which still survives.[2] Amongst the ministers that 'have a competent supply' in Devon are the Exeter men, listed as 'Mr. Gaylard, Mr. Hoppin, Mr. Trose, Hallet, Atkins, Ashwood'. The Hallett referred to now is Joseph Hallett II, his father having died in 1689, the son succeeding to the position of co-pastor at James' Meeting. Other familiar names appear at places in Devon, their owners having left the county town. Samuel Tapper was at Lympstone, and Robert Carel (or Caryll) at Crediton, while young Bernard Starr, the recruit ordained at Lyme Regis on 25th August, 1687, was by 1691 minister at Topsham. Among the men who were poor, whose people were unable to support them, was 'Mr. Crompton, att Exeter, an aged man and very poor'. He had been ejected from Cullompton in 1662, and had signed the petition against the Oxford Oath in January, 1666. Names of ministers destined to work later in Exeter also appear in this survey. Benjamin Hooper was in 1691 at 'Dauerton', Deliverance Larkham 'att Shepistor, has not above 10£ per annum needs encouragmt', and Mr. Withers 'att Lupton in Brixham'.

With the ending of persecution, therefore, the Dissenters accepted

---

[1] (i) Dymond, R., *Early records of Friends in Devonshire*, n.d. (ii) Thomasson, W. J. F., *Friends of East Devon*, 1928. MS.

[2] Gordon, A., *Freedom after Ejection*, 1917.

their freedom readily enough, but with no sign of jubilation at a victory gained. They felt no gratitude to the Anglicans who had at last, grudgingly, granted them toleration to worship in their own way. They realised that toleration had come more through political considerations than through any conviction by the Church party that it was a worthy end in itself. This belief was shown for at least the next fifty years in a consistent support of the Whig Party, and the Hanoverian Succession, in which it was clear their best interests were involved.

CHAPTER V

PROSPERITY ENJOYED, 1691–1717

WITH the coming of Toleration the old Exeter Assembly was revived. It was recognized that there was no immediate prospect of any scheme of comprehension within the Church of England being put forward acceptable to Dissenters, and that therefore steps must be taken both to organize their own communions and to ensure that there should be supplies of educated ministers for Nonconformist pulpits. To this end the Presbyterian and Congregationalist ministers of Devon and Cornwall agreed to meet twice a year in general Assembly, to discuss matters of common interest, to arrange for the ordination of qualified candidates, to raise money for the training of promising young men, and to hear a sermon. They referred to themselves as the United Brethren, seeking to avoid denominational labels. The first two meetings were held in Tiverton (17th March, 1691) and Topsham (23rd–24th June, 1691). In September, 1695, the meeting was at Plymouth. Apart from these early diversions, however, the place of gathering has always been Exeter: hence the name Exeter Assembly by which it has been customarily known. Its Minutes from 1691 to the present day are in existence, with the exception of the years 1717–21, 1729–33, 1753–63. These records throw much light on the history of Devon Nonconformity throughout the eighteenth century.

At the first meeting at Tiverton there were present 15 ministers of the County of Devon, 1 candidate for the ministry, and 5 delegates 'from the Western Divn. of Somerset'. All those present were Presbyterians. They proceeded to elect a Moderator and a Scribe 'to write such things as shal be transacted in the Meeting', and drew up a set of rules to govern their Association. Although these bear frequent resemblances to the rules of the Commonwealth Assembly, they were much more general in tone. The object of the Association was clearly stated in the first two articles, which read:

1. We are persuaded that it is not only lawfull but also very expedient that we frequently hold Meetings for mutual advice touching things pertaining to our Office, the right ordering of our Congregations, & the promoting of Purity & Unity in the Churches of Christ.'

2. We declare our hearty willingness & desire that others of our Brethren

in the County & City who are of godly life & sound in the ffaith should join with us in this Agreement, for the fuller demonstration of Universal Concord.

This desire for Universal Concord was further evident at the second meeting of the Assembly, at Topsham on 23rd–24th June 1691, when those present accepted 'cheerfully and heartily' the Heads of Agreement decided upon that year by the Dissenting Ministers of London, which for the time being brought about a Union between Presbyterians and Independents, the two most numerous of the Nonconformist societies. This Topsham Assembly was held under the moderatorship of John Flavel, the veteran scholar and preacher from Dartmouth, and it was largely due to his eloquent plea for unity that his colleagues followed the example of their London brethren. It was also his last public act: Flavel was taken ill at the Assembly and died on his way home. The union of Presbyterians and Independents in Devon and Cornwall lasted longer than the more publicized 'Happy Union' in London. Whereas the latter had already broken up by 1695, Congregationalists and Presbyterians continued to join together in the Exeter Assembly until the middle of the eighteenth century.

The remainder of the Rules of the Assembly were strictly practical guides to the handling of business. No specific doctrinal articles were included, unless the proviso that members should be 'of godly life and sound in the faith' be one.

The numbers attending the Exeter Assembly grew steadily as the years went by. In September, 1701, there were present 31 ministers and 13 candidates, and in May, 1706, 43 ministers and 14 candidates. In May, 1713, which was a very important occasion in the Assembly's history, there was an attendance of 57 Ministers and 13 candidates from Devon and Cornwall, 3 ministers from Somerset and 1 from London. The years from 1700–19 were those of the greatest influence of the Assembly, during which it really became the governing body of Devon and Cornwall Dissenters. The source of its authority lay in its control over the ordinations of candidates for the ministry, and in its Fund for the assistance of such candidates and the smaller country churches unable to support a minister by themselves.

No candidates for the Ministry in Devon & Cornwall were ordained without prior examination by, and approval of the Assembly, and such examinations were extremely thorough. As early as May, 1694, it had been 'agreed that no Candidate be ordain'd by any of the United Brethren of this County but by order of the Assembly'.

It was found in practice that there was no reason for the Independents to complain. There could have been very few cases of candidates being ordained until after they had received a call to the ministry of a particular congregation, which for the Independents was the important factor. There were complaints from time to time that candidates delayed applying for ordination, even after they had been licensed to preach and had settled with a congregation. This was regularised at the May Assembly of 1709 by the following Rule:

Resolved that for the future no Licence be given to any to Preach before they have promis'd before the Assembly to offer themselves to be ordained in a short time after they are constant preachers and have a call to take the Pastoral charge of some Particular Congregation.

The procedure to be followed in examining candidates for ordination was clearly defined in September, 1713:

That to prevent young men from entering upon preaching without due Qualification, for the future all candidates who propose themselves to be licensed be examined during the Assembly by some deputed thereby, and if so far approved, be obliged to state and defend a Theological Question in Latin, and to preach a Sermon on a Text given them before Four or more of the United Brethren in some private licensed house, where they are also to pass under such further Trials and Examinations as to their skill in Languages, Philosophy, Divinity, etc., as those Brethren shall think fit, before whom these exercises are performed, and notwithstanding such approbation and license to preach, whenever any Candidates offer themselves to ordination the Ordainers have liberty further to examine them and put them upon such further exercises as they think fit.

It is clear that great value was placed upon intellectual training at this time. These were no uneducated novices who were admitted to the ministry of the Protestant Dissenters, but men who could later be centres of cultural as well as of spiritual life in their neighbourhoods. A typical order of the Assembly on such matters occurred in May, 1714:

Mr. Stogdon examined in order to Publick Preaching, by Mr. Ball, Walrond, Withers, Enty, Evans, who gave a good account of his abilities. Ordered that he make and defend a Thesis on this Q: 'An Xtus. sit Mediator secundum utramque naturam?' That he preach on 'Fight the good fight of Faith'. That if the . . . Ministers approve his performances they give him a licence & recommend him to the Grace of God by solemn prayer.

In order to ensure a constant supply of suitably qualified candidates for the ministry, the Assembly from its earliest days organized a Fund, which had the twofold object of assisting the smaller country churches, and of making grants to young men judged suitable for education. There had been an Academy at Taunton under Matthew Warren for a good many years before 1687, and some of the Exeter Assembly ministers were trained under him.[1] Probably soon after the refounding of the Assembly Joseph Hallett II set up a modest Academy in Exeter, which he maintained until 1719. Although it is nowhere indicated in the Minutes that the Academy was set up at the request of the Exeter Assembly, it is impossible to doubt that the one institution did indeed spring from the other. Hallett himself had been educated by his father, who was a good Greek and Hebrew scholar. The Academy was open to both laymen and to candidates for the ministry, and the usual course took four years to complete. Theology, Classics, Hebrew, and a practical course in pastoral duties, formed the bulk of the curriculum. The names of 31 students who passed through the Academy are known, and one of the first who came under the influence of Hallett, although it is not known for certain whether he passed through the Academy or not, was Peter King, son of a Presbyterian grocer, cousin of John Locke. He later became Lord Chancellor. The importance of this academy should not be overemphasized, for it is unlikely that more than 6 pupils would ever have been undergoing training at one time there. Grants were also made to candidates for the ministry undergoing training at other centres of learning. By 1697 already grants to scholars totalled £138 in that year, an indication of the great importance set upon this part of the Assembly's work. Unfortunately the Minutes do not often mention the amounts paid in this way, and entries of later date were for much lower sums: £40 in 1709, and £31 in 1713, which suggests that by then support was confined to those receiving training in Exeter alone. Grants made to scholars varied from £4 to £10 a year according to their needs. That the Assembly could not, in any case, have kept up the high figure of 1697 is shown by the fact that the average yearly income of the Fund during the period 1691 to 1717 was about £80. By far the largest portion of this came from the Exeter Presbyterians. At the October, 1691, Assembly, for example, out of a total received of £60 15s 7d. the three Exeter Presbyterian meetings gave £30 2s. 6d.

Grants to ministers varied considerably. The incomes of many of the country churches were below £30 and some even below £20 a

[1] McLachlan, H., *English education under the Test Acts*, 1931.

year. Grants were normally made on the recommendation of neighbouring ministers more fortunately situated, and were given to avoid
real hardship. They were not always restricted to Presbyterian and
Independent causes, for the Huguenot Nonconformists were similarly
helped. Some ministers received grants also from the London Funds,
both Presbyterian and Congregational. The most well-to-do ministers
at this period were the Exeter Presbyterians. From 1708 to 1712 the
senior minister, George Trosse, received £72 each year while his
three colleagues had £64. From 1713 to 1719 the four ministers
averaged at least £80 each year, while in 1717 only this rose to exactly
£100.[1] At the same time the incomes of their church members would
in the majority of cases not exceed 12s. a week, an average weekly wage
for a master-craftsman in the first half of the century.[2]

It appears from the Minutes of the Assembly that the Exeter ministers
were highly respected, and looked upon to take the lead whenever
possible. A note in May, 1698, for intance, reads: 'Ordained that the
Exon. ministers shall inspect the Fund and as they find the fund will
bear, dispose of it for the education of young men.'

Instances of the Assembly intervening in the interests of professional
morality occur from time to time. In September, 1707, it was reported
that Mr. Bond, minister at Holsworthy, had not been receiving his
salary regularly, and as his wife was ailing, was considering leaving his
pastorate. 'Mr. Tross and the other Exon. ministers have writ to the
people to exhort them punctually to pay Mr. Bond his contribution.'

That it should not be thought that the members of the Assembly
were lacking in human weaknesses, the following extract is included,
referring to the May Assembly, 1699:

'Agreed that Mr. Toogood having continued above two hours in
Sermon all future preachers have warning given them to keep to their
hour: and that the Clark turn the Glass when the Text is named & take
it away as soon as tis run out.'

Despite the occasional criticism of the Independents it is unlikely
that the Nonconformists in Devon and Cornwall would have flourished
as they did in this period but for the co-ordinating work performed by
the Exeter Assembly. Some means of consultation and mutual help
was absolutely necessary if the freedom so hardly won were not to
degenerate into anarchy and indifference.

It was against this background that the Exeter Presbyterians

---

[1] The Accounts of the Committee of Thirteen.
[2] Hoskins, W. G., *Industry, Trade and People in Exeter, 1688–1800*, 1935, p. 130.

organized themselves in this period of their greatest prosperity. Until after 1713 there is little to record of them except the succession of ministers. Samuel Atkins died on July 4th, 1702. He was succeeded by Benjamin Hooper, who came from Silverton, was born on September 13th, 1649, and ordained by the Scotch Presbyterians at Rotterdam in 1676. The other pastor of Bow Meeting, John Hopping, died on 8th March, 1705, and was succeeded by John Withers, previously minister at Modbury, born in 1669, 25th March, and ordained (with Deliverance Larkham the Congregationalist) by Trosse and Hopping in Exeter on 26th August, 1691. Withers was not the first choice of the Exeter Presbyterians at this time, however. At the May Assembly of 1705,

These following questions were proposed by some people of Exon:
1. Whether a Ministers removal from one place to another on a clear call be not in some cases allowable? Resolv'd, N. Contrad., in the affirmative.
2. Whether there may not some circumstances occur which may make such a removal a probable dutie? Aff.
3. Whether in a Call of Mr. Walrond of Ottery by the Citizens of Exon such circumstances do not occur as make it his probable duty to accept of this Call?
This question was not debated because it appeared to the Assembly that Mr. Walrond had utterly refused to accept of that call.

Walrond was born on 25th August, 1673, and ordained in May, 1698, settling at Ottery in the next month.

A further instance of the part played by the Exeter churches is the invariable choice of an Exeter layman to act as Treasurer of the Fund. John Pym was thus chosen in May, 1709, to succeed Thomas Wood, who was a member of the Committee of Thirteen from 1689 until 1714. John Pym had been a member from its beginning in 1687 until his death in 1727.

At the beginning of 1713 died George Trosse, senior minister at James' Meeting. Trosse had for many years occupied a unique place in the affections of his people, and in seeking a successor they justifiably aimed high. Their choice fell on James Peirce, at that time minister at Newbury, Berkshire. While there (1706–13) he had indulged in controversial publications in defence of nonconformist ideas, and attracted a considerable amount of distinction. His character will be discussed later.

The call from Exeter was unanimous, and there is no room for doubt that Peirce from the first wished to accept it, as Exeter was one of the chief provincial centres of Nonconformity. He found it difficult,

however, for his Newbury congregation was most reluctant to let him
go, and appealed to the Lecturers at Salters' Hall, in London, who were
the leading Nonconformist ministers of the day. The Exeter people
also put their case to the Salters' Hall Lecturers, and Peirce said he
would be governed by their decision. The Lecturers were divided in
their opinions and a report of their proceedings was brought down to
the May meeting of the Exeter Assembly in 1713 by Dr. Edmund
Calamy, the Nonconformist biographer and historian. As soon as he
arrived in the city he was met by the leading Presbyterian laymen, and
they stayed with him until late in the evening.

Never before did I see such an earnestness in any people for a minister's
coming among them. They talked as if they were quite undone, if he did not
accept their call, and no one else could signify any thing to them, if they had
not him.[1]

Calamy was so impressed by their desire for Peirce that he warned
them against expecting too much from any one man, and rebuked them
for presumption.

The Assembly debated the matter at length. Yet the correspondence
before it showed well enough which way Peirce's mind was inclined, as
the following paragraph from the Minutes shows:

Letters from Exon people and Mr. Pearse's last answer read, in which he
shews a great inclination for Exon. He is afraid, tho' Newbury people subscribe for an Assistant, they would grow weary if the danger of Exon were
over. If any way could be found by wch. Newbury people might be satisfyd,
or there were any one on whom he might cast the blame of his removal,
he would come to Exon.

The phrase "cast the blame of his removal" may have been that of
the Scribe who wrote down the minute, but if it did in fact occur in
Peirce's letter to the Exeter Presbyterians, it was not a good augury for
his ministry among them. The debate in the Assembly continued until
candles were brought into the chapel, when the persistence of the
Exeter men won the day, and a letter was sent to Peirce with the
authority of the whole Assembly behind it. Peirce accepted the call to
Exeter, and began his ministry there in the autumn.

A further change in the complement of Presbyterian ministers in
Exeter occurred in 1715, with the death of Benjamin Hooper. The
Lavington family had been prominent amongst the three United

[1] Calamy, E., *Life*, Vol. 2, pp. 262–5.

Congregations from the beginnings, and now the family put forward as candidate for the vacant pastorate a younger John Lavington, who had first appeared at the Exeter Assembly amongst the candidates for the ministry in May, 1711. He was chosen, on a majority vote, to be the second minister at Bow Meeting.[1] The Exeter Assembly of September 1715 ordered that Lavington be ordained at Exeter, in company with Joseph Hallett III and James How, on 28th September. The Latin question he had to defend was 'An Foedus gratiae sit conditionatum?'.

The year 1715 saw Exeter (and Devonshire) Nonconformity at the height of its prosperity. By a stroke of fortune there is evidence for estimating just what proportion of the population at that time did adhere to the Nonconformist societies within the city. On the national scene the High Church reaction in the later years of Queen Anne had led to the passing of the Occasional Conformity and Schism Acts, which, taken in conjunction with the unrepealed Test and Corporation Acts of Charles II's reign, constituted a very real hindrance to the exercise of the Dissenters' rights as members of the nation. With the accession of George I and the assumption of power by the Whigs, a movement quickly developed to have these Acts repealed. To gather evidence of the strength of Nonconformist societies in the country, a survey was made by Dr. John Evans, minister of Hand Alley Presbyterian church in London. A letter noted at the end of Evans' Survey for Devon suggests that the correspondent for this county may have been John Vowler, an Exeter merchant who was a member of the Committee of Thirteen from 1714 to 1749. If it were not he, the most likely correspondent would have been the Rev. Isaac Gilling of Newton Abbot, to whose zealous transcription of the Minutes of the Exeter Assembly we owe most of our knowledge of the events of these years. The Survey estimates the number of 'Hearers' supposed to attend each Meeting. The figures for Exeter were:

1. By Southgate. (= James' Meeting)   1100 ⎫ These were all
2. Near John's Bow. (= Bow Meeting)   800 ⎬ Presbyterian.
3. Near Northgate. (= Little Meeting) 350 ⎭
4. Castle Street—Independents   400
5. French Protestants—place not stated 120
   And in a supplementary list of Baptist causes:
6. Baptists (then in Gandy St.)   300

It was further indicated that of these Exeter Dissenters 74 were County

[1] Peirce, J., *The Western Inquisition*, 1720, pp. 11–12.

voters, 478 had a vote in the city, and 47 in other boroughs not given by name.

This list gave a total of 3070 'Hearers' for the six Exeter chapels. To this should be added a small number of the Society of Friends, possibly making the total up to 3100. Exactly what is meant by the term 'Hearers' is not stated, but it may reasonably be understood to mean adults whose religious allegiance was definitely not given to the Church of England. In order to estimate these figures as a proportion of the population as a whole, an allowance must be made for children. A conservative estimate of the Dissenting population of Exeter in 1715, therefore, based on Evans' list, cannot come to less than 4500 persons. One qualification must be made. Although most historians have accepted the numbers given in the Evans manuscript as 'representing the number of those who were zealous Dissenters, realizing that there would be others who came within the ambit of Dissent',[1] it is possible that in the case of Exeter they may be exaggerated. James' Meeting was said to have had 1100 Hearers; yet it is unlikely that it could have held a congregation of more than 600 at one time, as has been shown above.[2]

Estimates of the total population of Exeter in the early eighteenth century vary from 12,000 to 16,000.[3] In either case, allowing for Evans' figures being a little inflated, in Exeter the Nonconformists must have formed between one-third and one-quarter of this total in 1715. Other Devonshire towns, notably Tiverton and Bideford, were not very different from this.

Added in note form to Evans' MSS. is a letter from John Vowler of Exeter to Mr. C. Taylor in London, dated 22nd December, 1716. The first part relates to conditions in Exeter.

In Exeter one Low-Churchman only to 3 Dissenters. The Votes of Dissenters in Elections more than two to one of the L.C., and the Low-Church never undertook to bear above an eighth of the Charges at any publick Election, the Dissenters advancing the other 7 parts.

On the choice of 40 Guardians for the new Hospitall (i.e. Work-house) erected in that City An. 1700 when the Law directed that every voter should pay 2d a week in their own right to the poor, the Whig interest carried every Member. Nor could the High-Church with their utmost efforts reach above half-way in any of the 4 wards, to the votes by which the lowest Guardian was chosen . . . Many of those reckon'd among Low-Church were formerly

---

[1] Bebb, E. D., *Nonconformity and Social and Economic Life*, p. 39.
[2] Evans' Survey, 1715 (MSS. in Dr. Williams' Library).
[3] Hoskins, W. G., op. cit., pp. 111–19. Pickard, R., *Population and epidemics of Exeter in pre-census times*, p. 18.

Dissenters & desirous to return again to them. The influence of Trading Dissenters very extensive over their Dependants in Business.

The concluding sentence was ominous for the future. When often the next generation of wealthy traders and manufacturers decided to forsake their Nonconformity, their dependants were carried with them, too, causing a marked decline in the fortunes of the meeting-houses. For the present, however, all was well, and if the Exeter Nonconformists could not, as their contemporaries in Bideford and Bridgwater are said to have done[1] take part in the official government of their city, it can hardly be doubted that the wishes of so large a section of the community had to be taken into account at every stage by the City Chamber.

[1] Cox, John, 'Memoirs', *Trans. Devon. Assoc.*, 1897, Vol. 29, pp. 86–94. Murch, J., op. cit., p. 178.

CHAPTER VI

DISRUPTION, 1716–1720

Up to this point little has been said of the theological basis of Nonconformity. One recent writer has gone so far as to claim 'There is not, and there never has been, any controversy between the Church of England and Orthodox Dissent in respect of the Articles of the Christian Faith'.[1] This is begging the question: if Dissent remains orthodox naturally enough it will be in agreement with the Church of England. But not only was there the obvious departure from orthodoxy by the Baptist denial of the efficacy of Infant Baptism, but all the Puritans emphasized Articles VI (of the Sufficiency of the Holy Scriptures for Salvation) and XVII (Of Predestination and Election) of the Church of England while they remained a part of it, and they carried this emphasis with them when they left the national church. Rejecting the Arminianism always present in the Church of England, the early Nonconformists stood by the full Calvinist teaching on Predestination and Election, including the complementary idea of Reprobation—that just as the godly are predestined to eternal life so God has equally chosen others for death and damnation.

Behind these differences of emphasis lay a basic difference of attitude to the religious life. The Nonconformist holds that 'The primary duty of the religious man . . . is . . . to secure for himself the presence and energising power of a religious life, and thereafter to let that work itself out into an organization which shall be at the same time the life's product and the life's new inspiration'.[2] In other words, Man's approach to God can be direct, and not through an institution already in existence. The Church, in this light, is composed of those who have received Grace and now come together for the purpose of worshipping God and to awaken other sinners to a proper sense of contrition. If the Church established in the land is in harmony with these beliefs, then conformity is possible. If not, then it is the duty of the truly religious man to witness to what he believes to be true, and to refuse to conform. But by 1660 the victory of the Laudian party in the Church of England was complete: the process of Protestant reform was halted, and the emphasis for the future would be on conserving rather than reform-

---

[1] Micklem, N., *Doctrine of our Redemption*, 1943, p. viii.
[2] Clarke, H. W., *History of English Nonconformity*, 1913, Vol. 1, p. 4.

ing, on the apostolical succession rather than on the extirpation of prelacy.

The Presbyterians and Independents of Exeter shared such beliefs without question until about 1710. The autobiography of George Trosse tells of his conversion in classical Calvinist terms: a dissolute and immoral youth at last brought to see the horror of eternal damnation, the agonized prayers and heart-searchings which followed, partial reform and relapse, and the final conversion, a flooding of his consciousness with a supreme wonder that he was, by no merit of his own but by the grace of Jesus Christ, saved from the consequences of sin and predestined to eternal life. Such was the witness he bore throughout his long ministry. The preaching of his colleagues would have been on similar lines: Trosse was the strongest personality among them, and there is ample witness to the veneration paid him by his colleagues.

The change from Trosse to Peirce as the leading minister in 1713 must have been felt with varying degrees of shock by the members of the three united congregations of James', Bow and Little Meetings. The difference between Peirce's teaching and that of Trosse is shown by the sermon preached by the former on 2nd June, 1717. The subject was 'The Satisfaction of Christ'. He criticized those who compare human sins with debts which have to be paid. 'They have represented sin as an infinite evil, and so our debts to be infinite, and that the punishment we deserve is infinite, and nothing less than an infinite punishment can be a satisfaction for it.' The corollary of this argument is that nothing less than the supreme sacrifice of Christ Himself is enough to redeem men from the consequences of such sin. Peirce, instead of this clear if extreme way of teaching, took the line

Sin ... exposes sinners to the righteous displeasure of God ... God would be injurious to his own perfections... to the soverain authority which he has over his creatures ... should he give any encouragement to his subjects to think lightly of it ... and therefore do's it seem requisite that he should some way or other testify his hatred against it ... The way that the gospel sets before us, his dealing as he has done with his own son, is what do's most fully and perfectly display the holiness of his nature, his hatred of sin ... He shews himself in his sufferings to be a righteous and sin-revenging God....

This was a tasteless draught to offer to a people brought up on the strong wine of Calvinism, with its drama of the soul's fight against the world and the Devil, so vividly displayed in Bunyan's writings. It spotlights the virtues and weaknesses of the chief figure in the drama which was about to unfold itself in Exeter, James Peirce. He was born in London, about 1673, of parents who belonged to the Stepney congregation which had Matthew Mead as pastor. On the death of both parents when he was only eight years old, Peirce remained under the guardianship of this minister, later going to Holland to study at Utrecht and Leyden universities, as did many of the sons of the wealthier Dissenters at a time when the English universities were closed to them. He spent some time at Oxford, as well, after this, despite not being able to take a degree there, and he was ordained in 1699. From 1701 to 1706 he was pastor of a mixed Independent and Presbyterian congregation at Cambridge, where he came to know William Whiston, who was developing Unitarian views at that time. From 1706 to 1713 he was pastor of a Presbyterian church at Newbury. By his writings during this period he emerged as one of the leading champions of Dissent against the claims of the Established Church.

It was with this background that Peirce came to Exeter, and it was for this reputation that the Exeter Presbyterians called him to their service. His record in 1713 was that of a scholar rather than an evangelist, a man far above his colleagues in the West of England in respect of intellect and learning. John Fox, a candidate for the ministry and a past student at Hallett's Academy in Exeter, said of Peirce in his Memoirs that 'He was one of those people who are never happy but when they are deeply engaged in thought, or in conversation which suits their way and manner of thinking.' Fox was only preparing for the ministry in order to please his father, is always very critical of ministers with whom he was brought into contact, and his evidence is not sympathetic towards Peirce, although there is no reason to doubt its essential truth.

He was not over generous, or much given to hospitality; he had very seldom his friends to eat or drink; . . . His love of money appeared at the time of the monstrous rise of the South Sea Stock; for he would not sell at 500 or 600 advance, and staid so long till it fell and missed his market . . . He was always close and secret about his own affairs, and, what is seldom, very incurious about the affairs of others. He used no manner of diversion nor any exercise, until the swelling of his legs and other disorders obliged him to it.

In another passage Fox wrote of Peirce:

He was a very good philosopher and mathematician, but what he chiefly bent his studies to was divinity and explaining the Scriptures . . . I never thought him a fine preacher; for his common discourses were loose and unstudied. . . . In his prayers he was often very jejune and dry, unless he happened to fall into a particular strain of thoughts which touched him, and then he would proceed with great elevation, without cant, tautology, or nonsense.[1]

The colleague whom Peirce found most congenial to his tastes at Exeter was John Withers, co-pastor at Bow Meeting. Withers was just four years older, and himself a pamphleteer of local reputation. Joseph Hallett II, with whom Peirce's name became more closely associated, was baptised on 4th November, 1656, and was therefore seventeen years older than Peirce. From his behaviour throughout the crisis of 1717–20 it seems that Hallett's faculties became rapidly weaker when he passed the age of sixty, and he at no time took a decisive part in events, although strong enough at the end to hold fast to what he had come to regard as the truth.

Despite the abrupt change in character from Trosse to Peirce in 1713 the Exeter Presbyterians had no cause but to congratulate themselves upon their new minister during the first three years of his pastorate. Their satisfaction is noticeable in the receipts of the Committee of Thirteen for those years. In 1712, the last full year of Trosse's life, their receipts for the Ministers' Fund came to just over £292. In 1713 this rose to over £359, in 1714 to £367, and in 1716 it rose to £384 odd, a figure which was never to be exceeded during the period when the Fund was dependent on regular personal subscriptions rather than on income from investments. This satisfaction was passed on by way of an increase in ministers' salaries. In 1712 Trosse had been given £75 and the other ministers £67. In 1714 all four ministers received £88, and in 1716 this was increased to £91 15s., rising in 1717 to £100. This was at a time when the yearly income of many country Nonconformist pastors did not exceed £30.

It was not long before the people of Exeter had an opportunity at first hand to sample Peirce's skill as a pamphleteer. A certain young man called Benjamin Read, brought up a Nonconformist and designed for the Ministry, decided to conform after all. He was persuaded that his original baptism was invalid, as it was given at the hands of one not episcopally ordained, and he was rebaptized in the parish church of Heavitree, one of the two godfathers on the occasion being the Rev. John Walker, compiler of 'The Sufferings of the Clergy'. Such a situation was irresistible, and Peirce burst into print with 'A Caveat against the New Sect of Anabaptists, lately sprung up at Exon, shewing the novelty and schism, the absurdity and dangerous tendency of their principles and practices, who were concerned in the rebaptization of

[1] Fox, John, 'Memoirs' (*Trans. Devon. Assoc.*, Vols. 28–9, 1896–7).

Mr. Benjamin Read' (London, for John Clark, 1714). In this 32-page leaflet Peirce had no difficulty in flaying verbally the clergy responsible for the affair, and in showing that non-episcopally-ordained baptisms were indeed valid by law and custom.

The validity of Dissenters' Baptism was a safe topic for debate. Next, however, the Trinity became the subject of discussion, a doctrine which while at the very heart of orthodox Christianity is at the same time the most difficult of all dogma to define accurately. The major heresies of the early Church were derived from attempts to explain the nature of the Trinity: Arianism, Sabellianism, Nestorianism, and Mono-physitism, all in turn were examined and rejected by Church Councils. It is not surprising that in the age of Newton and Locke when it was becoming fashionable to test beliefs by reason and experiment the doctrine of the Trinity should again be subjected to a searching examin-ation. There appeared in 1690 a work called 'The Naked Gospel', which showed a distinct leaning towards Arianism. Published anonym-ously it was the work of Dr. Arthur Bury, for whose pains came the reward of expulsion from the University of Oxford, and the public burning of his book. In the 1690s the controversy was contained within the Church of England, and this continued to be the case for some years longer. In 1708 came William Whiston's 'Essay upon the Apostolical Constitutions' in which he sought to prove that Arianism was the doctrine of the primitive Church. The work which set the pot boiling beyond control was Samuel Clarke's 'Scripture Doctrine of the Trinity' in 1712. Clarke, Rector of St. James', Westminster (now St. James', Piccadilly), does not seem to have gone further himself than to postulate the logical subordination of Christ as Son to God the Father, but he certainly did convey strongly to his readers the view that the Scriptures themselves nowhere insist upon the orthodox doctrine of the Trinity. It followed that it was not a necessary article of faith for salvation.

Clarke's book met with rapid success amongst Dissenters. From John Fox's evidence it was read in Hallett's Academy at Exeter very soon after publication, and similar ideas, derived from Whiston's writings, may have been discussed there before that time. The two candidates for the ministry who adopted the new outlook most enthusiastically were Hubert Stogdon and Joseph Hallett III, son of the Principal of the Academy. As for James Peirce, his contact with Whiston at Cambridge had led him to examine the writings of the Early Church on the Trinity, and he could not help being impressed with many of the arguments put forward on the opposing side. He wrote '. . . it made me . . . despair of getting clear notions of the Trinity, and so render'd me more averse to the study of the controversy.' This aversion led him to delay reading Clarke's 'Scripture Doctrine' until 'near a twelvemonth after the Doctor's book was publish'd'. Consequently he could not have read it until about the time in 1713 when he was considering moving to Exeter. Yet even then he was 'convinc'd that the common doctrine was not according to the Scriptures and was settled in my present opinion', and he therefore cannot be entirely absolved from the charge of not owning to unorthodox beliefs when he accepted the call. Peirce 'could not fall in with the Doctor in everything; but saw clearly, I must part with some beloved opinions, or else quit my notion of the authority of the holy scriptures'. He considered 'how widely good men had differ'd from one another upon the subject' and decided that God could not have made men's salvation to depend upon all holding the same notion concerning the Trinity. In practice he discarded the use of the common form of the Doxology, but kept very close to scriptural expressions in the pulpit, and ventured to say as little as possible on a matter about which he was in so much doubt himself.

Men who occupy a prominent position in a community seldom avoid committing themselves on controversial topics of the day. If they refrain from doing so when asked they will have opinions attributed to them which may not be their own. So it was at this time. Peirce's failure to condemn the new theology caused his conservative members to suspect that he was sympathetic towards it, and the indiscreet younger generation to claim openly that he was one of their party. The same was true of John Withers and Joseph Hallett II. It is from this viewpoint that we may understand the often repeated accusation from the orthodox side in the following years that some of Hallett's pupils claimed that most of the ministers in the City believed the new notions on the Trinity.

Although no contemporary minute books or similar documents have survived to form an unchallengeable account of the Trinitarian controversy in Exeter in these years, every stage of the debate is well documented by the pamphlets issued by the leaders on either side. Great care has to be taken to allow for the bias with which each was written, yet the astonishing conclusion which emerges from reading them is that they seldom conflict on matters of fact, only in interpretation. Occasionally dates becomes confused, but ambiguities are promptly seized upon by the next pamphlet on the opposing side and corrected with alacrity. By balancing one against the other, and confining oneself strictly to matters of fact, it is possible to reconstruct an accurate picture of the order of events between November, 1716, and mid-1719.

While the 'new theology' was known in Exeter from at least 1712 onwards, it does not seem to have become a public concern until November, 1716. Then Hubert Stogdon met John Lavington, the youngest of the four Exeter ministers, and talked with him about the Trinity. Stogdon had accepted the Clarkean viewpoint, but Lavington was strictly orthodox. Peirce later accused Lavington of stirring up trouble by telling everyone he met of the beliefs of Stogdon: Lavington himself denied having done so. In either case, the views of Stogdon and his friends at the Academy became the subject of common talk from this moment. In December, 1716, Henry Atkins (grandson of the founder of Bow Meeting) met

a considerable person now in communion with Mr. Peirce [who] declar'd himself (in the hearing of several persons at my house) of the same sentiments with Dr. Clark and Mr. Whiston; assur'd me, that some of Mr. Peirce's present hearers and communicants had embrac'd the same opinions, and was very positive, that the new scheme would universally prevail.

On 17th February, 1717, John Lavington, in the course of a series of lectures on the fundamental beliefs of Christianity, preached on the Trinity. 'The week after I had preach'd this sermon a poor woman came to me in great perplexity, and told me, That she knew not how to come to the Lord's-table; for that they told her, That Christ was not God, and the text I had preach'd upon, was not in the Bible.' His text had been I John v. 7. The individuals responsible for this incident were Stogdon, Joseph Hallett III, and another young man called John Spiring.

No mention was made of this controversy at the meeting of the Exeter Assembly on 7th and 8th May, 1717. Perhaps just because of this omission Henry Atkins felt it a duty to preach on the Trinity on Wednesday, 15th May, 1717, when he was asked to lecture at James' Meeting during Peirce's absence in London. According to Peirce's account Atkins charged some of his hearers with 'damnable heresies, denying the Lord that bought them.' His text must have been II Peter ii. 1. Atkins denied having used the words 'damnable heresies' but not the remainder of the phrase. On his return Peirce was so offended by this incident that he proposed to his colleagues that Atkins should no more be invited to occupy any of their pulpits: this was not accepted. Atkins' action had the effect of making the controversy come right into the open: it was not possible for ministers or laymen to ignore its existence any longer. Peirce was asked by the senior members of his congregation to preach on the subject of the 'Satisfaction of Christ', which he did on 2nd June, 1717, in the way already noted. He hoped that this would cause the dispute to die down once more, but his learned attempt to reconcile old and new Christianity very soon itself came under criticism. About a week after its delivery John Ball, minister at Honiton, met Peirce and plainly told him that 'he had it in his power, to prevent the spreading of Mr. Stogdon's opinions, and desir'd him to consider the consequence'. Peirce represented this as a charge that he was the man who had been the cause of Stogdon's lapse from orthodoxy, and naturally denied it. 'I told this reverend person then, that I knew no person in the county, who had been influenc'd by me to alter his opinion about the Trinity . . .'

At the Assizes that summer Judge Price 'spent most of his Charge . . . against those Errors, and own'd they had their rise from some Authors in the Church of England'. Thomas Lindford, Archdeacon of Barnstaple, in his address to his clergy, also alluded to the increase of Arianism among the Exeter Dissenters. The credit of Nonconformity was at stake. These people who had prided themselves on their superior virtue, on having to separate from the national church for conscience's sake, were being shown to be not quite as virtuous and sound in the faith as they had pretended.

It was alleged that the students at Hallett's Academy had been in the habit of meeting at the house of the Baptist minister for discussion, and the Baptists had soon after dismissed their minister on suspicion of heresy. Richard Sampson had died in 1716, and the Baptists had invited for one year on probation a young man called Lucas. Aaron Tozer, one of the Committee of Thirteen, interviewed members of the Baptist church about this matter, and established that certain of Hallett's students did visit Lucas in his rooms fairly regularly, and that Lucas was not appointed the permanent minister because 'not above five or six of the church express'd their desire of it'. By the time that the Baptists debated whether a permanent invitation should be sent, Lucas had already left for another church, and there was no question of dismissal. Nor was it established for certain that heretical doctrines were propagated in these discussion groups, though it seems likely that they were.

Meanwhile Hubert Stogdon, in the enthusiasm of youth and newly discovered truths, for so they must have appeared to him, was adding fuel to the fire. Both Thomas Edgley and Calvin Galpin, young ministers, were present at a discussion when Stogdon admitted 'I am an Arian, and glory in the name'. 'He spake his mind with a great deal of freedom and did not seem to be in the least upon his guard.'

Clearly something had to be done about Stogdon if Peirce was to succeed in laying the controversy to rest. Stogdon had intended to ask for ordination at the next meeting of the Exeter Assembly in September, 1717. It was sure to be strenuously opposed, and whatever the outcome the unity of Devonshire ministers would be shattered. Peirce therefore talked with Stogdon and persuaded him to admit that 'he had been imprudent in his management'. He also promised that 'should he remove anywhere else, he would apply himself wholly to (practical religion), without meddling with . . . points of speculation. All people were sensible of his abilities, and thought it pity they should not be employ'd for the good of the church; and therefore a project was form'd for the opening a way for his preaching in another county'. Accordingly, by a certificate dated 15th July, 1717, Hallett, Withers and Peirce testified that Stogdon had been approved as a suitable candidate for the ministry by the Assembly (this had happened in May, 1714) and that 'his conversation since, as well as before, his examination, has been . . . sober and christian; and that his preaching in these parts has met with good acceptance'. Nothing was said of his opinions, and the introduction later enabled Stogdon to obtain ordination and to take the pastorate of a small church in Somerset.

Stogdon having been removed from the scene things became quieter in Exeter for the rest of the year. The September Assembly certainly did not deal with the controversy. This period of calm ended in Christmas week, 1717. Then Peirce unguardedly used an expression in a lecture which was immediately taken by Lavington to be a reflection on the true nature of Christ. It needed only this spark to bring everything to a head once again. In January the Committee of Thirteen sent four of their number to each of the ministers to ask them to 'assert the eternity of the Son of God'. Peirce complied towards the end of a sermon on the Prodigal Son, in terms which were most likely above the heads of his Hearers. He concluded with a telling appeal for tolerance, which must have struck home.

Where we see mens lives answerable to the christian rule, let us learn not to judge one another; we are all the servants of Christ, and to him as our master we must each of us either stand or fall . . . There is one thing which I can't but think it just for men to insist on; that as the holy scriptures are the only rule in such matters, so men should not pretend to impose their notions upon others . . . Let him express himself as he thinks is most agreeable to the stile or sense of the scripture; only let him leave me the same liberty. And this liberty let others tamely give up as they please; I do, and will, insist upon it for myself, as a reasonable creature, a christian, a protestant, and a Dissenter.

But was it reasonable to expect the orthodox majority to sit calmly by while their most capable minister either ignored or only luke-warmly supported what they considered to be the essential item of the Christian faith?

It is at this point that Peirce's superior ability becomes very plain. The two Nonconformist ministers in Exeter who were free from all suspicion of heresy, John Lavington, and Deliverance Larkham (Congregationalist), preached often enough against the new ideas. Yet even their friends did not consider them able to manage the controversy efficiently. It was for this reason, and not with any desire to begin an Inquisition, that the Committee of Thirteen besought Peirce to preach in defence of the established doctrines in June, 1717, and January, 1718. When he failed to come down strongly on the orthodox side, and there seemed good reason to believe him infected with the new ideas himself, the orthodox party in Exeter was left without an adequate leader. Consequently, from the autumn of 1717 onwards the chief protagonist of the orthodox point of view became John Walrond, a member of an Exeter family who was at this time pastor of the Presbyterian church at Ottery St. Mary. He could not compete with Peirce in scholarship or oratory, but in the outcome proved a more skilful politician.

Matters dragged on unhappily for the first half of 1718. The controversy was again not dealt with at the Exeter Assembly in May, although Peirce's sermon which closed the proceedings (on Matthew xxviii. 20) did not pass without criticism. The ministers had a natural reluctance to debate a subject which it was known would bitterly divide them. If an open breach could be postponed many of them hoped that the trouble would gradually be overcome with the exercise of a modicum of Christian charity. The more perspicacious realized that a clash was bound to take place in the near future, and throughout these months there was taking place a jockeying for position, a grouping of resources and influence before the storm broke.

Peirce left for a visit to London at the beginning of July. This was his custom every year, but he had decided on this occasion to see what support he might obtain from his colleagues in London. It was the custom of country ministers to seek the advice of their more learned brethren in the Capital when serious problems arose. Peirce definitely received a report before leaving Exeter, that 'this affair would be brought into the Assembly in September'.

When Peirce returned to Exeter in mid-August, he learnt that John Walrond had been in correspondence with William Tong, one of the London Presbyterian ministers, giving his account of affairs in Devon, and asking advice. The decision to take this step was made when the news came that Hubert Stogdon was shortly to be ordained at the Rev. Matthew Towgood's meeting-house at Shepton Mallet in Somerset. John Ball of Honiton wrote in violent terms to Matthew Towgood's brother at Axminster:

I hear that your Mr. Stogdon is to be ordained at your brother's meeting-house. Doth your brother know what a confession of faith is carried about Exon as his, which all the ministers are against? . . . I am not willing my name should be mentioned, because Mr. Stogdon takes me as his enemy, which God is my witness I never was; but must I hold my peace, and see the church overrun with Arianism, to dethrone Christ, and bring in worship of a creature? These things should be considered, or where will faith be, and what will non-conformity end in? [1]

This news and a lamentation that the younger ministers in Devon were falling away from orthodox beliefs, were the main ingredients of Walrond's letter to Tong. The latter considered the matter serious enough to call together an unofficial meeting of Presbyterian and Independent ministers in London to discuss it. A reply was sent to Walrond signed by Tong and Benjamin Robinson (as chairman of the meeting) on 25th August, 1718. The advice was unexceptionable. It was

Not to suspect any among us to be infected with these Errors, unless we have good ground for it . . . Not to be harsh or hasty with those that are doubtful and wavering . . . Yet to represent to them faithfully and seriously the great Danger of denying the proper Godhead of Christ and of the Holy Ghost . . . To let them plainly know, that we cannot . . . recommend any to the Office of the Ministry by Ordination . . . who are known to maintain so great an Error . . . That if any already in the Ministry shall fall into that pernicious Error, and persist in it, and teach Men so, it will become our Duty . . . to warn People of them.

[1] *Monthly Repository*, XII, p. 581.

In addition to obtaining this clearcut advice from the London ministers, Walrond and Ball made sure that the orthodox party would be fully represented at the Exeter Assembly in September, 1718, by writing to their friends to warn them that they proposed to bring in a resolution on the subject of the Trinity. Peirce accused John Ball of sending 'circular letters . . . round the country'. Ball admitted to writing 'only to two or three ministers desiring their presence'. The latter was probably all that was necessary: those selected could be relied upon to pass the word to their neighbouring colleagues.

Meanwhile, to see whether an open trial of strength could at the last moment be avoided, Peirce and Withers visited Ball and Walrond, by invitation, at the latter's house at Ottery. Walrond announced that he definitely intended to call for a declaration of faith concerning the Trinity at the Assembly, a declaration which he considered absolutely necessary to clear from the ministers the suspicion of Arianism. 'Mr. Walrond profess'd then . . . that he had a very tender regard to my reputation in particular, that the usefulness of my writings might not be hinder'd . . .' There is no good reason for doubting Walrond's sincerity: his attitude is logical. The central doctrine of the Christian religion had to be defended at all costs, yet if the abilities of such a man as James Peirce could be retained for the orthodox cause, so much the better. Peirce could never endure criticism of himself, however, and attributed Walrond's action to jealousy and a desire to destroy his position in the country. In view of Walrond's refusal to accept the call to an Exeter pastorate in 1705 and his reluctance to accept a second call in 1730, it is difficult to accept Peirce's accusations as correct.

At this private meeting Peirce objected further to the calling of a preparatory meeting in Exeter on the Monday before the Assembly, to which he alleged only friends of Ball and Walrond had been invited. He secured an invitation for Withers and himself as well. The four ministers parted on a fundamental misunderstanding. Peirce and Withers imagined that the others had agreed to forego the formal declaration on the Trinity when the Assembly met, provided that in future all candidates should be examined very much more strictly concerning their beliefs. But the others had no intention of giving up the public declaration of orthodoxy, although they had been very pleased when Peirce and Withers accepted their suggestion for closer examination of candidates.

The Assembly met in the following week. The orthodox party met both on the Monday, and again on the Tuesday morning before the first formal meeting. Withers was invited to attend these gatherings, but not Peirce, and he attempted to defend his colleague. It now became clear that whereas the intention of Walrond and Ball was merely to clear those present of suspicion of heresy, and to discourage the trend towards the new theology, many of the country ministers were far less charitable in their intentions. Samuel Stoddon of Aylesbeare in conversation with friends in the City that day was asked, 'And what if some will not declare as you do? Then said the minister, we will set a mark upon them. And being ask'd what they would do afterwards, he reply'd, We will leave them to the people, who know what they are to do with them.'

Surprisingly enough Peirce and his supporters succeeded in electing a Moderator (John Cox of Kingsbridge) and Scribe (Isaac Gilling) favourable to themselves. Apart from this the first day's sessions did nothing except transact formal business and examine the two candidates for ordination. (Peirce was one of the examiners, Larkham another.)

The ministers got to grips with the situation only at an informal meeting on the Tuesday evening, at the house of John Pym, one of the Committee of Thirteen, and Treasurer of the Assembly's Fund. At this meeting 'it was proposed as very necessary, that we should purge ourselves and clear our reputation to the world'. Peirce immediately launched himself into the debate, and succeeded in tying up his opponents in verbal knots without altering their resolve in the least. His colleague John Withers received a more sympathetic hearing. He had prepared a detailed list of 'Reasons . . . why this following Declaration should not be brought into the Assembly: I believe the Father, Word and Spirit to be the one God.' His plea could be reduced to two essentials: that the proposed declaration was not in words of Scripture and that therefore any Dissenter would be justified in refusing to subscribe; and that the words used were just as heretical in the other direction as Arianism itself, being those of Paulus Samosatenus, condemned by the Council of Nice. Even Withers had to proceed through many hostile interruptions, and he certainly did not succeed in moderating the intentions of the majority.

At the formal meeting of the Assembly on the Wednesday morning, John Ball rose and said (in words reported by Peirce):

Mr. Moderator, I desire to know whether we shall declare against the errors of those, who deny the divinity of our Saviour. 'Tis thought necessary by several ministers here present, that we declare against the errors and heresies relating to the divinity of the Logos and the Holy Ghost.

Feelings on both sides were very strong, and the Moderator found it impossible to keep order. Propositions and amendments were brought forward without any votes taking place on them, and interruptions were frequent and noisy. The Moderator himself ran into trouble when he attempted to censure John Enty of Plymouth for departing from the usual method of speaking in the Assembly. But finally a vote decided in the affirmative that a Declaration on the Trinity should be made.

Further debate followed on the form in which the proposed Declaration should be made. Peirce made a final attempt to turn defeat into victory by suggesting that it would be enough to declare 'the holy scriptures are a sufficient rule of faith, without human additions and interpretations', but the decision was for everyone to declare his position either in his own or in Scripture words, as he thought fit. And so the ministers began, with the crowds gathering in the narrow street outside for the afternoon lecture. Joseph Hallett II, senior minister by ordination, began by declaring his beliefs (which seem orthodox enough) in Scriptural phrases, and ending with a deprecation of the imposition of tests of any kind. When his turn came John Withers made a declaration in his own words which was scrupulously orthodox, but he declined to use the form of words suggested by most of his brethren. Peirce openly declared his belief in the subordination of Son and Holy Ghost to God the Father, the first time he had done this in public. Matthew Huddy of Penzance, Samuel Carkeet of Totnes, and Edward Colton of Kingskerswell, all refused to make any declaration whatsoever. Not satisfied entirely with these personal declarations, which the Scribe had been ordered not to take down in the Minutes, it was then decided to make some record of what had been done. The Scribe was therefore 'required to write the following words, which were dictated to him by Lavington. "Tis the general Sense of this Assembly, That there is but one living and true God; and that the Father, Son, and Holy Ghost are the one God." '

The debate over, the Assembly ended with a public Lecture by Matthew Huddy on Jude, verse 3, 'It was needful for me to write unto you, and exhort you, that you should contend for the Faith which was once delivered to the Saints.' This text was extremely apposite to the situation, and was in substance a plea for the sufficiency of the Bible as a guide to matters of faith as against Creeds and Glosses made by Councils or Fathers of the Church. The Assembly refused to pass a vote of thanks to him, as was customary. The following morning,

Thursday, 10th September, Isaac Gilling preached another sermon at
6 a.m. before the ministers went home. Being on 'rash judging' this
also proved unpopular and only exasperated his hearers.

The orthodox party had achieved its object of declaring in favour of
the traditional doctrine of the Trinity, with one dissentient and three
abstentions, though the wording of some of the declarations may not
have been entirely satisfactory to its leaders, nor the manner in which
the debates had been carried on. It remained to be seen what the effect
of their action would be. What immediately followed was an outburst
of pamphlet skirmishing, which in itself showed that neither side was
satisfied with the position. It was not until November that Samuel
Stoddon's prophecy came true, and the people took action. Then the
Committee of Thirteen asked its four ministers to meet it, and to say
what they really believed on the disputed doctrine. Elected solely to
look after the Ministers' Fund, the 'Thirteen' had no authority to
demand these assurances from their pastors. Yet, being the men of
greatest wealth and influence in their societies they were the natural
people to take a lead if anything was to be done at all. They had
remained remarkably patient until this moment, almost two years
after the controversy had first broken out. It must have been apparent
to them by this time that unless Peirce publicly declared his views to
have altered, then he must go. The 'Thirteen' may have still hoped that
he would make such a declaration: in any case he had to be given the
opportunity. Of the orthodoxy of Withers and Hallett they probably
felt somewhat reassured since the Exeter Assembly of the previous
September, and hoped that they would fall into line without further
argument.

At the meeting the 'Thirteen'

Earnestly pray'd our Ministers . . . either to declare in the Sense of the said
Assembly . . . or in the Words of the Westminster Assembly of Divines, in
an answer to the Sixth Question of the lesser Catechism . . . Or in the words
of the First Article of the Church of England . . . which they had already
signed to and approved of: But we had no Satisfaction to either of the said
Proposals from three of our four Ministers; but instead thereof one of them
expressly declared for a Subordination.

This was Peirce, who also told the Committee 'that I could not satisfy
my conscience to lay down my ministry my self; if they would venture
to lay me aside, and that would make them easy, I should be satisfied,
and give them no trouble'. This promise can hardly have been made in
expectation that it would be taken up: in the event Peirce gave as much

trouble as he possibly could. Towards the end of the conference Peirce was given to understand that if he would return to the use of the form of Doxology ascribing Glory to Father, Son and Holy Spirit, and allow the teaching of the Westminster Catechism, this would help very much to put an end to the trouble which had arisen. He refused the first, on the grounds that he could find no example of it in the Bible. The second duty had been assigned to Hallett after Peirce's arrival, and he had only stopped catechizing the children because failing sight had made it difficult for him to teach them. He offered to try again if a 'more legible edition of the book' could be acquired. Peirce's speciality had been expounding the Scriptures: a similar division of duty had been customary at Bow Meeting.

The ejection of Roger Beadon by his congregation at Budleigh, which came soon after the September meeting of the Assembly, must have been ominous to Peirce. The idea of expulsion as the probable solution of the dilemma was already in the air. The 'Thirteen' may have hoped that favourable advice from London ministers might at the last moment influence Peirce to compromise with them, but after this November meeting they could have had little prospect that it would happen. The appeal to London and all the negotiations which followed are better understood as a further manoeuvring for position before making the final decision.

A letter dated 22nd November was sent to the London Ministers by the surviving members of the Committee. (Jerome King having recently died, there was one vacancy.) A brief outline of the state of affairs ended with the request that 'you will advise what becomes us as private Christians to do, and how we ought to behave ourselves in so critical a juncture'.

Reluctance to come to grips with so thorny a problem delayed a reply until 6th January, 1719. Then it was a polite refusal to 'interpose, at least till we see it further necessary'. This reply had advised the Committee to consult further with local ministers before taking any other action. It did this immediately, and the seven ministers of neighbouring churches invited to give advice were John Ball of Honiton, William Horsham of Topsham, Samuel Hall and John Moore from the two Tiverton churches, John Walrond of Ottery, Josiah Eveleigh of Crediton, and Joseph Manston of Lympstone. They met in Exeter on 19th January, 1719, and the next day went to see the three ministers under suspicion, Peirce, Hallett and Withers, clearly informing them what was being done. Again appears the complaint, so often made

G

throughout the whole crisis, that Peirce would 'not write or preach against these new notions'. They both desired his skill in defence of orthodoxy, and feared the sting of his pen if he should be expelled. Peirce later accused the Committee of only asking advice from those hostile to him, but this may be dismissed. The advice had to come from ministers outside Exeter, yet the Committee could not wait until the next meeting of the Assembly. The obvious course was to apply to those ministers who could come into Exeter conveniently, and this is exactly what was done. No neighbouring minister of the Presbyterian persuasion was omitted. One of them, indeed, Joseph Manston, had at one time deviated from complete orthodoxy, a fact known to Peirce.

The Seven agreed on three general resolutions, but requested the Committee to wait a further fortnight in order to give them time to obtain the opinions of colleagues in London, in Devon and Somerset. The resolutions were:

1. That there are some Errors in Doctrine which are a sufficient Ground for the People to withdraw from their Ministers holding such Errors.
2. That the denying the true and proper Divinity of the Son of God, viz. That he is one God with the Father, is an Error of that Nature; contrary to the Holy Scriptures, and common Faith of the reformed Churches.
3. That when so dangerous an Error is industriously propagated, to the overthrowing of the Faith of many, we think it the indispensable Duty of Ministers, who are set for the Defence of the Gospel, earnestly to withstand it; and to give reasonable satisfaction to their People of their Soundness in the Faith.

A copy of this letter was not sent to Peirce, and he had a justifiable cause for grievance when he only obtained one at second-hand.

The 'Seven' had agreed to meet again in Exeter on 9th February in order to give the Committee their advice. But by then they had received a request from London to postpone their meeting for the time being, as it was possible that a plan might be now devised to provide a peaceable solution to their problems. The Seven ministers agreed. What had happened was that Peirce had written to his own friends in London, requesting that their influence should be brought to bear. The most influential of these was John Shute Barrington, M.P., who had from 1714 onwards led the Parliamentary campaign for the repeal of the Test, Corporation, Occasional Conformity, and Schism Acts. On 13th December, 1718, Lord Stanhope had introduced a Bill in the House of Lords which aimed at removing these repressive Statutes.

The measure met with considerable opposition, to which the Trinitarian dispute raging at Exeter provided ammunition. Barrington therefore thought it highly desirable to attempt to compose matters there. His advice, laid before the Committee of the Three Denominations in London (an association for handling matters of common interest to Presbyterians, Independents and Baptists) was that any accusation of heresy should be proved by adequate witnesses, and that if a test of orthodoxy had to be imposed that test should be adherence to Scripture as the only rule of faith, and no other formula. These arguments were identical with those put forward in his own defence by Peirce at Exeter, and it is open to conjecture whether Barrington's proposals were not in fact drawn up by Peirce himself.

The Committee of the Three Denominations decided to lay the proposals before a general assembly of the London Ministers. This fateful decision resulted not in composing the situation at Exeter, but spread the controversy to the larger stage of the Capital. The London Ministers met in Salters' Hall on 19th and 24th February, and 3rd March. At the latter meeting they split up into two almost equal bodies, one in favour of accompanying their advice to Exeter with a subscription to the doctrine of the Trinity, and one against. The Subscribers met again separately on March 9th, and the Non-Subscribers on 10th March. The Subscribers sent their Advices to Exeter on 7th April: that from the Non-Subscribers had already been despatched on 17th March. Their terms were similar, and both began with the statement, probably suggested by the First Resolution of the 'Seven' which had been sent up to London at the end of January, that there were errors of doctrine which warranted and obliged their people to withdraw from Ministers who professed them. But whereas the Non-Subscribers continued on the lines of Barrington's suggestions, the Subscribers openly specified that the 'Denying of the true and proper Divinity of the Son of God and the Holy Spirit . . . is an Error contrary to the Holy Scripture.' [1]

Neither of these sets of advice reached Exeter in time to affect the situation. The 'Seven' waited four weeks for a reply from London, and then met on 4th March, handing their original three resolutions to the Committee of Thirteen as their formal advice. They must have heard of the course of events at Salters' Hall, and knew that whatever advice

---

[1] Powicke, F., 'Salters Hall Assembly and the Advices for Peace' (*Trans. Cong. Hist. Soc.*, 7, 1916–18, pp. 213–23). Thomas, R., 'Non-subscription controversy amongst the Dissenters in 1719' (*J. Eccles. Hist.*, Vol. 4, 1953, pp. 162–86).

eventually came from that Assembly would be divided and inconclusive. It would have been better if these ministers had shouldered their responsibilities firmly from the beginning and pronounced their decision at once. All through this controversy the tendency to pass responsibility on to someone else is most noticeable. The only result of procrastination was to spread the dispute on to the national plane, and to bring about the disruption of old-style nonconformity. No one on either side emerges from the situation with credit.

On 5th March the Committee of Thirteen asked the four ministers to meet again. The three Resolutions were read to them, and they were asked to own that 'the Son of God was one God with the Father'. Peirce asked the 'Thirteen' to wait until the advice from London was received: they would not agree. Peirce asked for time to consider his answer: he was told it must be given 'presently'. He then declared that he would not subscribe to any creed not specifically mentioned in Scripture. Hallett followed his example. Lavington, as expected, made a declaration acceptable to the Committee. Withers offered a declaration in the words of Bishop Pearson[1] but this was not accepted. The 'Thirteen' said that they 'were for withdrawing from us, but were for parting amicably'.

The Committee of Thirteen had no power to exclude any minister from the meeting-houses. But the Trustees had, and now used it. The Trustees of James' Meeting (where Peirce and Hallett were the accredited ministers) were appointed in January, 1705, and were Samuel Munckley, Thomas Jeffery, Jonathan Lavington and Andrew Lavington. Munckley was one of the Committee of Thirteen from 1702 to 1721; Jeffery from 1699 to 1742, being Treasurer of James' Meeting from 1705 onwards, and of the 'Thirteen' from 1721 to 1742. Members of the Lavington family would follow the lead of the Rev. John Lavington. So if the Committee of Thirteen decided that Peirce and Hallett should be expelled, the Trustees of James' Meeting would confirm this judgment without hesitation. That this is what happened is confirmed by Peirce himself in his 'Case of the Ministers ejected at Exon.' On Friday 6th March, 1719, the trustees locked the doors of James' Meeting, without notifying either of the ministers what they had done. On the Saturday, Peirce, wishing to go to the vestry to prepare his sermon, found he could not get in, and applied to one of the Trustees for the reason. From the nature of his reply, referring to his 'family' it is most likely that the person approached was Andrew

[1] Pearson, J., *Exposition of the Creed*, 1659.

Lavington. He received a most discourteous answer and was later told that he and Hallett might preach at Little Meeting, and Withers at Bow, as was the latter's custom. By this time John Withers had offered to subscribe to the Nicene Creed and to the First Article of the Church of England, and at the eleventh hour was spared from ejection.

On the following Tuesday the trustees of all the three chapels met and decided to close them to Peirce and Hallett from that time.

Action had been taken, but controversy continued. On Wednesday, 11th March, Peirce and Hallett attempted to call a General Meeting of Subscribers in order to put their case before them. About 31 attended this assembly in a private house. Soon afterwards the 'Thirteen' and the Trustees also called a meeting of subscribers, attended by 'at least eighty eight . . . who all agreed in the fitness of the measures that had been taken'. No record survives which tells how many subscribers there were at this time, but a list of 1708 totalled 250 exactly. If the figures attending these meetings are correct, neither was a truly representative gathering. As always, a large party abhorred controversy of any kind, and was ready to acquiesce in the actions taken by the Trustees, provided that the affair could be terminated. It is unlikely, either, that these people would ever have voted positively for the ejection of the two ministers, had a general meeting been called before the decisive action of the Trustees.

On the following Sunday after his ejection Peirce preached to those who had followed him (estimated at 300) in a private house on 'The Evil and Cure of Divisions.' His supporters included some men of wealth, for they were able to build at the beginning of the following year, 1720, a new chapel at the Mint, where Peirce and Hallett were appointed joint ministers.

By the time of the May meeting of the Exeter Assembly in 1719 the ejectment of the two Exeter ministers had caused feelings to run very high. The two partially contradictory sets of advice had been received from London. On the second day the large majority of those attending the Assembly followed the example of the London Subscribers by making a voluntary declaration of their faith in the Trinity. They did this by subscribing either to the First Article of the Church of England, or to the answers to the 5th and 6th Questions of the Westminster Shorter Catechism, or to the collective sense of the preceding Assembly, 'That there is one living and true God, and that the Father, Word and Holy Ghost are that one God.' 46 signed at the Assembly and 9 others assented later. 13 ministers and 6 candidates refused to subscribe, and do not appear at any later Assembly. The Non-Subscribers were headed by Joseph Hallett II, James Peirce, and Isaac Gilling of Newton Abbot. Joseph Hallett III, who succeeded his father at the Mint Meeting, was also one of them. In the years following 1719 subscription to the doctrine of the Trinity was required of all candidates for ordination, and from all new ministers coming into the county from elsewhere.

Throughout this tragic disruption neither side at any time appreciated the opposing point of view. Peirce and his associates did not consider the accepted doctrine of the Trinity to be of cardinal importance: variations of belief could therefore be accepted by him with equanimity. Ball, Walrond, Lavington, Enty, on the other hand, did hold that the Trinity was vital to Christian belief: departure from it would undermine the whole basis of their religion. In the light of subsequent history their instinctive reaction must be judged correct. Any attempt to reduce Christ to a subordinate position has always resulted in a drift to Unitarianism, and finally to regarding Him merely as a gifted human being. This is quite a rational position to hold, but it cannot be termed Christianity.

As for the actions of those most concerned, the Trustees of James' Meeting, although legally empowered to act as they did, were extremely highhanded in operation, and Andrew Lavington's arrogant assertion to Peirce on 7th March, 1719, that 'they were resolved upon having the place and ministers they liked, let the majority be ever so much against them; for they were able themselves to maintain them', was the worst possible handling of the situation which could be imagined. The Committee of Thirteen was patient and careful throughout. It did not take decisive action until November, 1718, when the controversy had already been raging for almost two years. Between then and the following March the Committee took competent advice and allowed themselves plenty of time to consider it. The attitude of the 'Thirteen' was quite simple: they were the leaders of the Presbyterian interest in the city, and it was their duty to safeguard the truths of religion as they had been taught to them. Granted that passions were running so high in Exeter, a division amongst the Presbyterians would have occurred in any case. From September, 1718, onwards many members of James' Meeting refused to attend the Lord's Supper when Peirce and Hallett were officiating, preferring to take Communion at Bow under Lavington. Some also refused to attend Lavington's services when he preached at James'. The accounts of the Committee of Thirteen show that subscriptions were held back in the last quarter of 1718 and the first quarter of 1719. The two districts which normally contributed most to the fund were South Ward within the Walls and South Without. In the last quarter of 1717 these had contributed respectively £23 14s. 3d. and £20 16s. In the last quarter of 1718 the figures had fallen to £18 16s. 3d., and £7 15s. In 1719 a total of £78 7s. 6d. was collected for the whole city for the first quarter, without specifying the districts, an indication that regular collections had broken down for the time being.

A secession had to take place, given the temper of both sides. Either the Trustees and the 'Thirteen' acted in the manner they did, and retained control of the chapels, keeping the secession as small as possible: or else they had to sit back and let affairs drift until Peirce and Hallett obtained complete control of James' Meeting, the orthodox members of which would have moved elsewhere, possibly to Bow Meeting under Lavington, but more likely to the Independents and Baptists, or to the Church of England.[1]

---

[1] A list of the pamphlets issued in the course of the Trinitarian dispute which have a bearing on the situation at Exeter are given in Appendix A.

CHAPTER VII

REAPING THE WHIRLWIND, 1720–1760

THE Trinitarian Controversy ended in the apparent victory of the orthodox party in Exeter and in Devon. At the cost of some 300 of their membership, estimated at 2250 in 1715, the Exeter Presbyterians had expelled the sources of the new theology from their midst, and the Exeter Assembly had raised up a barrier to future trouble in the shape of a Trinitarian test on all candidates for the ministry and on all ordained ministers entering the county from elsewhere.

The minutes of the Exeter Assembly become available again for September, 1721, and May, 1722, and then from May, 1723, until September, 1728. The attendances vary a lot but there are as yet no definite signs that the authority of the organization was on the wane. The May, 1723, meeting had a record attendance of 57 ministers and 18 candidates. All candidates and ministers were regularly made to declare their belief in the Trinity, in some cases being brought back again to retestify. Thus in May, 1725, George Denbury, recently come to be the minister of the Castle Lane Congregationalists, made the customary declaration, but in May, 1727, the following passage was recorded:

'Mr. Denbury having afresh renewed his confession of his firm believing of the Doctrine of the Trinity, we declared ourselves satisfied that he is no Arian.'

Candidates for ordination were still given the ordeal of close examination and required to present a Latin Thesis, which practice did not end until after 1753. One of the favourite questions was that given to Mr. Brush in September 1723 and to Mr. George Castle in May, 1746: 'An Spiritus Sanctus sit Deus? '

The minutes of the Assembly for 1729–32 and for May, 1733, are missing, and the records of those attending in the 1730s and 1740s reveal a definite decline. Usually between 25 and 30 ministers attended, with possibly half a dozen candidates and strangers. On one occasion only, in May, 1738, did the attendance reach its level of the period of prosperity, and that was because of the debate which took place then about giving support to the Taunton Academy.

Exactly what the motion originally brought in was, is not indicated, but it must have involved support for the Taunton Academy. The voting was 17 for and 20 against, but the preference of 14 was not given, presumably because they had either left the meeting or refused to vote either way.

A further indication of decline was the fall in the Assembly's income. Throughout the 1730s receipts were usually about £100 at the September meeting, and between £70 and £80 each May. In May 1742 only £60 was received (of which Exeter provided £41) and the minute appears:

It appearing to this Assembly that there are at present such defects in the contributions that have formerly been made to the Fund, & still likely to be greater if the Ministers don't make collects . . . tis desired of the Brethren present and of all that are members of the Assembly that they do make a collection at least once a year.

No improvement took place, however, for the receipts at the next few Assembly meetings were £78, £63, £90, £62. A clue to what may have been happening comes in a minute of the May, 1744, Assembly. 'Agreed that the money collected in the several Congregations be brought into the Fund to be disposed of by the vote of the Assembly.' This could mean that some churches had been sending their collections direct to needy causes, without reference to the Assembly. It would have been one way for the Trinitarian ministers to make sure that their collections only helped causes that were still orthodox.

Some slight relief came in September, 1746, with the collection of £119 3s. 2¼d. Every church had been galvanized into collecting on this occasion, and on top of all came 'From the Rev. Mr. Mudge of Plymouth as a grateful return for what he had formerly received from our Fund . . . £52 10s.' So the former student of Hallett's Academy, Headmaster of Bideford Grammar School, and Vicar of St. Andrew's, Plymouth, paid his debts to the memory of George Trosse, who had been his friend and patron as a boy. The improvement in the Fund was not maintained, and in May, 1753, the collections were £64 odd, of which the country churches only gave just over £28.

The next crisis in the Assembly's fortunes, which came in May, 1753, will be related later. Meanwhile it is necessary to resume the account of the Exeter Presbyterians. After the expulsion of Peirce and Hallett in 1719 the Committee of Thirteen settled down once more to its task of guiding the three united societies. Its minutes survive from its meeting on 2nd April, 1724, when the members are found discussing the amount which should be paid to 'Mr. John Handleigh' for collecting the subscriptions to the Ministers' Fund, and on 16th May following they began to 'consider how to dispose of those Legacys given by Benefactors . . . so as it may be perpetuated on good security'. No breath of controversy stirs the air: the events of 1717–20 might never have taken place for all the mention there is of them in the proceedings of the Committee.

The first task before the Exeter Presbyterians was to fill the gap left by the 'separation' of Peirce and Hallett, both of whom were paid in full to the end of the first Quarter of 1719. At the beginning of 1720 one of the vacancies in the pastorate was filled by the calling of Walter Furze. He had been a student at the Bridgwater Academy under the Rev. John Moore, and was ordained at South Molton in August, 1710, by order of the Exeter Assembly. He settled at Chulmleigh from 1710 to 1718, and then went to Bristol for two years, fortunately for him, as it meant that he did not become directly involved in the Trinitarian controversy. The Committee approved his orthodoxy, and paid the sum of £22 18s. for moving his household down to Exeter. The second minister chosen was John Enty, from Plymouth. Unlike Furze, Enty had taken a prominent part in the recent dispute, being one of the more frequent spokesmen of the orthodox side. In 1719 he had written a 'Defence of the Proceedings' of the May Assembly, which was promptly replied to by Peirce, and on 25th October, 1720, came Enty's pamphlet, 'Truth and Liberty Consistent', which sought to give a reasonable explanation of the position of the orthodox dissenters. He was now invited to Exeter to take the lead in trying to heal the divisions which still existed among those who had remained faithful to their churches. His able 'Answer to Mr. Peirce's Western Inquisition' which he set about compiling as soon as he moved to Exeter, has been quoted. It took the form of a collection of first-hand statements by the people concerned in the controversy, with Enty editing the whole and supplying the connecting narrative.

Furze died towards the end of 1722, and his place was taken in the second quarter of 1723 by James Green. He had also studied at the Bridgwater Academy under John Moore before being ordained in September, 1713. At the time of his call to James' Meeting he was at Shaftesbury.[1] In September, 1723, when the Assembly met,

Mr. Green, before he was desired to preach, did freely give an account of his Faith in the manner following, viz: 'I believe that there is but one living &

[1] *Trans. Cong. Hist. Soc.*, 1911–12, Vol. 5, p. 71.

true God & that the Father, Son & Spirit are that God'. And further he declar'd, that this Faith he would defend.

As has already been indicated, the Committee of Thirteen set about its job of raising money for the Ministers' Fund methodically enough. Collectors were appointed for each of the four Wards, East, North, South and West. In addition East and South Wards were redivided, 'Within' and 'Without' the walls, as Exeter had already begun to extend in these directions. The West ward included St. Thomas' parish on the other side of the Exe, and North Ward took in the parish of St. David's. The collectors were at first sometimes members of the Committee, but from 1712 the whole work was placed in the hands of one man, Thomas Norman, the Clerk of James' Meeting, for which he was paid 15s. a quarter.

Until after 1720 the Ministers' Fund depended almost entirely on personal subscriptions collected quarterly. Invested income was negligible. The accounts show just where in the City the main strength of the Presbyterians lay. South Within and South Without, which included the area around James' Meeting, the largest of the three chapels, at first provided the largest proportion of income. In 1712 they respectively subscribed £63 8s. and £55 0s. 6d. out of a total of £291 19s. In 1716 the figures were £118 9s. and £52 7s. 6d. out of a total of £384 14s. 6d. Even in 1720 after the secession had taken place, these two districts provided £86 17s. 3d. and £57 11s. out of £338 10s. 3d. It was in this South and West portion of the City in the seventeenth and eighteenth centuries that the cloth manufacturing industry was situated, and the bulk of the population lived.[1] Presbyterianism was very acceptable to successful merchants, for it gave them a degree of control over religious affairs which would have been impossible in the Church of England, or in the more democratic organizations of the Baptists, Independents and Quakers. It was only as the taint of heresy crept into the Presbyterian churches that the wealthy merchants one by one decided to return to the Church of England. Contributions from the East Quarter of the city, both Within and Without, were usually far below those from the other wards.

A list of those subscribing to the Ministers' Fund in 1708 was preserved in the Accounts Book. The figures were:

North:	44 persons.
West:	57 „

---

[1] Hoskins, W. G., *Industry, Trade and People in Exeter, 1688–1800*, 1935, pp. 111–50.

> East: 38 persons.
> South Within: 55   „
> South Without: 56   „

This made a total of exactly 250. John Evans' Survey of 1715 estimated the number of 'Hearers' at James' Meeting as 1100, at Bow 800, and at Little Meeting 350. It is evident that the Presbyterian Fund depended exclusively on the richer members of these societies. Furthermore, the amounts actually promised were not always forthcoming. The detailed list for 1708 shows that the amount promised by subscribers in the North Ward was £85 10s. For the years 1712–1713–1714 the actual sums paid were £57 14s., £64 10s., and £64 3s. 6d. Similarly South Without promised £77 12s. in 1708, but for these same three years actually gave £55 0s. 6d., £60 13s., and £61 3s.

Beginning in the 1720s the Committee of Thirteen found that it had surplus money to invest. This was the result of the first generation of Dissenters after the coming of Toleration dying off and bequeathing money to their churches. After some debate Polsloe Meadows, on the outskirts of the City, were bought in 1727 for £705 and tenants were secured. In 1742 this property, let in two portions, brought in an income of £35 each year. In 1736 another £500 was lent to a Mr. Edmund Carthew of Tiverton, at the interest of 4 per cent, and a mortgage was assigned to two members of the Committee on Carthew's estate. Other sums were invested in various stocks throughout this period, most frequently in Government Consolidated Annuities.

From 1730 the income from investments rose steadily, and by the end of the century it had become equal to the income from personal subscriptions. It is difficult to quote exact figures, because payment of rents and interest failed to be made regularly, and the accounts for one year may include payments for two or three years at one time. But it appears that whereas in 1717 only £6 5s. came from investments, later figures were:

1727: £26 1s.	1747: £61 16s. 11½d.
1737: £53 15s. 1½d.	1758: £69 6s. 3½d.

Despite this steady increase in investment income the Committee had periods when it was found difficult to meet its obligations. From a maximum of £384 received in 1716, income decreased more or less regularly until it fell below £300 in 1730. The receipts for 1742 and 1743 were £275 10s. 4½d., and £285 13s. 6d., and it was decided to 'advance' the subscriptions. The result was:

	1742.		1744.	
East Within.	£41 2s.	(21)	£66 6s.	(30)
East Without.	£11	(10)	£14 12s.	(13)
West & St. Thomas.	£33 15s.	(34)	£55 12s.	(39)
North & St. David's.	£28 12s.	(26)	£33 3s.	(28)
South Within.	£33	(21)	£47 1s	(28)
South Without.	£55 4s.	(22)	£66 4s.	(31)
	£202 13s. (134)		£282 18s. (169)	

The figures in brackets represent the number of individual subscribers in each division. The fall in the number of subscribers from the 250 of 1708 to the 169 of 1744 is a good indication of the effect of the Trinitarian Secession on the fortunes of the Exeter Presbyterians. The result of the 1744 financial adjustment was that total income rose again to £375 6s. 6d. But this level was not maintained and income again fell below £300 in 1749. There are frequent entries in the Accounts showing that Treasurers had to advance money themselves in order to pay the ministers at the correct times, in anticipation of interest and subscriptions due later. The inescapable fact was that while personal subscriptions were continuously falling from 1719 onwards, the situation was only partly redeemed by the increase in investment income. It is therefore not surprising that when John Lavington died in 1759 a successor was not appointed: the societies were content to be served by three ministers only. Ministers' salaries did not again reach the high level of 1717 (£100) until the end of the 18th century, but from 1720 to 1772 the figure aimed at was £80 for each minister, although for a time in the 1730s this was not reached, for the Fund did not allow it.

The upkeep of the meeting-houses depended on seat-rents. Records for Bow and Little Meetings have not survived, but the accounts book for James' Meeting is probably typical of the others. Like the Ministers' Fund, the income from Seat-rents became less as time went on. At intervals of five years throughout the lifetime of James' Meeting the income from this source was:

Year ending June 1694.	£14 1s. 0d.
June 1699.	£13 14s. 6d.
October 1704.	£19 12s. 0d. (included some from 1703).
October 1709.	Not recorded.
December 1714.	£11 14s. 9d.
„ 1719.	£10 14s. 6d.
„ 1724.	£13 5s. 9d.
„ 1729.	£10 17s. 6d.
„ 1734.	£8 8s. 6d.
„ 1739.	£9 4s. 0d.

December 1744.   £8 11s. 0d.
    „   1749.   £9 10s. 6d.
    „   1754.   £7 14s. 0d.
    „   1759.   Not recorded.

Outgoings were confined to repairs and ground rent. Typical entries were:

1714, October.   To Grinter the Masons worke about ye pulpit, etc.
  . . . . £1 2s. 0d.
1719, July.   To Js. Quick for pewter bason .   .   .   5s. 0d.
1723, Jan.   To Robert Walker, Esq. (ground rent) . . £2 5s. 0d.
1741, December. To Upjohn for 2 yrs. keeping the Clock . . £1 4s. 0d.

Fairly extensive repairs were necessary in 1746, costing £15 10s. 4½d.

The other financial commitments of the Presbyterians at this period were their annual contributions towards the Exeter Assembly Fund, and their own Poor Fund. Towards the Assembly the three Exeter churches were extremely generous. Between 1720 and 1753 sample figures are, at approximately five-year intervals:

Total from all sources.	*From Exeter alone.*
1723. £195 13s. 9d.	£96 12s. 10½d.
1727. £197 11s. 3¼d.	£99 13s. 0½d.
1734. £214 8s. 0¼d.	£105 7s. 9¼d.
1737. £194 7s. 4¼d.	£100 16s. 10d.
1742. £159 0s. 6¼d.	£82 2s. 2¼d.
1747. £141 11s. 2½d.	£76 6s. 7½d.
1752. £163 15s. 9d.	£82 17s. 7d.

From this it can be seen that the Exeter Presbyterians were contributing towards the stipends of the country ministers about one-third of the amount raised yearly for the payment of their own ministers, and about one-half of the total money received by the Assembly.

The Poor Fund was on a much smaller scale. Detailed lists are included in a ledger for the two years 1741–2 and 1742–3. The number of persons in receipt of relief from this fund in those years were:

	James'.	*Bow.*	*Little Meeting.*
1741–2.	50.	34.	15.
1742–3.	51.	42.	19.

Payment was made monthly and the amounts given were extremely small, even for those days. The most frequent sums were 9d., 8d., and 6d., but in a few cases only 1d. is mentioned, and the highest amount given was 14d. The total given out varied from £3 to £5 each month.

In 1742 the total was £3 9s. in March, and £4 14s. in November, for example. The money was obtained by special collections taken each month at the celebration of the Lord's Supper, a practice which is still customary in Nonconformist churches to this day. The figures for the period March to December, 1742, were:

	James'.	Bow.	Little Meeting.
March 7.	£1 11s. 1d.	£1 2s. 0d.	4s. 3d.
April 4th.	15s. 2d.	£1 15s. 4½d.	6s. 3d.
May 2nd.	£1 3s. 1d.	£1 3s. 8d.	7s. 2d.
May 30th.	18s. 2½d.	11s. 1d.	4s. 9d.
June 1st.	£1 5s. 10d.	19s. 0d.	5s. 6½d.
Aug. 2nd.	16s. 11¼d.	£1 17s. 6d.	7s. 8¾d.
Sept. 3rd.	18s. 5d.	£1 4s. 9d.	5s. 5d.
Oct. 3rd.	19s. 5d.	17s. 11d.	5s. 7d.
Nov. 7th.	18s. 2d.	£1 5s. 3d	7s. 4d.
Dec. 5th.	£1 4s. 3¾d.	8s. 8d.	1s. 4d.

In addition to these regular collections for the Poor Fund it was the custom for a Public Fast to be held at irregular intervals, usually about two months, at the end of which a collection was taken for the Poor. These were united meetings held at James' and Bow Meetings in turn. Such gatherings to implore God's blessing, to acknowledge His mercy, to confess one's own shortcomings, were very important in the lives of the seventeenth and eighteenth century Nonconformists of all sects. They could either be formal meetings of the whole society, as were these in Exeter apparently, or else gatherings of a few friends to cope with some private emergency: the loss of a child, the coming of age of a son, the departure of a family to new surroundings. They were all primarily meetings for prayer, but discussion of problems and an occasional sermon also took place. They would last from two to six hours normally, but on special occasions whole days would be set apart for the Fast.[1] The amounts collected for the Poor Fund at the Exeter Fasts in the period March–December 1742 were:

4th March	£1 3s. 9d.
29th April	£2 9s. 6½d.
1st June	£2 6s. 10¾d.
30th August	£2 3s. 2¾d.
5th November	£2 5s. 10d.
10th December	£4 9s. 2d.

Unlike the other Funds, the amounts received into and paid out of the

[1] Cragg. G. R., *Puritanism in the period of the Great Persecution*, 1957, pp. 163–5.

Poor Account remained fairly constant from 1742 until 1760, the end of the period at present under consideration.

The method by which Ministers should be chosen was nowhere clearly laid down, although it had been specified in the first Minute Book of the Committee of Thirteen, which was reported missing as early as 7th June, 1743. Illustrative of what happened in the early period is the calling of John Walrond, following the death of John Withers on 26th November, 1729. The vacant pastorate was at Bow Meeting. On 1st December 'Mr. Jeffrey & Mr. Vowler were appointed to desire our 3 ministers to spend some time in Prayer to seek Gods direction in filling the vacancy made by the Death of Mr. Withers.'

On 6th December, 1729, 12 members of the Committee met, and ten of them agreed that Mr. Walrond should be asked whether he would be willing to accept the call to the pastorate if the forthcoming general meeting of subscribers were to ask him. On 18th December, at 'a general meeting at the Bow . . . Mr. John Walrond was unanimously chosen'. On 7th January, 1730, 'Mr. Vowler read Mr. Walrond's answer to the Peoples call which was in the negative'. On 12th January, 1730, another General Meeting at Bow appointed a Committee to select Ministers 'to come and preach probationary'. On 13th January invitations to preach were sent to six ministers, including Stephen Towgood of Topsham, who was to become one of the Exeter pastors at a later date. The 'Thirteen' had meanwhile resumed negotiations with Walrond, for on 26th January, the Chairman of another General Meeting of subscribers read out a long letter from this minister in which he declared himself willing to come after all, if the Exeter Presbyterians were not able to be unanimous in their choice of anyone else. Consequently on 9th February the invitation was renewed and Walrond accepted. One phrase in the letter ran: 'Our societies having no rationall prospect of any one person in whom harmony is so likely to be preferred as in yourselfs . . . have unanimously agreed to renew their former invitation . . .'

The 'Thirteen' had cleverly played on the fear of further secessions taking place in order to secure approval of the candidate of their choice, and simultaneously to persuade the reluctant candidate himself. Walrond, having taken a prominent part in the 1717–20 controversy, was not anxious to become the minister of the societies which had formerly sat at the feet of Peirce, Hallett and Withers, and whose members would remember every detail of the lamentable disruption. Yet although the guiding hand of the Committee of Thirteen is so evident, the real power of choice lay with the General Meeting of all subscribers, which could, had it wished, have overridden any recommendation of the Committee. It should also be noticed that these were general meetings of subscribers to the Ministers' Fund from all three societies, and not merely those who happened to belong to Bow Meeting.

The situation was different in 1743, the next occasion when a minister had to be chosen, this time for James' Meeting on the death of John Enty. A note followed the 14th January, 1744, Minute of the Committee:

> In Jan. without any previous appointment or notice given as usual to proceed to an election of a Minister in the room of Mr. John Enty lately deceased yet on the meeting of the contributors to adjust the subscriptions . . . to advance the Ministers Funds it was incisted on that an Invitation should be forthwith sent to the Reverend Mr. Stephen Towgood of Topsham . . . this method is without precedent, and contrary to our Rules usually observed . . .

It is difficult to believe that such a coup d'état could have taken place without some members of the hitherto dominant Committee of Thirteen being accessories before the fact. A whole generation had now passed since the 1717–20 controversy, and the ideas of Peirce and Clarke no longer startled Protestant Dissenters. The idea of the Subordination of the Second and Third Persons of the Trinity to God the Father had been accepted by a large section of the Exeter Presbyterians, and the 'Thirteen' themselves were divided. When Walrond had been called in 1730 there were still seven of the Committee who had taken part in the controversy. But by 1744 only one of the 1719 members was still alive—John Vowler—while no fewer than six new members of the Committee had been appointed in 1742–3. This undoubtedly had much to do with the Committee losing the initiative in 1744. The tendency in Presbyterian societies throughout the eighteenth century was towards the autonomy of individual congregations: the overriding position of the Committee of Thirteen in Exeter was in opposition to this trend. At no later time is there mention in the Committee's minutes of the election of Ministers. There is no record of the procedure followed in 1749, when James Green, who died at the end of that year, was succeeded by Micaijah Towgood, nor in 1754, when Abraham Tozer followed John Walrond.

Occasionally an echo of the bitter Trinitarian controversy is heard. In September, 1731, Rev. William Nation, Presbyterian minister in

Puddington village, preached before the Exeter Assembly in terms that criticized the teaching of the Exeter ministers. The Committee of Thirteen took umbrage, and on 14th February, 1732, addressed a letter to its four ministers designed to remove all shadow of suspicion from them. In it they said:

> . . . As in the choice of our Ministers (ever since the Arian controversy broke out among us) we have had nothing more at heart than the electing such for our Pastors who gave us satisfaction of their soundness in the doctrine of the Trinity and Assurance of defending it, so there is nothing hath more endeared you to us than your defence thereof . . . (we) earnestly request the continuance of your care to fortify the minds of your people against the dangerous errors of those who deny the true & proper Deity of Jesus Christ and of the Holy Ghost as well as from all other attempts to subvert the truths and dutys of the Gospell . . .

It was not the accusation of Antinomianism which worried the Committee as much as the suggestion given in the address of William Nation that many of the subscribers to the Exeter churches were of the same mind as himself, a suggestion which was indignantly repudiated in this same letter.

By the beginning of 1750, when Micaijah Towgood joined his cousin Stephen as joint pastor of James' Meeting, the attempt to hold the Exeter Presbyterian societies to a rigid orthodoxy had failed. Micaijah Towgood, although a much more attractively human character, held roughly the same theological opinions as James Peirce had thirty years previously, and his cousin Stephen shared this outlook. Stephen Towgood was the son of the Independent minister at Axminster who had rebelled against the Assembly's control of ordination in the 1690s: Micaijah was the son of his brother. Stephen had been minister at Topsham (1727–43) before coming to Exeter: Micaijah at Moretonhampstead (1722–36) and Crediton (1737–49). There is evidence of Micaijah Towgood's beliefs on the subject of the Trinity:

> By considering how widely learned and good men had differed from one another upon the subject of the Trinity, Mr. Towgood was convinced that the commonly received opinion could not reasonably be esteemed so fundamental an article of the christian faith as it was generally represented. He did not call in question its truth, but the subject seemed to him so abstruse and difficult that he could not imagine God had made the salvation of men to depend upon entertaining exactly the same notions concerning it.[1]

[1] Manning, James, *A sketch of the life and writings of the Rev. Micaijah Towgood*, 1792.

He 'conceived of Jesus Christ as the very first Being whom the power of the Father called into existence', and because of this 'he concluded (Christ) to be a proper object of worship'. At the same time,

> . . . as many of the society with which Mr. Towgood was connected, considered all worship of Christ as improper . . . though he himself thought it defensible, he . . . very seldom . . . practised it in public, considering it as an obligation to conduct the religious addresses of a mixt society, in such a manner, as would be conformable to the sentiments of all his fellow-worshippers.

Micaijah Towgood was eminently fitted to hold together a religious society in process of transition from orthodoxy to Unitarianism. A less charitable man would have been in grave danger of bringing about a secession of one party or the other, as happened at Crediton in 1757, seven years after he left it, and as happened in Exeter in 1795, three years after his death.

In Exeter the influence of Micaijah Towgood was felt immediately, with the adoption of his proposal that there should no longer be any test for those wishing to take Communion. Henceforth, provided that the ministers were satisfied that the would-be communicant lived a godly life and understood the meaning of the service, that would be enough. From this time the members of Bow Meeting decided only to allow their own ministers (from 1759 onwards one only, Abraham Tozer) to officiate at the Lord's Supper there. Being for the most part Calvinist and Trinitarian—for there is no evidence that Bow Meeting was ever greatly affected by the Arian trend—they preferred to keep the customary examination before admitting new members to full Communion.[1]

In one other significant direction Micaijah Towgood made his presence felt. In the year 1757 was published: 'A Collection of Psalms and Hymns for Divine Worship. London, J. Noon & J. Waugh. Exeter, Aaron Tozer.' This contained 218 items, including selections from Watts, Addison, Tate & Brady, and Doddridge. It is said to have been edited by Towgood and used at George's Meeting. A second edition appeared in 1779, printed by W. Grigg at Exeter, which was enlarged to 345 items. Both these hymn books were extensively used by Presbyterian/Unitarian societies elsewhere in the country.[2]

Within a few years of the coming of Micaijah Towgood to Exeter

---

[1] Thompson, Josiah, List of Dissenting Congregations, 1715 and 1773. Dr. Williams' Library MS. 34.5. Contains letter about Exeter affairs written by Micaijah Towgood.

[2] Julian, J., Dictionary of Hymnology, 1892, p. 1191.

the Trinitarian test imposed by the Exeter Assembly was allowed to fall into disuse. For many years before his death in 1743 John Enty had been the Scribe of the Assembly, and then from 1744 to 1747 John Lavington usually recorded the proceedings. After that date the name of Stephen Towgood most often appears as Scribe of the Assembly: his writing records the proceedings in May, 1753.

It being proposed to take the sense of the Assembly on the following question—Whether the Assembly will recommend any Candidate to ordination who will not declare his faith in the Deity of the Son & the Holy Spirit? —it was previously queried whether or no the said question should be put, & was carried by a majority in the negative: 10 pro, 14 con.

A note in the handwriting of John Lavington followed, adding a list of those who voted for and against, with three names of ministers who did not vote at all. Heading the list of those who wished to retain the test were John Walrond and John Lavington, the two aged survivals of the more dramatic struggle of 1717-20: the names of their sons appear further down the list. Those against the test were led by Stephen Towgood and Samuel Merivale of Tavistock. The name of Micaijah Towgood does not appear amongst those present. The last candidate for the ministry to take the hitherto customary declaration of belief in the Trinity was Samuel Lavington, at this very Assembly, before the debate began. He belonged to the Exeter Lavington family, and became minister at the Great Meeting at Bideford, being ordained there on 4th July, 1753, and remaining until his death in 1807. Between 1856 and 1869 the Great Meeting at Bideford was rebuilt and renamed Lavington Chapel after its most famous pastor.

The effect of the debate in the May, 1753, Exeter Assembly was to place upon the individual congregations the onus of deciding whether any particular minister was sound in the faith as they saw it. This year marks the end of Presbyterianism in Devonshire and Cornwall. The name was retained for many years longer: yet each church was from this time completely independent in organization, allowing such outside bodies as the Exeter Assembly no authority whatever over its affairs. The Presbyterian congregations which remained orthodox in belief, such as those at Ottery St. Mary, Dartmouth, and Appledore, to name only three, gradually dropped the term Presbyterian, became known as Independent or Congregational churches, and today are members of the Congregational Union of England and Wales. Those which did not remain orthodox retained the old name until the beginning of the next century, when it became legally permissible to adopt the label of Unitarian without incurring any penalties thereby.

The story of the smaller Dissenting societies in the city has now to be resumed. The Independent Meeting in Castle Lane finally closed in the 1730s. There is no need to seek far for the cause of its failure. Adhering to a rigid Calvinist line in religion in an age of increasing scepticism and lack of religious enthusiasm, the society had little chance of thriving when faced with a long period when its minister was incapacitated by illness, as was the case with Robert Atkinson from 1730 until his death, which occurred sometime in 1744. Its surviving members are reported to have joined with the Presbyterians, most likely with Bow Meeting, which had remained orthodox.[1]

The fortunes of the Baptists similarly varied according to the abilities and enthusiasm of their pastors. The society increased in size under Richard Sampson (1692–1716), leaving its original home in St. Catherine's Chapel for larger premises in Gandy St. in 1712, and by 1715 it was said to have about 300 'Hearers'. Micaijah Towgood, reporting to Josiah Thompson on the Exeter Dissenters in 1772 referred to Sampson as a man of 'plain address and no great learning, but very successful'. Yet Sampson was acquainted with Sir Isaac Newton, who referred to him à propos of a discussion on the possibility of depriving Dissenters of their Bibles: 'They could not possibly deprive Mr. Sampson of his, for he has it all treasured up within him.'[2]

After two years in which the congregation heard without enthusiasm the services of certain candidates a call to the pastorate was sent to the Rev. Joseph Stennett, (1692–1758), eldest son of another Joseph Stennett, a Seventh-Day Baptist minister of extreme Calvinist views. Only 26 at the time of his coming to Exeter, this young minister proved an immediate success. Not only did he keep his people free from the disrupting effects of the Arian controversy which broke out in Exeter with major violence soon after his arrival, but he led his congregation to the decision, made in 1722, to build a very much larger chapel in the most populous area of the city. The land in South St., in the parish of St. Mary Major, was given by Benjamin Heath, a prosperous merchant of equal standing with any of the Presbyterian Committee of Thirteen, and the new church was opened on 31st January, 1725, at a cost of £600 odd. Two silver Communion cups of exquisite workmanship

[1] Murch, op. cit., p. 373.
[2] Ivimey, Joseph, *A history of English Baptists . . .*, Vol. 2, 1814, p. 132.

were made for the church at this time by the silversmith John Elston, junior: these still survive.

For the West of England Baptists the Arian controversy reached its height about 1733. Many of the General Baptist societies adopted the new ideas of the nature of Christ, and eventually became Unitarian; those at Honiton and Moretonhampstead were examples. The Exeter church belonged to the Particular Baptist group, and Joseph Stennett, its pastor, made a considerable impression upon his colleagues at the meeting of the Western Association of Baptists at Broadmead Chapel, Bristol, in 1733. This assembly instructed him in the following year to draw up a reasoned defence of their principles for circulation in a letter to all member churches.

In 1737 Stennett moved to Little Wild St. Chapel, Lincoln's Inn Fields, London, where he remained until his death in 1758. Once again the Exeter church experienced a difficult period, and a decline in membership. The society was without a minister until 1741, when a candidate for the ministry was invited from Bristol Baptist Academy, Edmund Jones. He was ordained in 1743 after two years' probation. He remained until his death in 1765, having 'sustained the pastoral office with great reputation and esteem for 22 years, at which time the Church consisted of 90 members—30 men and 60 women'.[1]

Even allowing for the difference between baptised members and the wider circle included in the term 'Hearers' these figures represent a sad decline from the estimate of 1715. They are supported by the Answers to the Primary Visitation Queries of Bishop Clagett in 1744, when the Exeter Rectors reported the presence of 18 families of 'Anabaptists' within the City Walls, and another 16 families in the neighbouring parishes of St. Thomas, St. David's, St. Leonard's, and Alphington. This would represent a total Baptist population, including children, of about 150.[2] The position of the Exeter Baptists in 1760 was one of stagnation; holding fast to the orthodox faith but showing no adventurous concern for the people around them, no evangelistic zeal to spread the benefits of the Gospel, little desire to brighten their own worship of God. Until 1759 no singing was allowed, even of Psalms, except at the Lord's Supper,[3] and the services each Sunday must have been without attraction to anyone not already convinced of his own Election.

[1] South St. Baptist Church Minute Book (MSS.).
[2] Devon Record Office: Answers to Primary Visitation Queries, Diocese of Exeter, 1744. Visitation of Nicholas Clagett.
[3] Thompson, J., op. cit.

The Society of Friends was last referred to at the opening of the new meeting-house in Wynard's Lane in 1691. Under the Friends' organization Quarterly Meetings were held for comparatively large districts, in our case for the whole of East Devon. Monthly meetings 'for discipline' covered one town or group of villages, while Preparative meetings took place each week wherever a group of Friends happened to be living. At the Quarterly Meeting at Kingsbridge in October, 1696, it was decided that the Friends who lived at 'Exon, Crediton, Sandfordcourtney, Tharverton, Shobruke, and Cristo' should in future have 'one Monthly Meeting for Discipline wch. was . . . ordered to be kept at Exon ye last first day in every month'. In June, 1704, the two separate Monthly meetings at Topsham and Exeter were joined into one. That a certain amount of missionary work still took place, although the first enthusiasm of Quaker history had long passed away, is shown by two Quarterly Meeting minutes for 1707. In September an Exeter Quaker, Joseph Sparkes, reported the renting of a house at Chudleigh for a meeting, at 40s. per annum, and at the next meeting Joseph Sparkes and Richard Hingston reported that the people of Chudleigh showed 'Agreeableness & willingness . . . to hear ye testimony of Truth declared.' More frequently came down to earth entries in the Minutes of Exeter Monthly Meetings such as:

'March, 1712: Going Holmes accepted the office of looking after ye boys to keep them quiet.' He was later given a less strenuous post as gravemaker, which he held until 1743.

'August, 1724. This meeting agrees to give the porter at Southgate half a crown a quarter for his civility in opening the gate to Friends.'

May, 1735. It was agreed to alter the week day meeting at Exeter to the 4th day 'at the time of every year when the several parishes of the city go about in procession, Friends having been generally abus'd in coming to meeting that day'. This referred to the practice of beating the bounds of the city parishes on 'Holy Thursday'.

The Exeter Friends had at least one noteworthy member in the early 18th century. At the July Monthly Meeting in 1717 it was noted 'Michael Lee Dicker intends to go for Laydon in Holland and desiers a certificate from this meeting, the which is this day given him'. This Dr. Dicker was born in 1693, spent a year under Boerhaave at Leyden, and returned to practise in Exeter. He was one of the first physicians at the Royal Devon and Exeter Hospital in 1741. He died in 1752 and was buried in the Friends' Burial Ground.

Many references occur in quarterly and monthly meetings to Quaker activity in commerce, showing that although most of them were good business men they did have an active social conscience which bade them take concern for the welfare of others. At Topsham in December, 1699, it was decided 'for preventing scandell & reproach to be cast on Truth & friends, yt. sutch friends as imploy poore peopell doe not impose on them to take goodes or wares for their worke or labor, but to pay ym, with mony'. This was an intelligent anticipation of the anti-truck legislation of the nineteenth century: payment by goods was used quite extensively in the Devonshire woollen industry in the 18th century, with not always happy results.

A meeting at Exeter in December, 1710, rendered judgment that 'those who take lands covenanting to defray outgoings (including tithes) do not bear a faithfull testimony . . .' Payment of tithes was a sore point with Quakers from the earliest days of their existence: the other Nonconformist bodies only joined in the attack much later.

Other entries occur which throw light on some of the occupations of the Exeter Quakers in the eighteenth century.

November, 1705. James Goodridge to be advised to give up the retailing of brandy and strong liquors in his house at the bridge as it does tend to the dishonour of truth.

January, 1706. Emblem Sympson, inclining to set up a school in this city for teaching Friends' children, she is encouraged to do so.

A clear picture of the type of behaviour at which Friends particularly aimed was given at the Topsham Quarterly Meeting of January, 1713. Here it was laid down that the Friends appointed to visit families were to inquire 'whether meetings are duly maintained, and sleepiness & all manner of unbecoming behaviour' therein is avoided, that when Friends have occasion to be in a Tavern 'they be carefull not to exceed ye bounds of moderation in staying, drinking, smoaking & unnecessary talking'. They must also avoid ostentation in dress, 'p'ticularly unnecessary and unbecoming perriwigs, superfluous buttons and buttonholes & unecessary folds on ye sides and behind their coats, with hatts cock'd up in an unbecoming manner'. They must also keep to plainness of language, 'using thou and thee to a single person'.

There were also Women's Monthly Meetings held in Exeter in the early years of the eighteenth century. Monthly in name only, they were held at irregular intervals, seldom oftener than two months. In 1733 an attempt was made to define the business to be transacted by such meetings:

1. To take cognis of Proposals of marriage.
2. To appoint Representatives from our Mo.ly to our Quarterly Meeting.
3. And to make collections for all the poor women friends among us.

Allowances made to the Poor were on a moderate scale, although in excess of allowances made by the Exeter Presbyterians at the same period. A Prudence Mineard received 10s. a month: in 1740 8s. a month was paid to Dorothy Hobbs, and another 1s. to a woman for looking after her. It is somewhat surprising to find also the item of 7s. 1d. for 'ale before and at the funeral' of this same woman in 1750.

Reference to taking cognisances of marriage proposals illustrates the great care the Quakers took over such engagements. There is in the Exeter Monthly Meeting minutes a full record of a wedding in 1693, which shows the procedure usually followed. In July, 1693, John Cook reported that he wished to marry Temperance Tapper, both being present. At the next meeting, in August, two members, George Feay and Edward Limbrough, reported that John Cooke 'is cleare from being concerned with any other woman as fare as they can understand, & Alis Ruell likewise informs this meeting the same in the behalfe of said Temprance Tapper'. Both the young people then had to produce certificates of the consent of their parents & relations, and the meeting then allowed the marriage to be approved.[1]

The first and only indication of the number of Quakers living in Exeter and its environs comes in 1744, with the Primary Visitation of Bishop Clagett. The Exeter Rectors then reported the existence of 15 families of Quakers within the city, and a further 12 (with one more half Quaker and half Church of England) in the parishes of St. David's, St. Thomas, and St. Leonard's. This represented a total of about 120 souls.

The Mint Meeting, opened by the followers of James Peirce and Joseph Hallett II in 1720, proceeded quietly enough side by side with the orthodox Presbyterians. Joseph Hallett II died in 1722: his faculties had been weakening for some years before the secession took place. He was succeeded by his son, the third minister to bear the name in Exeter, who had been in the thick of the controversy. He was an able man, but of a cold authoritarian personality, very insistent on the dignity of the ministry. His most important publication was 'Critical Notes and Observations on the Scriptures'.[2] On 30th March, 1726,

[1] Dymond, R., Early records of Friends in Devonshire, n.d. (Contains verbatim extracts from Minute Books of Devonshire Meetings of the Society of Friends.)
[2] Fox, John, 'Memoirs' (Trans. Devon. Assoc., 1897, Vol. 29).

died James Peirce, only in his 53rd year, a very disappointed and
depressed man. John Fox wrote in his memoirs: 'After he was ejected,
he removed from the city into a retired house in the suburbs; but he
retired in a very ill-humor, for . . . he had not sufficient greatness of
mind to despise his enemies, and he suffered the triumph they gained
over him in his ejection to break his heart.' [1]

No successor to Peirce was appointed until 1728. Then a Thomas
Jeffery was called to share the pastorate with Joseph Hallett III. It is not
recorded how long he remained, but afterwards only one minister was
appointed at one time for the Mint Meeting.

In 1727 a passage in a letter of Samuel Crellius, dated Amsterdam,
17th July, after a visit to England, read:

But at Exeter the Presbyterians do not allow Arians in their body, on
which account the Arians, to the number of about three hundred, have
formed a separate congregation, and have their own preachers. There they
meet openly and in peace, to attend sermons and their sacred rites, without
being disturbed by the magistrate. [2]

The successor to Joseph Hallett III was William West, who was
minister at the Mint from 1744 until 1761. He had been one of the very
few students to study under Matthew Towgood at Shepton Mallet,
between 1716 and 1729. He was extremely interested in mathematics.

A further indication of the size of the Mint congregation may be
taken from Bishop Clagett's Primary Visitation Returns in 1744. The
Exeter Rectors told him that there were 21 Arian families within the
walls, and about 13 in the neighbouring suburbs. This represented a
total population of around 150 persons. It is probable, also, that some
other families classed as Presbyterian, especially in the parish of
St. Olave's where the chapel was situated, should be counted with the
Arians.

To conclude this section an estimate needs to be made of the proportion of Dissenters to the total population of the city in the middle of
the eighteenth century. This may be done by using the Answers to
Primary Visitation Queries of Bishop Nicholas Clagett in 1744, to
which reference has already been made. Among the questions he
addressed to all incumbents within the Diocese were some aimed at
finding the total number of families in each parish, how many Dissenters there were, and how many Nonconformist Meeting Houses.
The information given is tabulated on the opposite page.

[1] Murch, op. cit., p. 428.   [2] Ibid., p. 401.

Parishes.	Total families.	Presby- terian.	Arian.	Baptist.	Quaker.	R.C.
West Quarter:						
Allhallows-on-the-Wall	107	36	—	—	1	—
St. Edmund's. (300–400)	350	3	2	—	1	—
St. Olave's	134	13	—	—	—	—
St. Mary Arches . . .	80	9	—	—	—	—
South Quarter:						
St. Mary Steps . . .	200	4	—	—	—	—
St. John's Bow . . .	72	15	—	—	2	—
St. George . . .	94	16	—	2	1	4
St. Mary Major . . .	412	75	8	6	1	2
Holy Trinity . . .	357	95	—	4	7	—
East Quarter:						
St. Petrock	55	12	6	2	—	1
St. Martin	57	6	—	1	—	—
St. Stephen	56	5	—	—	—	—
North Quarter:						
St. Lawrence	50	—	—	—	—	—
Allhallows, Goldsmith St. . .	26	4	—	—	2	—
St. Pancras	31	1	—	—	—	—
St. Paul	51	5	—	—	—	—
St. Kerrian . . .	40	5	5	3	—	1
	2172	304	21	18	15	8
Population at 4·5 persons per family.	9774	1368	94	81	67	36

Total number of Protestant Dissenters = 1610, or 16·5 per cent

Certain qualifications must be made at once. The returns were all by Anglican clergymen, none of whom would be anxious to overestimate the number of Dissenters within their parishes. When William Barter, Rector of both St. Mary Steps and St. Edmund's wrote on his return, 'I thank God, I have not more than 5 or 6 families of Dissenters of every kind', and this in a most populous area of the City, one is led to suspect his report to be slightly less than the full truth. Some of the estimates of population are extremely vague: the same William Barter reported 'Between 3 and 4 hundred families' for St. Edmund's, and most figures are prefixed by the word 'about'. It is unlikely that the Anglican clergymen distinguished clearly between the still orthodox Presbyterians of James' and Bow Meetings, and those who met at the Mint. The Rector of St. Olave's, in which parish the Mint Meeting was placed, reported merely '13 families of Dissenters and one Meeting House'. Where such families are not clearly designated as Arian, they have been assigned to the Presbyterians: but there is a wide margin of error to be allowed for. The picture of the total population which emerges from this survey is much smaller than one would have expected from other sources. It is dangerous to assume a ratio of more than 4·5 persons per family in calculating population in pre-Census England.[1] By this measure, the population of Exeter in 1744 according to these returns was only 9,774. (It must be remembered also that part of the parish of Holy Trinity, here included, was actually outside the city boundaries.) Col. Ransom Pickard has shown that the population of Exeter did fall considerably in the middle of the eighteenth century, but his estimates ranged from 16,000 in 1710, to 12,300 in 1750, thereafter rising slowly to 14,200 in 1770, and quickly again to 17,412 in the 1801 Census.[2] But whatever the merits of these Visitation Returns as an estimate of the total population of Exeter, they do provide the minimum proportion of Dissenters in the city at mid-century. Even by the hostile assessment of the Anglican Rectors, Protestant Dissenters were 16·5 per cent of the inhabitants of Exeter in 1744. The actual proportion may have been nearer 20 per cent, or one-fifth. This is a decline from the period of prosperity of 1715, but not a surprising reduction in view of the demoralization of the Presbyterians as a result of the Trinitarian controversy.

The 1744 returns provide figures for the four neighbouring parishes without the walls. They are:

Parish.	Families.	Pres.	Arian.	Bapt.	Quaker.	R.C.
St. David's	140	8	1	2	4	2
St. Thomas	327	21	2	11	8	—
St. Leonard	19	4½	—	2	½	—
St. Sidwell	430	80	—	—	—	—
	916	113½	3	15	10½	2
Total population at average of 4·5 per family	4122	510	14	67	47	9

Total number of Protestant Dissenters = 638, or 15·4 per cent

A similar Primary Visitation was made by Bishop Frederic Keppel in 1764, which, but for one defect, could have served as a further check upon the proportion of Protestant Dissenters in the City of Exeter. This defect was, however, the complete omission of any figures for the

[1] Hoskins, op. cit., p. 114.

[2] Pickard, Ransom, *Population and epidemics of Exeter in pre-Census Times*, 1947, p. 18.

most populous parish in the city, St. Mary Major, and this would make any statistical summary absurd. As far as may be observed from the figures given for the other parishes, however, the slow fall in the numbers of Dissenters had continued, but it had not gone far enough to make any significant change in the situation.

CHAPTER VIII

WHITEFIELD AND WESLEY

Sat. 24th. (November, 1739). We accepted an invitation to Exeter . . . and on Sunday, 25th, . . . I preached at St. Mary's, on 'The Kingdom of God is not meat and drink; but righteousness, and peace, and joy in the Holy Ghost.' Dr. W—— told me, after sermon, 'Sir, you must not preach in the afternoon. Not', said he, 'that you preach any false doctrine. I allow all that you have said is true; and it is the doctrine of the Church of England. But it is not guarded; it is dangerous; it may lead people into enthusiasm or despair.'

I did not readily see where the stress of this objection . . . lay. But upon . . . reflection saw it plain. The real state of the case is this: Religion is commonly thought to consist of three things,—Harmlessness,—using the means of grace,—and doing good, as it is called: that is, helping our neighbours, chiefly by giving alms. Accordingly, by a religious man is commonly meant, one that is honest, just, and fair in his dealings; that is constantly at church, and sacrament, and that gives much alms . . .

Now . . . I was . . . led to show, that religion does not properly consist in any or all of these three things; but that a man might both be harmless, use the means of grace, and do much good, and yet have no true religion at all . . .[1]

This extract from the journal of the Rev. John Wesley, is an apt summary of the religious situation in Exeter in the year 1739. What the Rector of St. Mary Arches, the Rev. Robert Wight, remarked after morning service on 25th November, expressed better than he intended the wide difference between the formal religion of churchgoing people and the intense personal conviction of Wesley and his helpers. The temperature of both Anglican and Nonconformist life had fallen extremely low. The revolution in thought caused by the acceptance in the western world of the philosophy of Newton and Locke had turned men against persecution and intolerance of any kind. Led by reason instead of by tradition and superstition man could yet reach an earthly paradise. Meanwhile if he could not agree on religious dogmas he should keep his uncomfortable notions to himself. It was this mental atmosphere which gave Arianism its strong attraction in the eyes of the learned divines of the early eighteenth century. It is possible that only the anchor of the Thirty-nine Articles saved the Church of England from the shipwreck which was the fate of the Presbyterian churches.

[1] All quotations from the Journal of John Wesley are taken from the standard edition, ed. by Nehemiah Curnock in 8 vols., 1909–16.

The only religious alternative was the unattractive Calvinism of the Particular Baptists and the Independents. These could expect no accession of strength in the conditions of the eighteenth century while they continued to preach the complementary doctrines of Election and Reprobation, particularly the latter. No party was likely to welcome the Wesleys, whose uncomfortable emphasis on the necessity for re-birth, and free grace for all who desired it, disturbed Anglican, Arian and Calvinist alike. It is true that the Wesleys' most outstanding partner, George Whitefield, accepted the Calvinist views on Election, but he was always much more interested in calling sinners to repentance than in indulging in theological controversy, and in practice there was little difference in the effect he and the Wesleys had on the unconverted masses, those masses who could never be reached by cold reason, who might be controlled by fear, but who could only be won over voluntarily to the Church by a gospel of love, available free to all who cared to accept it.

Methodist influence first began to bear fruit in Exeter in 1743. Early in July came Charles Wesley and his first blast on the trumpet was quickly followed by George Whitefield, who came to Exeter on 30th July and stayed for three days. He preached on both Saturday and Monday evenings, the latter occasion being on 'Southernhay Green, to upwards of ten thousand'. The difficulty of correctly estimating numbers in the open air should be borne in mind here: it is not easy to believe that two thirds of the city's population turned out to hear one whom their clergy condemned as a dangerous agitator.[1]

John Wesley spent Sunday, 28th August, 1743, in Exeter, on his way to Cornwall. Following the afternoon service in the Cathedral he preached in the Castle Yard to 'half the grown persons in the City'. He did his best to remedy the defects of the services he had heard earlier in the day, of which he wrote in his journal: 'The sermon we heard at church was quite innocent of meaning; what that in the afternoon was, I know not, for I could not hear a single sentence.' He was again at Exeter on 21st September, on his way back to Bristol. 'In the evening I came to Exeter, and preached in the Castle; and again at five in the morning, to such people as I have rarely seen; void both of anger, fear, and love.'

It was George Whitefield whom the people of Exeter found most to their liking, and on 25th October he paid his second visit, remaining for almost two weeks. He wrote to a friend on 6th November: 'The

[1] Tyerman, L., *The life of the Rev. George Whitefield*, 1877, 2 vols., Vol. 2, p. 67.

Lord makes this place very comfortable to me. Prejudices fall off daily, and people begin not only to discern but to feel, the doctrines of the gospel.' [1]

Whitefield left behind in Exeter a small group of people who continued to meet together in spite of unpopularity and physical violence directed against them. In his reply to Bishop Clagett's Primary Visitation Queries of 15th May, 1744, the Rector of Holy Trinity parish reported: 'I know of no unlicensed Place of Meeting except Mr. Kennedy's House, where Mr. Whitefield and his Brethren assemble the Mob, & pretend to teach and expound the Scripture'.

The two men probably referred to as Whitefield's brethren were John Cennick and Thomas Adams. Cennick had been one of John Wesley's earliest lay-preachers. He then became a Calvinist, and a follower of Whitefield, whom he succeeded at the Tabernacle in London in 1744, while Whitefield was in America. But in 1745 he had a further change of opinion, and joined the Moravians, with whom he remained until his death in 1755. His preaching was most effective, particularly in his tour of the West of England in 1744, and as a hymn writer his name is still remembered. His best known hymn is:

> Children of the Heavenly King,
> As ye journey sweetly sing.

Thomas Adams was a Gloucester man, converted by one of Whitefield's first open-air sermons, and he had already experienced persecution and physical violence.[2]

Cennick spent ten days in Exeter in September, 1744, and excited the Dissenting ministers (Stephen Towgood, James Green, John Lavington and John Walrond) into activity. At any rate they circulated leaflets denouncing Whitefield and his disciples as 'false prophets, unlearned, and Antinomians'.[3] On Cennick's return to London his place as superintendent of the Devonshire groups was taken by Thomas Adams. Visiting Exeter, Kingsbridge and Plymouth in November, 1744, Adams preached in this city in 'the society room' at five in the mornings, and in Mr. Kennedy's house at seven in the evenings. Kennedy's house was in Rock's Lane (now Coombe St.), while the 'Society room' was in Waterbeer St. It is also referred to as the 'playhouse' in letters of Thomas Adams and John Cennick, and it would

---

[1] Tyerman, L., op. cit., p. 78.
[2] Ibid., pp. 63–4.   [3] Ibid., pp. 113–14.

seem that the early Methodists had rented the first Exeter Theatre, and used it as a meeting-house.[1]

First curiosity satisfied, the large crowds which had come to hear Whitefield and the brothers Wesley vanished, and only a handful remained loyal. The attitude of the Anglican rectors hardened into open hostility, while old-style Nonconformists looked on critically. The climax came in serious rioting in May, 1745, occasioned by the visits of both Cennick and Adams in that month. There are three accounts of the affair, one by Cennick, one by Adams, and the third by 'An Impartial Hand'. Adams' account is not dated, but appears to refer to events immediately following Cennick's visit. News of the latter's coming spread in advance, and rioters disturbed the meeting in Waterbeer St. on both the 1st and 4th of May. On Sunday the 5th, the morning service was held without more than shouting from outside, but after the evening service the mob beat and insulted the little group without anyone trying to stop them. On the following day the Methodists tried to get their meeting-house licensed for worship, but the Mayor refused. That evening the whole group was severely beaten up, several of the women being stripped and rolled in the 'kennel', the gutter which ran down the centre of the street. Cennick and a few others obtained protection from a Justice of the Peace, but he was unable to quell the riots, which continued until after midnight. The next day some of the chief sufferers took out warrants against the leaders of the trouble, who were bound over until the next Quarter Sessions. But the warrants were served negligently and the rioters realized that the authorities were in no hurry to put an end to the disturbances.[2]

When Adams came he experienced similar treatment, including a stay of some six hours in the Southgate prison before he succeeded in convincing the constables that no charge would lie against him. One evening he preached in the 'playhouse' against a background of so much disturbance that he sent two of his staunchest followers to the nearest J.P. to ask him to come and disperse the mob. He agreed, but delayed for a long time before arriving with the Mayor and Town Clerk to perform their duty. The following day, being a Sunday, Adams confined his preaching to Mr. Kennedy's house in Rock's Lane,

---

[1] Cotton, W., Story of the drama in Exeter, 1887, pp. 1–3. (But according to this the first Theatre began in 1749: this incident indicates that a still earlier play-house existed in Waterbeer St.).

[2] Cennick, J., *An account of the late riot at Exeter*, 1745.

I

rather than risk visiting the old theatre once more. On the Monday he was summoned to appear before the Mayor, who attempted to intimidate him, and threatened him with imprisonment. Adams knew there was no charge which could legally be brought against him, and he finally obtained his dismissal, but on the way home from the Mayor's house in South Street

a mob of some hundreds gathered together, who pelted us with cabbage-stumps, and whatever they could find, until we came almost to Southgate, which was near a furlong; when one opened a door, and desired us to come in, which we did. By this time, I was ready to fall down, by reason of the violent blows I received on my head, and other parts of my body. O Good God, forgive these cruel men.[1]

'The Impartial Hand' confirmed the truth of these reports, and gave his opinion that Adams would have been killed on that last day had he not been given shelter near Southgate.[2]

This outbreak of mob violence in May, 1745, effectually purged the city of the bitterness which had arisen, for there is no record of any further major disturbance against the Methodists. In considering the attitude of the magistracy and upper classes in Exeter in this period it must be remembered that the country was at war, living under the threat of invasion, and aware of the preparations of the Stuart Young Pretender which resulted in the Jacobite rebellion beginning in July of this same year. Any movement which disturbed the established order in church and state was therefore suspect to them, even if they had not already a dislike of Methodists on personal grounds.

The small band of Methodists steadily pursued their way from that time free from all but petty outbreaks of unpopularity on rare occasions. John Wesley passed through the city on 16th September, 1745, and his brother Charles in June, 1746, but there is no record of services being held then, nor on 25th June, 1747, when John again passed through the town. There is little evidence, indeed, that either of the Wesleys cared very much for Exeter at this time in comparison with their untiring efforts elsewhere, especially in Bristol and Cornwall. The original Exeter Methodist society owed its allegiance to Whitefield, and the Wesleys were always extremely careful not to do anything which might cause trouble between the two wings of the Methodist movement.

[1] Tyerman, Vol. 2, pp. 116–19.
[2] 'A Brief Account of the Late Persecution and Barbarous Usage of the Methodists at Exeter, by an Impartial Hand', Exon . . . 1745.

From August, 1744, until June, 1748, Whitefield was in America, and the affairs of the 'Calvinistic' Methodists were in the hands of men like Cennick, Adams, Daniel Rowlands, and Howell Harris. Whitefield's connection with Exeter was resumed in 1748 soon after his return to this country, through the person of George Lavington, appointed Bishop of the Diocese in the previous year. A malicious anonymous wit had circulated a fraudulent 'Charge' to the clergy of the diocese of Exeter, in the Bishop's name, including many of the sentiments known to be most prevalent among Methodists. Not unnaturally the Bishop was annoyed, and charged the Methodist leaders with being connivers at the fraud. Whitefield had no difficulty in disclaiming this accusation, and the Countess of Huntingdon obtained its withdrawal by the Bishop. But the offence was not forgotten, and Lavington's *Enthusiasm of Methodists and Papists compared* (3 parts, 1749–51) was inspired by it. Whitefield journeyed to Plymouth in February, 1749, calling at Exeter on his way in both directions. He found the affairs of the society here in confusion, but his visit put new heart into its members. Immediately on his return to London he brought out his answer to the first part of Bishop Lavington's attack on the Methodists. In reply to Lavington's claim that Methodism was 'A composition of enthusiasm, superstition and imposture', Whitefield stated that his aims were

To awaken a drowsy world; to rouse them out of their formality, as well as profaneness, and put them upon seeking after a present and great salvation; to point out to them a glorious rest, which not only remains for the people of God hereafter, but which, by a living faith, the very chief of sinners may enter into even here, and without which the most blazing profession is nothing worth.

The second part of Lavington's book came out in August, 1749, but Whitefield decided that he had nothing further to say in reply, and suggested that Wesley, as the more directly attacked person, should undertake this duty. But, again on a journey to Plymouth and back, he preached in the open air at Exeter on Sunday evening, 27th August, reporting to Lady Huntingdon:

. . . I preached twice at Exeter, and, in the evening, I believe I had near ten thousand hearers. The bishop and several of his clergy stood very near me, as I am informed. A good season it was. All was quiet, and there was a great solemnity in the congregation; but a drunken man threw at me three great stones. One of them cut my head deeply, and was likely to knock me off the table; but, blessed be God! I was not at all discomposed . . .

One cannot help hoping that the Bishop had left before this distressing incident occurred.[1]

The early spring of 1750 saw Whitefield once more in the South West peninsula. He passed through Exeter on 23rd February, on his way to Cornwall, returning on 19th March after a most exhausting but successful mission in that county. He remained in the city until 23rd March, the last visit of any great consequence which he made. Exeter did see him again in the course of his journeys, but he never stayed long enough to make a major impression. These occasions were 11th April, 1751; 8th September, 1757; June, 1761, and December, 1762.[2]

A leader for the Exeter society had already been provided. While Whitefield had been waiting at Plymouth in July 1744, for a ship to take him to America for the second time, he had preached regularly in the open air. One of those who came to scoff and remained to worship was Henry Tanner, an Exeter man who had knocked about the world quite a lot already.[3] According to his own memoirs he was a man of whom Paul's saying was true: 'The evil that I would not, that I do.' He married unwisely at Bath in 1740, but soon returned to Exeter as a brickmaker, and prospered for a while. Disaster came in the shape of the collapse of his brick kilns, and, his money gone, he moved to Plymouth in 1743 to seek employment as a ship-builder. Thus he came to hear Whitefield, was completely converted, and joined the Plymouth Calvinistic Methodists, led at that time by Andrew Kinsman, with whom Whitefield always stayed while in Plymouth. His troubles were far from ended, for his wife had become a heavy drinker, scorned his new beliefs, and in 1747 was drowned while dramatically eloping to Ireland with a Marine. Tanner, a widower with three small children, did not falter in his new course. In 1754 his uncle offered him employment in Exeter again, and he returned there at the age of 36. He linked up with 'Mr. Kennedy's' group of Methodists in Rock Lane, and by sheer perseverance and strength of character became acknowledged as its leader. There is no evidence that he was ordained as a minister, even in the manner of the Independents by the authority of the particular church alone, yet in his published *Memoir* he was described as 'The Reverend Henry Tanner'. A second marriage in 1756 was very successful.

By 1769 this society had grown enough to be able to afford a

[1] Tyerman, op. cit., Vol. 2, pp. 201-2, 215, 217, 220-2, 230-2.
[2] Ibid., pp. 250-4, 270, 398, 443, 456.   [3] Ibid., p. 104.

permanent meeting-house, called as so many of the Calvinistic Methodist churches, a 'Tabernacle'. This was still in the unfashionable situation of Coombe Street. Tanner preferred this 'because it was near the spot where his labours had been so much blessed; and chiefly because it was the residence of the poorer classes of society, to whom he particularly wished to be made useful. He undertook the building himself . . . and frequently said, "The Tabernacle was built by Faith and Prayer".' His instinct was sound, and the number of his hearers increased considerably. His influence on the poorer section of the city was recognized by the magistrates, who are reported to have said on occasions when they were faced with persistent and unrepentant offenders, 'We know not what to do with them, unless we send them down to Old Tanner's.'

The conditions under which Tanner worked are shown clearly in a letter of his dated 1st May, 1789.

I preached eighteen years and did not receive eighteen pence: but laboured hard with head, heart, and hands, as in some measure you was acquainted with, to the support of my family and the necessity of the church, because they were poor. Since that, one year, with great difficulty they raised for me twelve pounds six shillings . . . then it was reduced to four pounds ten shillings; until last year, 1788, when two or three members who are in better circumstances in life were added to the church; these raised, and caused to be raised, twenty-two pounds ten shillings and sixpence . . . But this year it will be some pounds deficient, because some payers are gone from Exeter.[1]

Evidence that the Coombe Street Tabernacle and the South St. Baptists co-operated on many occasions is supplied in the Answers to Bishop John Ross's Primary Visitation queries of 1779. The rector of St. Mary Major reported that there were two meeting-houses in his parish, 'one said to be Methodist, the other Anabaptist. But the reputed founder of the former sometimes officiates at the latter. . . .' Apart from the insistence on adult baptism, the Baptists were completely agreed on doctrine with the Calvinistic Methodists. The emphasis of both was on a personal religious experience: the learning of their ministers was a secondary consideration.

Tanner lived until 31st March, 1805. The main stream of Methodism, however, had long set in another direction. Neither John nor Charles Wesley was eager to interfere in Exeter during the lifetime of George

[1] Tanner, Henry: *Memoirs of the life and writings of the late Rev. Henry Tanner, of Exeter, with a selection of his letters . . . published . . . by Robert Hawker*, 2nd edn., 1811.

Whitefield, yet they could not be expected to leave the city completely
to the ministrations of the Calvinists on the one side, and the Arians on
the other. The Rector of St. Mary Major reported to Bishop Ross in
1779:

'I have been inform'd that a Conventicle is held within this parish in
a private House; the Teacher's name is Gidley (an Exciseman). But
of what Denomination as to religious tenets I cannot learn.'

The Rector could not have tried very hard to find out. George
Gidley, an Excise Officer, was transferred to Exeter from Port Isaac in
Cornwall, early in 1776. He was already known to John Wesley, as
the following letter shows:

London, January 18, 1776.
My Dear Brother,
I am glad to hear that you are ordered to Exeter: There seems to be a
particular providence in this. We have a small society there, which is but lately
formed, and stands in need of every help; so that, I doubt not, your settling
among them will be an advantage to them.[1]

There is evidence of a society of Methodists distinct from Whitefield's
followers as early as 1762. J. Wesley Thomas, in his reminiscences
recalled that 'Their second place of meeting was a room over Northgate',[2] the first having been the old play-house in Waterbeer Street.
Northgate was taken down in 1769, and it is probable that this was 'the
room' in which John Wesley had preached on Saturday, 28th August,
1762.

'When I began the service, the congregation (besides ourselves)
were two women and one man. Before I had done the room was about
half-full: this comes of omitting field preaching.'

The next day he remedied this by preaching twice in the open air on
Southernhay.

The circuit organization which has ever since been the distinctive
feature of Wesleyan Methodism was first set up in May, 1746, at the
annual Conference held at Bristol. Seven circuits were formed named
after London, Bristol, Cornwall, Evesham, Yorkshire, Newcastle, and
Wales. Devon was not mentioned in any of these divisions, but in
1748 it was part of the Bristol circuit (excepting Plymouth, which
was grouped with Cornwall.) By 1753 a Devon circuit had emerged,
based on Tiverton. Itinerant preachers based here, walked or rode on

[1] Wesley, John, *Works*, 3rd edn., 1830, Vol. 12, p. 497.
[2] Thomas, John Wesley; *Reminiscences of Methodism in Exeter*, 1875, p. 10.

horseback throughout the county encouraging and exhorting the humble folk whom they considered it their privilege to serve.[1]

With the demolition of North Gate the tiny society found another meeting-place in a room in the 'Ten Cells', almshouses which stood near the top of Preston Street. Numbers were still small and the members poor. The travelling preachers had to be given hospitality each week, and, not without hardship, this was performed from the 'Ten Cells' days until the end of the century by John Eastlake and his family.[2]

The first indication of numbers was given in 1778. Exeter was at that time part of a separate circuit whose centre was Tiverton. To the Lady Day Quarterly Meeting Exeter sent its first contribution of 6s. to circuit funds. At Midsummer the same amount was given, and the number of members recorded as 26. At the same time Tiverton reported 55 members and Cullompton 101.[3] It is not surprising that Wesley wrote to George Gidley from Dublin on the 4th of July, 1778: 'I am glad to hear that the work of God begins to increase even in poor Exeter.' [4]

Nonconformist experience has shown that while open-air preaching is the only way (until the advent of radio and television) of attacking the unconverted in large numbers, a permanent religious society can only be organized satisfactorily when it has a permanent place of meeting. This the Exeter Methodists had lacked. At this point, 1778, under the leadership of Gidley, they exerted themselves to provide this essential. A lease was obtained from the Dean and Chapter of Trinity Chapel, in Trinity Lane, a turning off High Street opposite Bedford Street. The purchase of the property was under discussion as early as 4th July, 1778, when John Wesley wrote to Gidley:

'As to the house, it would, undoubtedly, be a means of much good, if it can be procured. All the difficulty is, to procure the money. We cannot do much, because of the building at London.' [5]

By the beginning of 1779 the property had been bought, for the advice of Wesley was sought in the matter of obtaining a licence for the new chapel. He wrote to Gidley on 25th January, 1779:

'Any house is ipso facto licensed, if the demand is made either at the Bishop's Court, the Assizes, or the Quarter-Sessions. The Act of

[1] Thomas, J. W., pp. 9–13.   [2] Ibid., pp. 13–14.
[3] Chick, Elijah, A History of Methodism in Exeter and neighbourhood, 1907, pp. 29–30.
[4] Wesley's Works, 3rd edn., Vol. 12, p. 497.
[5] Ibid., p. 497.

Parliament licenses, not the Justices: They can neither grant nor refuse.'

And to Mr. Samuel Wells, Gidley's colleague, on 28th January:

I advise you to go once more to the Sessions, and say, "Gentlemen, we have had advice . . . We desire nothing at all of you; but we demand of your Clerk to register this place, and to give us a certificate thereof; or to answer the refusal at his peril. . . . P.S. You led the Justices into the mistake, by your manner of addressing them. Beware of this for the time to come: You have nothing to ask of them.[1]

Yet it was not until 15th October, 1779, that Roger Thomas and John Dunn brought in a certificate to the Principal Registry of the Diocese of Exeter, for a 'room in Musgrave's Alley commonly called the High School', and this was registered on the 25th.[2]

These letters show John Wesley in his later years, sure of his position, ruling Methodism dictatorially through the weight of his immense prestige. He wrote again to Gidley on 11th April, 1779:

It seems to me, that this is a very providential thing, and that you did well not to let the opportunity slip. There is no doubt but our brethren at the Conference will readily consent to your asking the assistance of your neighbours for your preaching-house. And the time appears to be now approaching . . . when poor Exeter will lift up its head . . . .[3]

He preached in the new chapel for the first time on Tuesday 31st August, 1779, recording in his Journal:

'I preached at Exeter in a convenient room, lately a school; I suppose formerly a chapel. It is both neat and solemn, and is believed to contain four or five hundred people.'

Musgrave's Alley Chapel, or Gidley's Meeting, as it was sometimes called, was obtained on a lease of 21 years from 1780 at a rental of £2 2s. per annum. The lease of the chapel was surrendered again in 1787, and renewed for a further 21 years at the same rent.[4]

The period between the acquisition of the Musgrave's Alley Chapel, and the promotion of the Exeter society to the headship of a separate circuit in 1808,[5] was one of painfully slow development. The reminiscences of nineteenth-century Methodist leaders in the area do not add to the impression recorded at the time by John Wesley in the 1780's.

---

[1] Wesley's *Works*, 3rd edn., Vol. 12, pp. 496–8.

[2] Meeting House Licences, Diocesan Registry, 1779–1851. Register in County Record Office, Exeter.

[3] Wesley's *Works*, 3rd edn., Vol. 12, p. 498.

[4] Chick, op. cit., p. 34.   [5] Thomas, op. cit., p. 27.

This is seldom enthusiastic. On 16th August, 1780, he wrote: 'It is still a day of small things here for want of a convenient preaching-house.' 24th August, 1781, saw him pass through without preaching, but the following year, 1782, he remained in the city from 15th to 18th August, combating the influence of Hugh Saunderson, a former Methodist preacher who had not risen to Wesley's high standards, and consequently forfeited his confidence, being in the Conference Minutes for 1777 among those who had 'desisted from travelling'. On 15th August, 1782, Wesley recorded in his Journal: '. . . in the evening at Exeter. Here poor Hugh Saunderson has pitched his standard and declared open war. Part of the society have joined him; the rest go on their way quietly to make their calling and election sure.' He does not seem to have considered the affair very serious: but in so small a society any defection must have been felt sadly, and this helps to explain the very slow development in Exeter.[1]

Wesley did not return to the city until 1785, when he passed through twice in March without staying, and then on 17th August he preached there in the evening. Eighteen months later he again preached in Musgrave's Alley Chapel on 5th March, 1787, on 'By grace are ye saved through faith.' He enjoyed the experience, ending the entry in his Journal with the words, 'I know not that I ever saw such an impression made on the people of Exeter before.' Another visit on 13th September that year led to the record: 'In the evening we had a crowded congregation, that drank in every word. This society likewise increases both in number and strength.'

John Wesley's final visit to Exeter came in the summer of 1789, when the picture was again unfavourable. He preached there on 12th August, and again on the 31st, on his way to and from his beloved Cornwall. On his final appearance he wrote:

Here the scene was much changed. Many of the people were scattered, and the rest faint and dead enough. The preaching-house was swiftly running to ruin, the rain running through the roof into it amain; and five or six tenants living in the house were noisy enough, having none to control them. We called earnestly upon God to arise, and maintain His own cause.

No explanation for this deterioration is given in the 'Journal'. The date should, however, be borne in mind. The French Revolution had just begun, and revolutionary ideas were in the air. In such circumstances there would have been a danger that the extreme liberals would

[1] Ibid., pp. 17–18.

have become discontented with the separation of religion from politics which was Wesley's rule, and timid members would tend to return to the established Church of England. That this was the case in Exeter is hinted at by John Wesley Thomas, whose father, John Thomas, together with John Eastlake and George Flamank, was one of the three most prominent figures amongst the Exeter Methodists of that time. He quoted the case of a 'Mr. Cross, of the Butcher Row', who had been an enthusiastic Methodist until he read Tom Paine. Then, 'as his republican zeal increased in warmth and fierceness, his religious ardour abated in the same proportions, until he became an avowed unbeliever'. Even the long-established Presbyterian cause in Exeter suffered from the same conflict of political interests at this time.[1]

Officially no Methodists could be termed Nonconformists until after the death of John Wesley in 1791, for he certainly had no desire to leave the church in which he had been ordained. Such a separation as he had agreed to had been forced upon him by the attitude of the Church of England authorities. The first year in which Methodists must be definitely classed with the Nonconformists is 1795, when at the Manchester Conference the decision was made to allow Methodist ministers to dispense the sacraments of Baptism and Holy Communion in their own chapels.[2] Most Methodists had gone to the Anglican churches for these sacraments, but by this time the bulk of their ad-herents had been recruited either from the Dissenters or from no Church at all, and they demanded that their own clergy should celebrate the Sacraments with them in their own chapels. In Exeter John Thomas' eldest son Elias, born in 1791, was baptized in his parish church; but his son John Wesley Thomas, born in 1798, was baptized in Musgrave's Alley Chapel by a Methodist minister.[3]

The situation of the Methodists by 1800 was such that the society could consider itself over its most difficult period. Yet numbers were still small, and there were no signs of the rapid expansion which was to come later in the nineteenth century. The Rev. Thomas Taylor, preaching in Exeter in 1800 in the Musgrave's Alley Chapel commented, 'Yet there are a few sensible lively souls even in Exeter'.[4]

[1] Thomas, op. cit., p. 22.   [2] Ibid.   [3] Ibid., p. 22.   [4] Ibid., p. 24.

CHAPTER IX

FROM PRESBYTERIANISM TO UNITARIANISM, 1760–1790

THE minutes of the Exeter Assembly from May, 1753, until September, 1763, have not survived, but from then onwards the impression gained from reading them is very different. The volume of business is much less, mainly concerned with allocating the reduced funds available to the poorer churches which still adhered to the disunited Brethren. No further mention of Ordinations or of Ministerial Candidates is found, which indicates that the Independent method of leaving candidates to be ordained by the individual churches had been accepted, in place of the Presbyterian conception of ordaining men to the Ministry as a whole. Occasional resolutions appear in favour of religious toleration, especially in 1778–9 when a Bill was before Parliament which extended the scope of the Toleration Act in a way calculated to admit Unitarian ministers to its benefits. After that, to obtain a license under the Act they had to affirm their belief in the gospel as revealed in the Scriptures: a clause which they had no scruples in accepting.

The numbers of those attending the meetings of the Assembly were not always given, but by the end of the century they usually varied between 12 and 20. In 1789, it is true, a list of ministers considered as being members numbered 31, but the highest recorded attendance during the period was 25 in September, 1793. Attempts at reviving interest, and exerting stricter discipline over ministers who already belonged to the organization, were made from time to time. In September, 1763, there was a reference to an order made at the previous Assembly 'that no Minister who does not acknowledge himself a Member of the Assembly by giving his attendance shall receive any exhibition from the fund'. This would have been aimed at those few, poorly paid, parsons, who whilst needing money to survive hesitated to join in the proceedings of an Arian Assembly.

In May, 1784, it was further resolved 'that no Minister shall be considered as a member of this assembly, or receive from its funds, who shall not bring with him what shall appear to this assembly a satisfactory testimonial'. This was repeated in May, 1789, and the Moderator was then requested to send a copy of the resolution to every new minister entering the county.

The Assembly's Fund had less money to distribute than in its prosperous days. At five-yearly intervals from 1765 to 1800 the amounts handed in were:

From Exeter churches.	From County churches.	Total
1765. £57 2s. 4d.	£50 4s. 6d.	£107 6s. 10d.
1770. £56 15s. 8¼d.	£49 11s. 5½d.	£106 7s. 1¾d.
1775. £65 19s. 6d.	£47 11s. 9d.	£113 11s. 3d.
1780. £64 2s. 8d.	£34 9s. 2d.	£98 12s. 5d.
1785. £66 7s. 10d.	£32 14s. 6½d.	£99 2s. 4½d.
1790. £66 6s. 2½d.	£30 0s. 8d.	£96 6s. 10½d.
1795. £49 13s. 8d.	£24 13s. 4d.	£74 7s. 0d.
1800. £37 17s. 4½d.	£21 14s. 0d.	£59 11s. 4½d.

While the total receipts did not fall seriously until after 1790, the money subscribed by the country churches had dropped sharply between 1775 and 1780, the balance only being restored through increased giving by the three Exeter churches, George's, Bow, and Mint Meetings. The end of Bow Meeting in 1794 meant a loss of about £10 a year, and at the same time the members of George's Meeting ceased to be as generous as before. In the last decade of the eighteenth century, therefore, the income of the Exeter Assembly fell catastrophically by about 50 per cent. Those country ministers who had previously depended upon assistance from the Fund must have been extremely hard hit by this failure.

Finally, in September, 1801, it was decided that in future only one Assembly should be held each year instead of the customary two, a clear indication of the value placed upon its work by those ministers who still remained loyal.

The figures quoted above show that Presbyterianism in Devon in the last half of the eighteenth century was dependent upon the support of the Exeter churches, and on George's Meeting in particular. This tendency had always been present, even in the most prosperous period of Nonconformity at the beginning of the century, and now, with the weakening of Presbyterian causes in other important towns, at Plymouth, Newton Abbot and Tiverton in particular, a position had arisen where the only church whose minister remained a member of the Exeter Assembly, whose position was strong and prosperous, was George's Meeting.

Reorganization had taken place in Exeter following the arrival of Micaijah Towgood in 1750. What happened was that the Little Meeting in Waterbeer St. was closed altogether, while James' Meeting was replaced by a new chapel in South Street, one of the main thoroughfares of the City. Its opening coincided with the first year of the reign of King George III, and it was named George's Chapel in remembrance of the benefits English Protestantism, and the Dissenters in particular, had gained from the Hanoverian Succession. It is probable that the old James' Meeting, at that time more than seventy years' old, was in need of substantial repairs, and the Trustees preferred to spend what money was available on a new structure altogether.

The one entry in the Minutes of the Committee of Thirteen which refers to the new building comes under the date of 19th April, 1759.

Resolvd ... that Mr. Tozer do pay four hundred pounds ... to Mr. John Duntze to be applycd towards the expence of building a new Meeting house as soon as a mortgage of the said house and for securing the payment of four per cent interest on the said sum together with the Principal shall be properly executed and also fifty pounds given formerly by Mr. Benj. Brinley towards erecting a new Meeting house should be paid by him to said Mr. Duntze for that purpose.

In other words £400 was now to be lent from the Ministers' Fund to the trustees of George's Meeting at the rate of 4 per cent interest per annum. Entries in the accounts of the Ministers' Fund show that this was paid regularly. Benjamin Brinley had been the last surviving member of the original Committee of Thirteen, and had given his £50 now mentioned shortly before his death at the end of 1735, and he therefore has the distinction of being the only man who contributed towards both James' and George's Meetings, in 1687 and 1760.

For the building of the new chapel it is probable that much the same procedure was followed as in 1687. Apart from the capital sum gained by the selling of the two old meeting-houses, and the £400 borrowed from the Ministers' Fund, the remainder of the cost was subscribed by members of the congregation, and sympathizers. There is no mention in the accounts of the Trustees of George's Meeting of payments of interest on a debt, except for the £400 already mentioned, so we may assume that the total cost was covered by subscriptions before the end of the year 1760.

There has survived a list of subscriptions to the new building, and it contains a total of 110 names, with another 20 additions, some of whom had already subscribed once before. 33 of the sums mentioned were for £20 or more. The names of those in this latter category are:

Mr. Duntze	.	.	.	£100
Mr. Duntze, junr.	.	.	.	50
Jno. Tozer	.	.	.	50

Her. Katenchamp [sic]	. .	£50
Jno. Conant	. . . .	52 10.
James White	. . . .	52 10.
Jno. Stephens	. . . .	50
Mrs. Baring	. . . .	50
Mat. Lee	. . .	52 10
Geo. Coad	. . .	55 5.
Willm. Fryer	. . .	52 10.
Jno. Gifford	. . .	26 5.
Mrs. Honour Gifford	. .	20
Jno. Stoodly	. . . .	31 10.
James Seely	. . . .	50
Sam. Coad	. . .	40
Jonath. Green	. . . .	26 5.
Mrs. Shepheard & daughters	.	20
Benj. Withers	. . .	36 15.
Mrs. Gould	. . . .	20
Willm. Kennaway	. . .	31 10.
Abraham Kennaway	. .	30
Willm. Kennaway, junr.	. .	20
John Walrond	. . . .	20
Mrs. Hilman & Son	. .	20
Mrs. Lee & daughter	. .	20
Willm. Clark	. . . .	25
Mrs. Burgess	. . . .	21
Stephen Towgood	. . .	20

(Micaijah Towgood and Abraham Tozer gave £15 each.)

In the list of additional subscriptions the following items were for more than £20 each:

Mr. John Duntze and Son	. .	£50
Mrs. Baring (née Elizabeth Vowler)	.	£20
Mrs. Gould	. . . . .	£20
John Stephens	. . . .	£20

The total sum subscribed, according to this list, was £1693 11s. If to this be added the £450 already mentioned, and the price obtained for the sale of the two old chapels, something like £2500 to £3000 must have been available for the building of George's Meeting in 1760.

No time was lost in setting the financial side of the new meeting-house in order. On 29th April, 1760, comes the minute:

The Committee met at the New meeting house in Southgate Street to settle the sittings in the gallerys and to ascertain their several annual prices —Likewise the Pews Seats and sittings for single persons.

Unanimously agreed on:

First. That all who contributed towards the building shall chuse according to their subscriptions.

Secondly. They who pay towards the support of the Ministers.

Thirdly. The Wives & widows of Tradesmen.

Fourthly. The Servants of the principal subscribers according to their Master or Mistresses subscription.

Annual Prices: For the Long Seats 6/- per year, the 4 small seats near the entrance 4s per year. All the large Pews under the Gallerys and in the body of the House 10/-, the 4 small pews adjoining the table pew 7/-. Sitting for single persons 2/- per year. Front seats in the gallerys 2/- each person. Second do, 18d., Third seats 12d.

The collector of seat rents and subscriptions was to be paid three guineas a year and the caretaker a similar sum.

It is clear from this that we are dealing with a social order very different from that of the twentieth century. This was a society where all members were carefully graded according to their wealth and importance. The Exeter Presbyterians may have been receptive to new ideas in theology, but they were intensely conservative in all other ways, a factor which was to prove of significance when the ideas of the American and French Revolutions began to be aired in Exeter.

On 21st July, 1767, 'It is the opinion of this Committee that a new Mahogany Pulpit shall be forthwith made and sett up in the sd. Meeting.' Nothing came of this direction, for we read on 18th April, 1770: 'Ordered ... by the Committee that a new Canopy only is ordered soon.' No mention of this came in the accounts for this period and neither pulpit nor Canopy were replaced. By this accident was preserved the magnificent pulpit which had been transferred from James' Meeting to the new building. It is unlikely that any replacement would have equalled it.

A further addition to the chapel was made in 1781 by the erection of a small vestry for the use of the ministers.

At the first meeting of the Chapel Committee after the building of George's Meeting, the following members were recorded as being present: 'John Duntze, Esq., James White, Esq., Jno. Stephens, Esq., Mr. Herman Katenkamp, Mr. Benj. Withers, Mr. Sam. Coade, Mr. John Gifford, Mr. Wm. Kennaway, and Mr. Abraham Kennaway.'

There is no mention of how this Committee was chosen, nor is their conduct of necessary business questioned until the beginning of 1782. Then their normal procedure of filling vacancies on the Committee by co-option was queried, and a General Meeting of Subscribers belonging to George's Chapel was called for 3rd March. This meeting decided to dissolve the Committee then in being, and to form a new one of 'such Gentlemen as do at present, or shall at any time hereafter, subscribe the annual sum of Forty shillings or upwards toward the salary of the Ministers; and also of such Gentlemen as have contributed the sum of twenty pounds towards the Building this Meeting house'. Public notice of all business had to be given by the Clerk on the Sunday preceding meetings of the Committee, so that all should know what was going to be discussed. The Committee was to meet regularly on the first Tuesday after every Quarter Day. Applications for seats were to be made by sealed letter to the Clerk, and 'no person be permitted to be present at the Committee when any claim or application of his own shall be under consideration'.

This arrangement did not last many years. A General Meeting of the 'Payers' on 3rd June, 1788:

Resolved unanimously, that, upon perusing the deed of settlement dated the 24th day of June, 1776, it appears to this meeting that there is a Committee regularly nominated and appointed by the said deed consisting of the several persons following, namely

Sir John Duntze, Bart.	John Withers.	James White.
John Walrond.	Edward White.	John Vowler Parminter.
Samuel Coade.	Abraham Kennaway.	John Katenkamp.
William Gifford.	John Stoodly.	Thomas Gearing.
John Gifford.	William Kennaway.	Jonathan Green.
William Clarke.	Henry Bielfield.	Samuel Mandrot.
Richard Davis.	William Kent.	Abraham Kennaway, Junr.
James Green.	John Gifford, Junr.	William Kennaway, Junr.
Philip Moore.	John Skinner.	William Grigg.

for the express purpose of regulating and disposing of the seats, for directing the terms upon which they shall be lett, and disposing of the produce of the same, and that therefore the resolution entered into by a general meeting held here on March 3rd 1782—appointing a Committee for the Regulation of Seats, be rescinded—but that the several orders and resolutions of the said Committee down to this time be confirmed.

This return to legality made a considerable difference to the personnel, as only six of the people named had been mentioned as members of the Committee in the previous ten years. Sir John Duntze and William Kennaway, Senr., had been on the original 1760 Committee. While no ruling on the matter of co-option is recorded at this time, it is clear from the proceedings of these two General Meetings that the main body of subscribers was prepared to step in and make its authority felt whenever necessary.

A similar questioning of the powers of the Committee of Thirteen had arisen in 1771–2. At this time the scope of the Committee was abruptly narrowed. In previous years its Minutes had always included a direction to the Treasurer to pay the Ministers' salaries, at whatever figure prevailed at the time. In 1773 and later comes the phrase similar to 'Mr. Parminter is desired to *pay the balance* . . . to the three Ministers'. The amounts raised by direct subscriptions ceased to be recorded in the Committee's accounts, the former Collector, a Mr. Gribble, resigned through old age, and Mr. Benjamin Withers, a somewhat unmethodical accountant, died, and a new Treasurer was appointed. Withers had been Treasurer of the Ministers' Fund since 1758, and the accounts became from that time less and less intelligible. There may have been some justification, therefore, for criticism of the Committee's handling of its finances.

The method of paying the Ministers was now changed, and henceforth the 'Thirteen' had charge only of the invested funds, the income from which they divided equally among the ministers. Quarterly subscriptions must have been collected directly by the clerks of George's and Bow Meetings. The reason is not far to seek. While George's Meeting had been changing slowly from orthodoxy in the early part of the century to the semi-Arianism of the Towgoods, and to complete Unitarianism by 1800, Bow Meeting had remained orthodox. There were only four different ministers of Bow between 1715 and 1794, which helps to explain the continuity. These were John Withers, 1705–29; John Lavington, 1715–59; John Walrond, 1730–54; and Abraham Tozer, 1754–94. Each meeting may now have preferred to pay its own contributions directly to its own minister(s), leaving the balance from invested income to be divided equally. The amount obtained from direct subscriptions had been falling steadily since 1719, as has already been pointed out. In 1771, the last year when they were received by the Committee of Thirteen, these came to only £179 10s. 9d., whereas as recently as 1744 subscriptions had amounted to £282 in the year. By 1821, despite a big drop in the value of money, subscriptions were only averaging £185 each year, although this was for George's Meeting only, Bow having ended in 1794. Reduction of the number of Ministers to three in 1759, after Lavington's death, enabled the Committee to maintain the average aimed at of £80 each year for each minister, and even to raise this figure slightly by the 1780s. When Timothy Kenrick became pastor in 1783, he was led to expect 'between 90 and £100'.[1] When the number of ministers was reduced to two in

[1] Kenrick Papers, No. 11, 4th November, 1783. The Kenrick Papers were printed in the Record Section of the Transactions of the Unitarian Historical Society, Vols. 3–5, 1923–34.

K

1797 it was possible to increase individual salaries considerably, and at the same time, due to wartime inflation, investment income rose by almost 100 per cent.

Like the Committee of Thirteen, the George's Chapel Committee ran into financial difficulties as time went by. The original seat rents were sometimes found inadequate to meet expenses, and either a general increase had to be imposed, or else a special levy made. Examples taken from the records are:

1785, June 30. Resolved unanimously that the Bill of Costs now produced by Mr. Stoodly for business done for this society . . . amounting to the sum of £22 5s. 1d. be defrayed by an assessment of one years additional and extraordinary payment of the sum annually paid as seat money by those subscribers only who have pews or seats on the ground floor of the Meeting House . . .

1800, Feb. 23. . . . it appearing that seventy three pounds eighteen shillings and threepence is wanting to discharge the Tradesmens' Bills . . . also two years Intrest Money due to the Ministers at Midsummer next, Resolved unanimously that an assessment of one years additional of the sum annually paid as seat Money by the subscribers who have Pews & Seats on the ground floor of the Meeting . . . (be made).

1807. May 31st, General Meeting. . . . recommended, that in order to discharge the present debt, & to meet future exigencies, one quarter of the subscriptions paid to the ministers should be collected, for the former purpose, and for the latter, that the rents of the seats should be advanced to the following,

Pews under the Galleries	.	.	.	£1 4s. per annum.
The other Pews	.	.	.	£1 0s.
Seats under the Galleries	.	.	.	12s.
The other seats	.	.	.	10s.

From the evidence already given it is possible to arrive at a fair picture of the position of the Exeter Presbyterians in the period 1760–95. The two 'united congregations' of George's and Bow Meetings were drifting quietly apart owing to doctrinal differences, the peace being kept by the efforts of a gifted series of ministers. The stronger of the two congregations, George's Meeting, remained prosperous, but there were within it severe tensions, inevitable in a society of mixed beliefs, which occasionally broke out in unpleasant incidents. If subjected to further strain, serious trouble might be expected, and this is indeed what happened in the 1790s when to the already existing doctrinal differences were added political disagreements at the time of the French Revolution.

Before passing to this second critical period for Exeter Noncon-formity certain other events must be related. At the same time as the reorganization of the chapels took place in 1760, Micaijah Towgood formed a second Nonconformist Academy at Exeter. This new venture was an attempt to revive the Taunton Academy in more congenial surroundings, the latter institution having finally collapsed in 1759, on the departure of its chief tutor, Thomas Amory, for a pastorate in London. It is unfortunate that the minutes of the Exeter Assembly for this year have not survived, for the venture must have been planned there first of all. It was decided to train young men 'for the ministry and other learned professions as well as for commercial life'.[1] William Mackworth Praed, of Teignmouth, father of the poet Winthrop Mackworth Praed, presented the Academy with a house in Paris Street for its headquarters.[2] To this house the library of the Taunton Academy was transferred. Towgood himself lectured on Biblical interpretation and Greek literature, while he secured the services of Samuel Merivale for the Divinity lectures, and of John Turner, a 'graduate' of Hoxton Academy, for mathematics and science. Easily the most qualified tutor of the three was Merivale, a former pupil of Philip Doddridge at Northampton, who had become minister at Tavistock in 1744, and was ordained after examination by the Exeter Assembly in that year. A letter to Merivale by the three Exeter ministers shows what impor-tance they attached to his co-operation.

Exon. Feb. 7, 1761. Revd. and Dear Sir, Being persuaded that you are thorowly impressed with a Sense of the great Importance of some Academical Institution in this City, . . . we have now to represent—That all attempts to accomplish it are like to prove utterly abortive, if this Application to you . . . should prove unsuccessful. . . . In the character of a Tutor, and an occasional Preacher, residing in this City, you will . . . be far more essentially useful to the Church, and more extensively beneficial to Society in general, than even in that of a Pastor to your present Congregation. The losing the Profits of your present Salary is a Thing, we know, of no Moment to a Person of your Circumstances and Temper. . . .[3]

This latter remark shows that no official salary was attached to the post. Merivale was in comfortable circumstances through his first marriage with Elizabeth Shellaber (9th August, 1748), through whom the Merivales acquired valuable estates at Bideford and Annery. She

---

[1] McLachlan, H., *English education under the Test Acts*, 1931, pp. 230–2.
[2] Lysons, S. & D., *Magna Britannia*, Vol. 6, Devonshire, p. 449.
[3] Merivale, Anna W., *Family Memorials*, 1884, pp. 42–3.

only lived until 30th March, 1761, however, and a desire for a fresh field of work may have been the deciding factor in Merivale's removal to Exeter. Towgood's letter had emphasized the importance of Exeter as the centre of Westcountry Nonconformity: the attitude of a layman in another part of the county was somewhat different, as shown in a letter of a friend of Merivale's, Pentecost Barker of Plymouth:

Feb. 25. 61. . . . I don't like your going . . . The Exonians are a prag-matical censorious set of People, and void of Charity. You write, I would not be an Exeter minister. But let them get you there, and preach you must, or your house will be besieged . . . .[1]

John Turner died in 1769, and was succeeded both as tutor and as pastor of the Lympstone Presbyterians by Thomas Jervis, another former student at Hoxton Academy. He left in 1772 to become tutor to the sons of the Earl of Shelburne. Merivale died in December, 1771, and although John Hogg of the Mint Meeting may have for a short time taken over Merivale's position, the Academy came to an end in 1772. The names of 48 students educated during its existence are known.[2] They included Joseph Bretland and James Manning, later to become pastors of George's Meeting, and John Merivale, son of Samuel. Only twelve of these students are known to have become ministers, the rest going into trade, the professions and the services. The library remained in Exeter until 1786, when it was lent to Hackney College. When this failed in 1796 the books were returned to Exeter, where they came into use once more for a Third Academy, organized by the Rev. Timothy Kenrick.

After the death of John Lavington in 1759, no further change in the personnel of the Exeter Presbyterian ministers took place until 1777, when Stephen Towgood died. He had been assisted for the previous year by James Manning, stepson of Samuel Merivale. Merivale had married for the second time, on 5th October, 1766, at Northampton, a Mrs. Betsy Manning, whom he had known in his student days at Doddridge's Academy. He greatly influenced his stepson, who studied under him at Exeter before going to Hoxton Academy in 1774 for a year. Manning was an Arian in belief, but never pressed his doctrinal opinions where they were not liked. He was a man 'in whom the moral qualities are more conspicuous than the intellectual'.[3]

---

[1] Merivale, op. cit., p. 43.   [2] McLachlan, op. cit., p. 232.
[3] Murch, Jerom, *History of the Presbyterian and General Baptist Churches in the West of England*, 1835, p. 450.

In 1782 old Micaijah Towgood decided to retire from the ministry, though he remained resident in Exeter until his death ten years later. An invitation was issued to Timothy Kenrick, at that time a part-time tutor at Daventry Academy, and only 24 years of age. From James Manning he learnt confidentially that only four subscribers 'withheld their names from disapprobation' and they ultimately fell in with the majority. Kenrick began his ministry in the New Year, 1784. He was the first complete Unitarian to become minister at George's Meeting. He gave worship to God the Father alone, and regarded Christ as entirely human, albeit divinely inspired. He was influenced considerably in his early career by his uncle Samuel Kenrick, a banker at Bewdley (1728–1811), who wrote to him on 27th September, 1790:

As to Unitarianism I cannot help thinking it is the belief, tho' not professed, of nine-tenths of the body of Protestants who have no pre-established creeds or prayers to the contrary repeated every Sunday. The Confession of Faith & the Assembly's Catechism keep a kind of shadow of a Trinity, while the substance of unity is maintained in every prayer, addressed in public and private worship to the supreme God of all.[1]

At the end of 1785 Kenrick married Mary, daughter of John Waymouth of Exeter, to whom he had become engaged in the previous March. From London on the 23rd of April, 1785, he had written to her . . . '. . . on Thursday I intend to set out for Exeter in company I believe with ye two Miss Peckfords, if my Heart was not already engaged I should not think it in great danger on this Occasion.' [2]

Throughout his life, as will emerge from quotations to be given later from his letters, Timothy Kenrick believed in speaking out what he believed. There is no trace of humbug or hypocrisy to be found in him, a rare quality amongst eighteenth-century divines. It was this directness of his character which at once attracted many followers, and repelled those who did not hold the same religious views. He was not the man to preside without conflict over a society of mixed religious beliefs. The Towgoods had successfully held the 'united congregations' together, and James Manning proved himself equally adept, but Kenrick, although he never deliberately provoked his Hearers, seldom attempted to conceal his own advanced Unitarian beliefs.

[1] Kenrick Papers, No. 16.
[2] Chronicles of a Nonconformist family: the Kenricks of Wynne Hall, Exeter, and Birmingham, ed. by Mrs. W. Byng Kenrick, 1932, pp. 52–3. All further quotations from Kenrick's letters are taken from this work or from the Kenrick Papers (see p. 137, n. 1).

CHAPTER X

CONTROVERSY RENEWED, 1791–1804

WHEN to a potentially explosive religious situation was added the political dynamite of French Revolutionary ideas, trouble was certain, and from 1791 until the end of Kenrick's life a succession of crises rocked the Presbyterian/Unitarian societies of Exeter. Timothy Kenrick was in sympathy with democratic ideas, and made little secret of his feelings. In a letter of 15th May, 1791, he reported to his uncle Samuel that Paine's 'Rights of Man' had been read in Exeter 'with great avidity'. Then on 14th July, 1791, came the Birmingham Riots, when a mob attacked Joseph Priestley's house, and burnt down the new chapel near by. Kenrick on the 24th of July preached a sermon in George's Meeting on the subject of the Birmingham riots, which he condemned in no uncertain manner. Immediately 34 gentlemen of the congregation demanded a meeting of subscribers 'to consider the propriety of requesting the Rev. Mr. Kenrick to avoid the discussion of subjects of a political nature from the pulpit'. On the appointed day, 27th July, only 22 attended, but they proceeded to pass a very respectfully worded resolution to that effect.

Their minister replied on 30th July, denying the charge of habitually introducing political subjects into his sermons, and stated quite uncompromisingly: 'Whenever I am called upon by a just occasion, which you admit may sometimes exist, to treat of any Political duty in the Pulpit, I shall do it in that manner, to which my judgment and conscience shall direct me at the time.'

A further General Meeting of subscribers on 7th August accepted Kenrick's reply, and 'with regard to his future conduct . . . they have the fullest confidence in his Judgement and his Prudence'.

So ended the first crisis of the 1790s, whose pattern was similar to those to follow.

The next difficulty arose in October, 1792. Kenrick had in one of his extempore prayers prayed for the success of people struggling for their liberty, and he admitted later that he had the people of France in mind. John Merivale instantly took exception, and withdrew himself and his family, a not inconsiderable loss, from the Meeting. He wrote to Kenrick on 6th October, 1792:

. . . it is so utterly repugnant to my Conception of what is right to join in prayers offer'd up to the God of Mercy for the further success of a wretched Faction which has already involv'd a whole country in a most deplorable state of Anarchy & Distress,—that I feel myself obliged to seek some other Place of Worship than that to which I have been pretty regularly accustomed for many years.

Kenrick replied very promptly, stating that he certainly did not approve of 'the late horrid murders committed at Paris'. He went on to distinguish between the 'ferocious mob at Paris and the French Nation'. Towards the end of his long letter he made a very important confession for our understanding of the tensions inherent in the situation at Exeter at this time. He referred to

. . . the rule which I universally lay down to myself for conducting Public Worship—to use language in which the Society may all conscientiously join, altho' everyone cannot . . . apply them in exactly the same manner, this has long appeared to me the only equitable way of conducting joint addresses to the Divine Being: . . . & upon this plan Mr. Tozer, Mr. Manning & myself may publickly pray for the spread of Christianity, altho' we each of us affix different ideas to the phase—the first meaning by it Trinitarianism, the second Arianism, & the last Unitarianism.

Such a situation was too precarious to last indefinitely. In a further letter to his uncle Samuel of 26th February, 1793, Kenrick reported that John Merivale and his family 'continue to absent themselves whenever I preach'. Merivale did not go so far as to quit the Committee of Thirteen, however, of which he was at that time the Treasurer, for he did not resign from that until 1802. His granddaughter, L. A. Merivale, described her grandfather as '. . . a sturdy conscientious Dissenter of the old school; combining with his dissent an absolute horror of Radicalism and disloyalty'.[1]

By the beginning of 1793 Kenrick was becoming depressed in face of the difficulties which confronted him. This position was not improved by the death of his beloved first wife Mary in mid-1792 after the birth of her fifth child, George. For the remainder of that year his sister Martha came to look after Timothy Kenrick and his young children, but early in 1794 he married again—a marriage of convenience which proved to be very successful. His second wife was Elizabeth Belsham, sister of a prominent Unitarian minister, Thomas Belsham, of Essex Street Chapel, London.

It was at this time, when his personal affairs were sufficient burden

[1] Merivale, Anna W., *Family Memorials*, 1884, p. 129.

for any man to cope with, that the French Revolution reached its
climax, with the Terror raging in Paris from September, 1792, until the
fall of Robespierre in June, 1794. Anglicans and Dissenters alike
united in expressing their horror at these events. On 26th February,
1793, soon after the execution of Louis XVI, Kenrick wrote:

Most of the Dissenters in this part of the County have joined with the
members of the Establishment in making professions of attachment to the
Constitution & of their abhorrence of all attempts to overturn it by seditious
writings. In the list of subscribers I have often been mortified to see names
which I little expected to behold there. . . .

Kenrick seriously began to think of following Priestley's example
and emigrating to America. His brother-in-law Ralph Eddowes wrote
to him on 16th June, 1793:
'. . . the number of emigrants from Liverpool in every Vessel is
immense—let us cast in our lot among them & leave this detestable
country which its present corruption & vices of every kind have
marked out for the object of the divine judgments . . .'

A year later, on 1st August, 1794, Eddowes, his wife and Kenrick's
brother John, sailed in the *Hope* from Liverpool, arriving at Philadelphia after a journey of 3 months and 1 day. Timothy Kenrick wrote
to his father (13th August, 1794):

We have had several emigrations from this town and neighbourhood &
others talk of following their example, it is easy to perceive that unless ye.
situation of affairs in this country takes a favourable turn soon it will lose
great numbers of its inhabitants. Ye. prospects in America are so inviting in
themselves that a few inconveniences in this country will drive away ye.
sufferers.

Kenrick had the example of others on his very doorstep, for on
12th June, 1795, he wrote to his father:

Mr. Blackford of Topsham, a Dissenting Minister at a place three miles
from Exeter, preached a farewel sermon to his people last Sunday, previous
to his embarking for America, in wch. country he has been invited to settle
with a Congregation, fourteen other emigrants sail in ye same ship.

The only significant clue to the reason why Kenrick did not emigrate
himself comes in a letter from Ralph Eddowes in June, 1795, where
he said: 'I fear an obstacle will arise in the delicate state of your wife's
health.' With a family of young children to care for, this would have
been sufficient reason for Kenrick's decision to remain in England, a
decision which was confirmed possibly by a letter from Priestley of

28th October, 1796, when the latter stated that he would personally like to welcome Kenrick in Philadelphia, but pointed out the risks he would run in so doing.

The period from 1793 to 1796, during which Kenrick was considering emigration was one of continual strife among the Exeter Presbyterians. On the outbreak of war with France on 1st February, 1793, the Government appointed a 'Fast Day' on which loyal subjects were asked to pray for success in the struggle then beginning. Although his two colleagues agreed to conduct services on the appointed day, and almost all his 'Hearers' desired him to do so as well, Kenrick refused to take part, to the annoyance of a large section of his congregation. James Manning disliked the controversy intensely, and was unwise enough to state publicly 'if this state of things continued I should probably be obliged to remove'. This was by the laws of gossip reported to Kenrick as meaning 'if he did not remove I must'.

Kenrick brought his critics up sharply with the offer of his resignation on 28th April, 1793. It was not an easy task for a congregation of divided religious beliefs to find a minister of whom all could wholeheartedly approve, and the General Meeting called on 5th May quickly passed a resolution requesting Kenrick to withdraw his resignation, and sent him a letter expressing their complete confidence in his 'integrity and ability in the discharge of the various duties of the ministerial office'.

In a letter, to his Uncle Samuel, dated 1st June, 1793, Kenrick said: 'Considering how obnoxious my political & theological sentiments are, I was not a little surprised to find I had so many & such warm friends.'

Kenrick was always interested in education, from his carliest days at Daventry Academy, and at the beginning of 1792 he had secured the co-operation of his fellow ministers in forming a Western Unitarian Society, whose object was to circulate literature of a religious nature in the West of England, and he remained Secretary of the Society until his death. The annual meeting of the Society in 1794 was planned to take place at George's Meeting, in Exeter. The approval of the Trustees was first given, then withdrawn, at the protest of

One Gentleman who has distinguished himself, altho' a dissenter, by his zeal in supporting all the vile measures of a vile Court, & by his antipathy to every species of innovation. He assembled the Trustees of the Meeting house, represented to them the dangerous consequences of holding such meetings, & persuaded them to refuse us the use of the place.

The situation was redeemed by a generous gesture from the Trustees of Bow Meeting, who sent to Kenrick the following note:

The Trustees & others of Bow Meeting present their respects to the Revd. Mr. Kenrick and request that himself and his friends will make that use of the Bow Meeting house on the morrow which their ancestors have been accustomed to glory in, Worshipping the Great God according to the dictates of their own Consciences.

This, in spite of the fact that the members of Bow Meeting were Calvinist in belief. Bow Meeting had by this time come to the end of its history, and it is welcome to find it finishing on such a charitable note. A manuscript survey of Devon Nonconformity preserved in the earliest minute book of the Exeter Assembly, which compares the situation in 1715 with that in 1794, gives the approximate number of those attending this meeting house in 1794 as 150, a sad falling away from the 800 of 1715. The orthodox society of Bow had suffered more than the Unitarian society which worshipped at George's Meeting. In 1794 George's Meeting had about 700 Hearers, compared with the 1100 for James' Meeting in 1715. The death of Abraham Tozer, which took place in June, 1794, the last orthodox minister of the Exeter Presbyterian churches, led to a most serious crisis.

A postponed General Meeting of Subscribers to 'the two united Congregations of Protestant Dissenters' was held at George's Meeting (not Bow) 27th July, 1794, and invited the Rev. Joseph Bretland to fill the vacant pastorate. The invitation was signed by 95 subscribers to the Ministers' Fund, certainly a large majority of them, although the exact total at this time is not recorded. (It was 136 in 1783, at the time of Kenrick's invitation.) Bretland was of an Exeter family, and was 52 years old at this time. One of the more promising students of Towgood's Academy, he became minister of the Mint Meeting from 1770 to 1772, and then kept a school in the city until 1790. He returned to the Mint as minister from 1789 to 1793, when he resigned over a difference about the Liturgy used there. He was a Unitarian in belief, and just the colleague with whom Kenrick might be expected to work amicably. Yet the orthodox attenders at Bow Meeting were now faced with the unpalatable fact that their Trinitarian minister (who alone had been allowed by them to administer the Lord's Supper in their chapel) had been replaced by a Unitarian, and there was no minister of orthodox views left to lead their worship. They refused to accept this position, and parted finally with their former Presbyterian traditions.

Their chapel was closed in 1794, and pulled down soon after.[1] In the following year a Rev. John Giles appeared on the scene, whether by invitation or not is uncertain, the seceders accepted him as their pastor, and on 2nd June, 1795, formed themselves into a Congregational Church. On 5th June the names of 68 members were enrolled, and the first 3 deacons elected. These were John Coward, John Cox, and Samuel Lake.[2] Coward had been one of the Presbyterian Committee of Thirteen since 1791, and his resignation was reported at the meeting of that committee on 22nd September. Another member of the 'Thirteen', Benjamin Peckford, was probably amongst those who joined the new church. When visited by their attorney, he had stated that he was 'no longer a member of the United Congregations & therefore having nothing to do with the business'.

The fortunes of the new Congregational church will be followed later. For the present it is sufficient to study the effect of this major secession upon the fortunes of the main body. The immediate effect was to make James Manning's conscience overactive again. At what must have been a long and arduous meeting of Subscribers at George's Meeting on 5th July, 1795, two letters of resignation were read. The first was from Manning, on the grounds that in the present state of their society (i.e. since the secessions) three ministers were no longer required, and there were several other churches in the county who were without a pastor at all. The second was from Bretland, who knew of Manning's scruples, and offered to resign himself, as the latest comer. The General Meeting refused to accept Bretland's offer, and asked him, with a select committee, to visit Manning and try to persuade him to stay as well. After a prolonged argument they succeeded, and on 26th July, Manning agreed to remain as minister, although he still thought that three ministers were unnecessary in one congregation. The incident was uncharitably summed up by Timothy Kenrick in a letter to his uncle Samuel on 9th August:

Some persons who pretend to be in the secret, say that Mr. M. had no intention of leaving the Congregation but intended making one of his colleagues do so, & finding that they could neither of them be removed was willing to resume his office again.

The decline in prosperity of George's Meeting did, however, result in the reduction of the number of ministers to two in 1797. The method by which this was brought about was deplorable. On accepting the call

---

[1] Murch, Jerom, op. cit., p. 373.
[2] Southernhay Congregational Church, Exeter: *Centenary Yearbook*, 1895, pp. 3–4.

in 1794 Bretland had offered to stand down again if any section of the society considered it would be advantageous to their cause for him to do so. In June, 1797, seventeen of the subscribers took it upon themselves to send him a letter asking him to resign:

We . . . have observed with much regret the interest declining, many of the society occasionally or entirely withdrawing themselves since you have been settled among us. It is with no small uneasiness we think ourselves call'd upon to declare, that we consider your ministry as the occasion of this declension.

Bretland naturally took offence at the abrupt way in which this notice had been served on him, and although a General Meeting begged him to reconsider, he held firmly to his decision to resign. The letter of the seventeen had referred to the probable agreement with their views of William Kennaway, who acted as Chairman of General Meetings at this period. In a letter on behalf of the meeting to Bretland dated 23rd July, he denied this agreement, while at the same time referring to the unfortunate necessity of 'advancing the salaries of the ministers, or reducing their number'. This was the motive, conscious or unconscious, which lay behind this final crisis of the 1790s. A society declining in numbers and wealth was faced with the necessity of increasing the Ministers' salaries to meet the rising cost of living during the Napoleonic Wars. Increased demands upon subscribers would lead to more resignations: the only solution which would once more place the society on a stable foundation was the reduction of the number of ministers serving it to two. By this means salaries could be raised immediately by 50 per cent without further increase in revenue.

Following these convulsions the reduced society meeting at George's Chapel settled down quietly. The transition from Presbyterianism to Unitarianism had been completed, leaving a more homogeneous body than at any time since 1719. Kenrick, approaching middle-age, and possibly disillusioned by the course of events in France, avoided any further grounds of provocation, and came to be one of the most loved of all the ministers of his society. Manning worked well with him now that his point had been carried.

The remainder of Kenrick's pastorate was occupied with two main subjects: the provision of a new hymnbook, and his project of a Third Exeter Academy. The first shows the attitude of eighteenth-century Nonconformists towards hymn provision in general. The first mention of Hymn books of any kind in the minutes of General Meetings occurred on 10th August, 1794, when it was:

resolved, that as a new Collection of Psalms & Hymns are now publishing in London by the Rev. Andrew Kippis, Abm. Rees, Thos. Jervis and Thos. Morgan,[1] that . . . the Chairman is desired to call a meeting of the united Congregations, to consider of adopting the use of said Psalms and Hymns in one or both of the united Congregations.

This proposal proved abortive, and it was not until 18th November, 1798, that there came a general meeting 'for the purpose of considering of the propriety of adopting a collection of Psalms & hymns for divine service, in the room of that now used'. This meeting asked for copies of four different hymnbooks to be circulated for examination: Capp's collection, that formed by Messrs. Belsham and Kentish, and 'Those called the London, and Birmingham Collections'.[2]

Nothing further was done until 9th February, 1800, when it was resolved 'that neither of the collections . . . proposed be adopted'. Instead they decided 'that the present collection be revised and re-printed; leaving out therefrom all objectionable hymns, and adding thereto any of approved excellence that have been omitted'. A sub-committee of 12 was appointed, to include both the ministers. The Committee met on 23rd February, 1800, when Kenrick declined, by letter, to assist in the revision, on the grounds that several of the hymnbooks already in existence were of sufficient merit for their purpose. The Committee got down to its labours despite this, and reported on 1st June, that it had completed its work. It was then resolved 'that the intended collection should remain at the Vestry for one month for the inspection of the members of this society'. Five men proposed no less than 27 alterations, involving the removal of no less than 19 hymns, of which six were to be replaced by hymns from other collections. The revised version was approved on September 28th, and ordered to be printed. This was not quite the end of the process, how-ever, for the Revs. Manning, Kenrick, Bretland, and Mr. Samuel Pope, were asked to superintend the work through the Press, and in the course of this they recommended the substitution of a small number of other hymns, 'to render the whole perfectly unexceptionable'. The subscribers agreed without protest.

Well-to-do members of the chapel were expected to buy their own copies, and copies for the use of their servants as well. A subscription

[1] 'A Collection of Hymns and Psalms for Public and Private Worship, selected and prepared by Andrew Kippis, Abraham Rees, Thomas Jervis, and Thomas Morgan', 1795.
[2] 'A Selection of Psalms for Social Worship', ed. Newcome Capp, York, 1786. 'Psalms and Hymns for the use of the New Meeting in Birmingham', 1790.

list was opened for the purchase of extra books for the use of the poor.
A note of 17th June, 1802, shows that 123 were provided in this way.

The hymnbook was further revised in 1812, the original edition
having by then become out of print.[1]

As illustration of the type of alterations usually made, three hymns
by the most famous of eighteenth-century hymnwriters are given
below, with the George's Meeting version following:

Philip Doddridge, 1702–51

1. Hark! the glad sound! the Saviour comes,
   The Saviour promis'd long;
   Let every heart prepare a throne,
   And every voice a song.

2. He comes, the prisoners to release
   In Satan's bondage held;
   The gates of brass before Him burst,
   The iron fetters yield.

3. He comes, from thickest films of vice
   To clear the mental ray,
   And on the eyeballs of the blind
   To pour celestial day.

4. Our glad hosannas, Prince of peace,
   Thy welcome shall proclaim;
   And heaven's eternal arches ring
   With thy beloved name.[2]

George's Meeting, 1812

1. No change.

2. On him the spirit, largely shed,
   Exerts its sacred fire;
   Wisdom and might, and zeal and love
   His holy breast inspire.

3. He comes from galling chains of vice
   To free the captive mind;
   He comes to pour the cheering light
   Of truth upon the blind.

[1] 'A Collection of Psalms and Hymns for Social and Private Worship', 1812. Mainly
edited by Dr. Lant Carpenter.
[2] Original text taken from Julian's *Dictionary of Hymnology*, p. 489.

4. Our songs of joy and gratitude,
   His welcome shall proclaim,
   Who comes with messages of grace,
   In God his Father's name.

Isaac Watts, 1674–1748

1. Jesus shall reign where'er the sun
   Doth his successive journeys run;
   His kingdom stretch from shore to shore
   Till moons shall wax and wane no more.

2. For him shall endless prayer be made,
   And praises throng to crown his head;
   His name like sweet perfume shall rise
   With every morning sacrifice.

3. People and realms of every tongue
   Dwell on His love with sweetest song;
   And infant voices shall proclaim
   Their early blessings on His name.

4. Let every creature rise and bring
   Peculiar honours to our King;
   Angels descend with songs again,
   And earth repeat the long Amen.[1]

George's Meeting, 1812

1. To God let fervent prayers arise
   With every daily sacrifice,
   The great Messiah's reign to spread,
   And with new honours crown his head.

2. Soon may he reign where'er the sun
   Doth his successive journies run;
   His kingdom stretch from shore to shore
   Till suns shall rise and set no more.

3. Great God! may realms of every tongue
   Dwell on thy love with grateful song;
   And with united hearts proclaim,
   That grace and truth by Jesus came.

[1] Original text taken from 'Hymns Ancient and Modern', Historical edn., 1909, No. 373.

4. Parent of good! to thee we trace
   These boundless stores of richest grace;
   All have their source in love divine,
   And be the praise and glory thine.

Charles Wesley, 1707–88, John Cennick, 1718–55,
and Martin Madan, 1726–90

1. Lo! He comes with clouds descending,
   Once for favoured sinners slain;
   Thousand thousand saints attending
   Swell the triumph of His train:
       Alleluia!
   God appears on earth to reign.

2. Every eye shall now behold Him
   Robed in dreadful majesty;
   Those who set at nought and sold Him
   Pierced and nailed Him to the tree,
       Deeply wailing,
   Shall the true Messiah see.

3. Those dear tokens of His passion
   Still His dazzling body bears,
   Cause of endless exultation
   To his ransomed worshippers;
       With what rapture
   Gaze we on those glorious scars!

4. Yea, Amen, let all adore Thee
   High on Thine eternal throne:
   Saviour, take the power and glory,
   Claim the kingdom for Thine own:
       Alleluia!
   Thou shalt reign and Thou alone.[1]

George's Meeting, 1812.

1. Lo! he comes from heaven descending,
   Sent to judge both quick and dead;
   Midst ten thousand saints and angels,
   See our great exalted Head;
       Hallelujah! !
   Welcome, welcome, Son of God!

[1] 'Hymns Ancient and Modern', Historical edn., No. 52.

2. Full of awful expectation
    All before the Judge appear;
    Truth and justice go before him;
    Now the joyful sentence hear;
        Hallelujah!
    Welcome, welcome, judge divine!

3. 'Come, ye blessed of my Father,
    Enter into life and joy;
    Banish all your fear and sorrow;
    Endless praise be your employ:
        Hallelujah!
    Welcome, welcome to the skies!'

4. Now at once they rise to glory;
    Jesus brings them to the King;
    There, with all the host of heaven,
    They eternal anthems sing;
        Hallelujah!
    Glory be to God on High!

It was too much to expect that Unitarian hymn-revisers would not tamper with the work of Charles Wesley and his fellow-Methodists, but it is difficult to forgive them for their literary murder of Isaac Watts' miniature masterpiece. Whatever the merits of the compilers of Unitarian hymnbooks at the beginning of the nineteenth century, a feeling for poetry was not one of them.

We have seen in Kenrick's promotion of the Western Unitarian Society his interest in educational affairs, and religious instruction in particular. Soon after his arrival in Exeter, on 28th October, 1785, Kenrick wrote to his uncle giving a summary account of the previous attempts to found a lasting Academy at Exeter. He then stated that the old library remained available, and that Messrs. Hogg (of the Mint) and Bretland would be available as tutors, but funds were not available to maintain such an institution at present. Possibly Kenrick's decision to make the attempt sprang from an invitation he received on the 5th February, 1798, to become Theological Tutor at the Manchester Academy. 'The Theological Professor may very reasonably calculate upon receiving the value of £270 per annum with an increase of emolument rising in proportion to the number of Pupils exceeding 20.' Kenrick did not accept this invitation, attractive though it must have been to him financially. Instead in the following year appeared proposals for an Academy in the West of England, under the joint tutorship of Bretland and Kenrick. Pupils must be at least 14 years of age at entry, and the time to be spent at the Academy would be between 3 and 5 years. Kenrick proposed to take a large House and to board students at £40 a session. Fees to tutors were to be from £10 10s. each session, but considerable reductions would be made for all intending ministers. No articles of faith would be imposed, and students would be allowed to attend whatever places of worship they might wish. Bretland and Kenrick would teach Latin, Greek and Hebrew together. Geography, Geometry, Algebra, Mathematics, Natural Philosophy, General Grammar, Oratory, and History, would be taught by Bretland alone: while Logic, Metaphysics, Morals, Natural and Revealed Religion, Jewish Antiquities, Ecclesiastical History, and Critical Lectures on the New Testament all fell to Kenrick. The library of the Towgood Academy, lent to Hackney, was to be returned to Exeter in time for the first session of the new Academy.

To focus local support for the institution public meetings were held, which came to the following decisions:

1. That a Society be formed for the purpose of forming a Seminary in the West of England, for the Education of Ministers among Protestant Dissenters, and that no subscription to doctrinal articles of religion shall be required as a condition of admittance.

2. That every Subscriber of One Guinea or upwards per annum be considered as a member of this society . . . and that every Benefactor at one time of Ten Guineas or upwards, be considered as a member for life . . .

3. That the whole of the sum subscribed, and two-thirds of the interest arising from benefactions, be expended in paying for the board and instruction of young men intended for the christian ministry among protestant dissenters. . . .

11. That, at every annual meeting, two Ministers, members of this society, be requested to examine the proficiency and conduct of each student, supported by the funds of the society, and to report the result of their examination to the next meeting.

The remainder of the Rules of the Society, which were 16 in all, dealt with administrative matters of no special significance. Whereas the Academy itself was designed to prepare youths 'for the Christian ministry . . . or . . . for commercial and active life', this Exeter Society was designed to help the ministerial candidates only.

On 21st October, 1799, Kenrick reported to his father:

I have taken ye. house adjoining to my own for one year from Michaelmas,

& I have now two pupils at my house as Boarders, besides one more who boards with his parents in ye. town . . . Ye. students are to be placed under my care, & to receive instruction from us both . . . Our people do not enter into these schemes wth. all ye. zeal I could wish, but they do perhaps as much as could be expected. . . .

The type of student with which Kenrick was dealing is illustrated by a further passage from the same letter, referring to one of his first three pupils: 'Mr. Shute is ye. son of a Gentleman, who was lately in business as a grocer, but having a very handsome fortune left him has retired. Ye. son was for a few years with his father but discovering no turn for trade he intends to bring him up as a minister.'

This Academy was designed on a small scale, owing to the small resources available to it. The fees which had to be charged were such as to prohibit all but the sons of well-to-do parents from taking advantage of the undoubtedly valuable education offered. Only eleven students had completed their courses in the Academy when it closed on the 25th March, 1805, while four others went on to complete their education elsewhere, including John Kenrick, Timothy's son, who went to Glasgow after private study at Plymouth with John Kentish.[1]

The brief remainder of Kenrick's pastorate at Exeter was calm and prosperous. His 'Hearers' had by this time grown into a warm affection for him, and the stormy episodes of a decade before were becoming a memory. He was requested to have printed his sermons on 'the suspension of all consciousness at death, and to the objections of modern unbelievers'. It was, however, at the beginning of 1803, when it became known that Kenrick had received an invitation to the pastorate of the New Meeting, Birmingham, that the hold he possessed on the affections of his Exeter friends became truly apparent. A General Meeting was called on the 23rd January, from which a letter was sent couched in extremely appreciative terms requesting Kenrick to stay in Exeter. But at a further meeting on 6th February it was reported that Kenrick had accepted the Birmingham invitation before their petition had reached him, and the subscribers then decided to appeal direct to Birmingham New Meeting to release him from his promise. This was done in very tactful terms, stressing the affection in which Kenrick was held at Exeter, and the importance of George's Meeting as the most substantial Dissenting society in Devon and Cornwall, upon which many of the smaller country chapels depended. The reply from Birmingham of 18th February was sympathetic, but refused to release

[1] McLachlan, H., *English education under the Test Acts*, 1931, pp. 232–5.

Kenrick voluntarily, on the principle that their need was as great as that of Exeter. As Kenrick had still not sent in his resignation the Exeter men did not give up hope, but made a further appeal to Kenrick. Their perseverance won the day, and a General Meeting on 13th March was told that Kenrick had disengaged himself from his obligations to the Birmingham Meeting. He had obviously been doubtful of the wisdom of going all along, and the unanimity of the Exeter members in desiring him to stay made the move impossible for a man of his strong sense of duty.

Kenrick's ministry was not greatly prolonged by this incident. On his usual summer visit to his relations at Wrexham, he died suddenly on 22nd August, 1804, probably of a cerebral haemorrhage. The Academy was temporarily carried on by Joseph Bretland alone, but he found the task too much for him, and brought it to an end in the following March, with the consent of the Committee which supported it.[1]

The society meeting at George's Chapel at Kenrick's death had thus survived the disturbances and controveries arising from the transition to complete Unitarianism, and the aggravation caused by political movements of the age. It was weaker by far than it had been in 1760, with the total number of subscribers to the Ministers' Fund about 120 (these would be the wealthy section of the society) and 'Hearers' may have been from 500 to 700. Yet it was easily the most prosperous of the causes which remained loyal to the Exeter Assembly, and its adherents more numerous than those of the other Nonconformist societies in Exeter at that time.

The 'Arian' meeting at the Mint continued its placid existence until just after the end of the eighteenth century. No reliable figures are available relating to attendance there after 1744, but a gradual decline in prosperity took place there as in the other heterodox Dissenting societies. The chief subject of interest lies in the use of a revised Liturgy at the Mint Meeting. By mid-century some ministers had begun to feel the lack of form in their services. This took place mainly among the Presbyterians, and the first instance of a revised liturgy being used was at the Octagon Chapel, Liverpool, in the early 1760s.[2] This formal order of worship was introduced at the Mint Chapel by David Williams, minister there from 1761 to 1770. He was succeeded, for two years only, in 1770 by Joseph Bretland, then a young man fresh

---

[1] Murch, op. cit., pp. 442–4, 447, and Kenrick Papers 74–7.
[2] Coomer, D., *English Dissent under the early Hanoverians*, 1946.

from Towgood's Academy, who did not care for the Liturgy and persuaded his congregation to put it aside. From 1772 until 1789 the minister was John Hogg, and there is no evidence that the liturgy was used during this period. It is recorded that 'the duration of this gentleman's ministry was shortened by his engaging in business', which is sufficient indication of the state of his congregation. The minister of a thriving church has no time for engaging in business, and if its members discharge faithfully their obligations to him he will not need to augment his stipend by such means. Once again Joseph Bretland was invited to take on the pastorate at the Mint, he meanwhile having kept a classical school. In 1792, at the repeated request of his congregation, Bretland agreed to reintroduce the Liturgy.[1] Timothy Kenrick, in a letter to his uncle dated 1st June, 1792, wrote:

2 or 3 Societies of Dissenters in this neighbourhood have lately adopted Liturgies, taken principally from the Book of Common Prayer, but altered so as to render it entirely consistent with the principles of Unitarians . . . The Mint Meeting Congregation which has adopted this mode of Worship in Exeter is considerably increased for the present. . . .

The differences between this 'Liturgy for the use of the Mint Meeting in Exeter' and the Book of Common Prayer are best illustrated by comparing the General Thanksgiving, and the General Confession in each of them. It is perhaps surprising that so few changes were made by the eighteenth-century Arians, though there is a world of difference between the phrases 'in Christ' and 'by Christ'.

Book of Common Prayer. General Thanksgiving.	The Mint Liturgy.
Almighty God, Father of all mercies, we thine unworthy servants do give thee most humble and hearty thanks for all thy goodness and loving-kindness to us, and to all men . . . We bless thee for our creation, preservation and all the blessings of this life; but above all, for thine inestimable love in *the redemption of the world by our Lord Jesus Christ*; for the means of grace and for the hope of glory. And, we beseech thee, give us that due sense of all thy mercies, that our hearts may be unfeignedly thankful, and that we shew forth thy praise, not only with our lips, but in our lives; by giving up ourselves	Almighty God, Father of all mercies, we thy unworthy servants give thee most humble and hearty thanks for all thy goodness and loving-kindness to us and to all men . . . We bless thee for our creation, preservation and all the blessings of this life; but above all, for thy inestimable love *in sending our Lord Jesus Christ to save sinners*: for the means of grace, and for the hope of glory. Give us, we beseech thee, that due sense of all thy mercies, that our hearts may be unfeignedly thankful; and that we may shew forth thy praise, not only with our lips, but in our lives, by giving ourselves up to thy service,

[1] Murch, op. cit., pp. 402–3.

to thy service, and by walking before thee in holiness and righteousness all our days; *through Jesus Christ our Lord, to whom with thee and the Holy Ghost be all honour and glory, world without end. Amen.*

and by walking before thee in holiness and righteousness all our days, *according to the precepts of Jesus Christ, thy son our Lord. Now to thee, O Father, the only Living and true God, be everlasting praises.*

General Confession.

Almighty and most merciful Father; We have erred, and strayed from thy ways like lost sheep. We have followed too much the devices and desires of our own hearts. We have offended against thy holy laws. We have left undone those things which we ought to have done; And we have done those things which we ought not to have done; and *there is no health in us.* But thou, O Lord, have mercy upon us, *miserable offenders.* Spare thou them, O God, which confess their faults, *Restore thou them that are penitent*; According to thy promises declared unto mankind *in Christ Jesu our Lord.* And grant, O most merciful Father, *for his sake*; That we may hereafter live a godly, righteous, and sober life, To the glory of thy holy Name.

Almighty and most merciful Father! we have erred and strayed from thy ways like lost sheep. We have followed too much the devices and desires of our hearts. We have offended against thy holy laws. We have left undone those things which we ought to have done; and we have done those things which we ought not to have done; and *we justly deserve to be punished for our transgressions.* But do thou, O Lord, have mercy upon us. Spare thou those, O God, who confess their faults. *Receive thou those who are penitent into thy favour,* according to thy promises declared unto mankind *by Christ Jesus our Lord.* And grant, O most merciful Father, that we may hereafter live a godly, righteous, and sober life, to the glory of thy holy name.

It is probable that the Liturgy continued in use at the Mint until it closed in 1810, but Bretland's patience with it was soon exhausted. The facts were given by Kenrick again in another of his periodical reports to his uncle Samuel, of 1st July, 1793.

Mr. Bretland, who preached to perhaps the oldest Society of Unitarians in the kingdom . . . has lately resigned. The cause . . . is singular,—he objects to the use of 'We' in public Prayer, because the Minister answers to the Almighty for the dispositions of the people which he cannot know, & has no reason to presume, instead of 'We thank thee', 'We beseech thee' etc., he would substitute 'Thanks be unto thee, Let the Lord be besought', but the congregation being unwilling to have their Books altered, for they use a Liturgy, he has been obliged to resign.

Bretland's place at the Mint was taken by Theophilus Edwards, who had been minister at the Abbey Church, Tavistock, for 22 years. Once again there is no evidence of affairs at the Mint in the closing years of its life. It probably declined rapidly in the 1790s owing to the unpopularity of Dissenters generally during the Revolutionary and Napoleonic era, and in 1810 the handful of members remaining decided to join with George's Meeting. Their chapel was sold to the Wesleyan Methodists, pulled down, and rebuilt on a larger scale.[1] The memorial to James Peirce was removed to George's Meeting, and installed in the large Vestry there in 1812. The remaining endowments of the Mint were likewise transferred to the other society, and used to provide an organ, which was installed before February, 1815.

By 1810, therefore, the sole inheritor of the Presbyterian tradition in Exeter was George's Meeting in South Street, now with one possible exception completely Unitarian. The exception was the Rev. James Manning, who never went the whole way towards Unitarianism, and who had not been particularly happy at the vigorous propagation of the new ideas by Kenrick, his fellow minister. The transition may be said to have become complete by 1810. However, it remained to be seen whether, in spite of its unorthodoxy, George's Meeting would keep its leading position among Exeter Nonconformist societies in the new century.

[1] Murch, op. cit., p. 403.

CHAPTER XI

BAPTISTS AND CONGREGATIONALISTS, 1760–1824

FOLLOWING the general pattern of eighteenth-century Nonconformity, the Exeter Baptists experienced a further slow decline after the death of their Pastor Edmund Jones in 1765. Now followed a most unpleasant episode in their history, as a result of which their early church records were destroyed, records which would otherwise have served as a valuable comparison with those of the Presbyterians. In October, 1765 a Thomas Lewis was asked to become the minister, but the invitation was not unanimous.

'Mr. Lewis and the Church met with no small trouble from a disaffection in some of its members relative to Mr. Lewis' settlement, which issued in a number withdrawing themselves and setting up a separate interest. They had a Mr. Twinning for their Minister.'[1] It is not known what were the causes of disagreement: the most likely would have been the reaction of a strong minority against the strict Calvinism hitherto accepted in the church. Both sections supported the petition in the early 1770s to remove subscription to the 39 Articles from Dissenters who did not enjoy State emoluments: this was recorded in Josiah Thompson's Survey of English Nonconformity, made in 1773. All the Presbyterian ministers in Exeter signed the petition, together with Thomas Twinning, Joseph Twinning, and Thomas Lewis. The two Twinnings would have been father and son.[2]

In 1770 a temporary reunion of the two sections of the church was brought about. Its success was short, for division took place for the second time in 1771. The minority then applied to the Western Association of Baptist Churches for recognition as a separate church. The reply of their General Assembly of 1772 was:

It is the opinion of the Association that you cannot be acknowledged as a Church until you are regularly constituted such, having first sought dismission from the Church to which you lately belonged; but when you have taken such steps, should you appear to be animated by a love of truth and

[1] Gabb, Arthur, *A history of South Street Baptist Church, Exeter*, 1955, p. 39.
[2] Thompson, Josiah, 'Survey of English Nonconformity', MSS. in Dr. Williams' Library, London. Printed in *Trans. Cong. Hist. Soc.*, Vol. 5, 1911/12.

holiness, we shall think it our duty to give you such countenance and assistance as may be in our power.[1]

This never took place, and as the Twinnings left the church in 1772, Thomas Lewis was left as sole pastor until his death on 4th December, 1774.

There is little else to record of the South St. Baptist society until the beginning of the nineteenth century. The disastrous split between 1765 and 1772 had weakened the little church and it showed few signs of revival for long afterward. The minister from 1776 until 1789 was Enoch Francis, and under him a close co-operation grew up between the Baptists and the Calvinistic Methodists of Henry Tanner, meeting in the nearby Coombe St. Tabernacle. Ministries became shorter than those of the early part of the century, when it was the custom for pastors to settle permanently for a lifetime's work in one place. William Clarke was minister from 1791 to 1793; William Mannering from 1796 to 1799; Daniel Sprague from 1800 to 1808; Thomas Clarke Edmonds from 1809 to 1812; and Samuel Kilpin from 1812 to 1829. Answers to the Primary Visitation Returns of Bishops Ross (1779), and Henry Reginald Courtenay (1798), give no indication of the number of families of Dissenters of any denomination, nor are the few figures given in reply to the similar Visitation of Bishop William Carey in 1821 sufficient to estimate the support given to the Exeter Baptist society at that time.[2] The only indication from an outside source comes in Jenkin's 'History of Exeter' (1806) which referred to 'the Anabaptist Meeting House, very commodious and frequented by a large and genteel congregation'.

If this passage from Jenkin is to be taken literally, it can only mean that the impetus born of the Methodist movement in the eighteenth century had begun to affect the Nonconformist societies which had remained orthodox. A forward movement by the Exeter Baptists certainly did come with the ministry of Samuel Kilpin. For almost the first time there is noticeable a concern with the poverty and squalor which was the lot of so many of the inhabitants of every city in those days. A decade or two later this concern spread to the civic authorities and led to improvements in sanitation and medical services. Kilpin lived in St. Sidwell's parish, which at that time contained some of the more disreputable inhabitants of the city, and 'fastened a notice to his

[1] Gabb, op. cit., pp. 36–40.
[2] South St. Baptist Church Minute Book, 1812–68, with notes on earlier periods. Preserved at the Chapel.

front gate which read: "Reading and prayers from eight o'clock till half past eight every morning. Neighbours of all classes are respectfully invited to attend; preaching every Wednesday evening." ' His actions were ridiculed but he persisted, and gradually achieved positive improvement in the conduct of the people who came.[1] His house had to be licensed still, to obtain the benefits of the Toleration Act, and there is an entry in the Diocesan Registry of 1815, 21st March, 'St. Sidwell's, House & premises of the Revd. Samuel Kilpin.'

As a reaction against the eighteenth century drift towards Unitarianism, the Exeter Baptists had accepted an extreme Calvinism, often tending towards Antinomianism. There was in the years following 1815 a Calvinist revival in the West of England, both inside and outside the Church of England, and during the early years of Kilpin's pastorate there arose considerable controversy amongst the Exeter Baptists on the subject of Antinomianism. Kilpin was not a man interested in theological disputes: like most evangelists his faith was expressed in living rather than in words. He refused to remain unless those dissatisfied with his preaching left the church. In a letter to Church Meeting of 5th January, 1817, after referring to his happiness with the members until that time, he said:

'But it is not so now. I no more come among you as a Pastor highly esteemed for his works sake, but as a Criminal to be judged by the standard orthodoxy of the times'. He had been advised to go on as before. 'But belov'd, I cannot go on. Shackled and fettered I will not attempt to go on.' He withdrew from the city until the church decided what to do. He asked those who were dissatisfied to

respectfully and peaceably withdraw and form another Society, and choose a Pastor after their own heart. The City is large enough for another Baptist Church, and so far from resenting their non approving of me, I would say from my heart, Go and the Lord be with you. . . . They have a right to differ from me, and have an equal right to express that difference . . .

The members asked Kilpin to return and take services until the end of March, 1817. On 9th March, he took three well-attended services, and such was the impression he made that the church decided it could not lose him after all. A letter asking him to return was signed by 104. At the same time 54 people asked to be considered as no longer members, and later that year they formed another cause, which came to be known as the Bartholomew St. Baptist Church. The letter inviting Kilpin to return had included the passage:

[1] Gabb, p. 45.

Considering the doctrines you have with great success preached are the great truths of the gospel; promoting humility, gentleness, meekness & every Christian grace; truths distinct from those sentiments which are generally known by the appellation of Arminian, and from those which are termed Antinomian, we . . . express our . . . desire you again take on yourself the Pastoral Office over us. . . .

This secession was never acrimonious. The South Street church sent a letter more in sorrow than in anger to those who were leaving, expressing the hope, as in the event was the case, that the new church might increase the number of professing Christians within the city. Yet this division severely reduced the numbers in communion at South St. The early years of Kilpin's ministry had seen a remarkable growth in the parent society, until at the time of the crisis the membership was 169. The 54 who now withdrew were followed by others as time went on, and when Kilpin's successor revised the membership list in 1829 there were then only 99 members of the South St. church. The enthusiasm of the early days was never regained.

Kilpin's return put him in a much stronger personal position than before, and he dictated his terms from then on. He demanded that the 'pulpit be considered as the pastors own, & none permitted to preach in it, except by his invitation or consent'. He asked that 'a strict impartial & scriptural discipline be immediately acted upon and kept up uniformly as it respects choice of officers, admission, dismission, or exclusion of members'. Yet the Church was not unduly narrow in outlook at this time, for on 15th February, 1819, a resolution was passed 'To admit as Occasional Communicants with us Paedobaptist friends who are members of other parts of Christ's church.'

Some expansion took place in the form of a small Mission in St. Sidwell's where Kilpin lived. In a letter of August, 1818, Kilpin wrote to a friend about 'the conversion of at least thirty precious souls to God. . . . My further plan is to establish two Sunday schools and to make a kind of depot or rendezvous for any Sunday School children.' [1]

This he did, for under the date of 23rd December, 1818, the Diocesan Registry recorded a licence issued for 'St. Sidwell's. Dwelling house, Chapel and rooms adjoining . . . situate in a garden adjoining Jeffery's Row in St. Sidwell's'. This was given the name of the Refuge Chapel, and survived until Kilpin's death.

A closer co-operation than before is also seen between the orthodox Nonconformists of the City. Such institutions as united Missionary

[1] Gabb, p. 46.

Prayer Meetings, and the Exeter Sunday School Union, date from this period, and when the Castle St. Congregational church was inviting a young student, John Griffin, to its pastorate in 1820, he recorded in a letter to his father: 'The baptist minister, a very respectable gentlemanly man, said to me, the other day, "I sincerely hope you will come to Exeter: there are indications of the divine will, in the feelings of the people, which there have not been before." ' Such an encounter would have been unusual in the eighteenth-century scene.[1]

The one other major incident in Kilpin's ministry at South St. was the rebuilding of the chapel itself in 1822–3. The foundations of the building were declared unsafe, and the only wise solution was to level it and build again. Much of the old material could be re-used, but the church had to face expenditure of about £1800. Subscriptions and loans from Deacons were enough to meet the whole cost, and no debt was incurred. In fact, by the terms under which the land and chapel had been given in 1725 by Benjamin Heath, the property had to be kept 'free of all incumbrances for ever', and could therefore not be mortgaged.

In 1828 Kilpin's health began to break down, and E. H. Brewer, from Shaldon, was appointed as his assistant. Kilpin gave up some of his salary to pay for this. The next year in March, Kilpin resigned and went to live permanently in St. Sidwell's, where he died four years later.

The foundation of the Baptist church in Bartholomew Street in 1817 was the result of the convergence of two separate forces. The membership came from a secession from the South St. Baptists, and the first entry in the minute book of the Bartholomew St. church runs:

1817, March 31. Seventy two persons members of the Baptist Church South St. Exeter under the pastorate of the Rev. Saml. Kilpin withdrew themselves from that communion & hired a room in Bartholomew St. for public worship, and formed themselves into a Church professing the doctrines of Three equal persons in the Godhead—Eternal and Personal Election—Original Sin—Particular Redemption—Free Justification by the Righteousness of Christ—Efficacious grace in Regeneration—the final perseverance of the Saints—the Resurrection of the Dead—the future judgment—the Eternal Happiness of the Righteous and the endless misery of the Impenitent.

These articles of belief were identical with those held by the parent church, yet they were always interpreted in an extreme manner, tending to the Antinomianism of which the members had been

---

[1] Griffin, John, *Memoirs and remains of the Rev. John Griffin, Jun., late minister of Castle Street Chapel, Exeter*, Portsea, 1822, p. 382.

accused by their former pastor at the time of the separation. They chose six of their number to be their leaders, or Deacons. The names were Enos. Welsford, Edwd. Buxton, Wm. Davies, Thos. May, Nathanl. Welsford, and Joseph Greswell.

The second factor in the foundation of this church was the practical interest shown by the Rev. George Baring, youngest son of Sir Francis Baring, founder of the London branch of the Baring family, which had originated in Exeter 100 years previously. Until 1815 he had been a clergyman of the Church of England, but then, with at least three others whose surnames were Snow, Evans, and Bevan, he decided that 'many things in the established church were inconsistent with Scripture' and he seceded. These four at first settled in Taunton, acquired the Octagon Chapel by purchase from the Methodists, and preached there to a congregation attracted by their extreme Calvinism. Evans soon removed to London, and Snow to Cheltenham, and the other two came to accept the doctrine of Believers' Baptism by immersion. This step meant that their views were identical with those of the seceding Baptists in Exeter, and both Baring and Bevan were invited to preach to them. Baring secured a substantial following in the city, and came back to live in the summer of 1817. It was by Baring that the pleasant Regency building in Bartholomew St. was constructed, opened for use on 16th August, 1818. Baring provided by far the larger part of the £4000 the chapel cost, and it remained his property entirely. 'As the people had not contributed any thing toward the expense of the building, he would never allow them any control over it.'

Baring recorded in the Church Minute Book a statement of the doctrines which he personally held. The statement ended with:

It is wished to preserve the due administration of the Ordinance of Baptism by Immersion: & also that believers only should be partakers of it —It is therefore suggested that, while every believer inclined to unite with the Church shall be allowed the general privileges belonging to the body, yet (that the choice of a Minister, Deacons & all public servants shall be vested with the Baptized Members only) that no unbaptized person shall be eligible to fill a public situation.

The beliefs of Baring and his followers were not orthodox on the doctrine of the Trinity, the chief difference being that they did not consider the Holy Spirit to be a distinct person, but 'an influence or energy of the One God, the Father'. Their beliefs on the person of Christ, as far as they are intelligible at all to the twentieth century, fell short of the orthodox Catholic teaching of three equal persons in the

Godhead. They all emphasized the value of faith for obtaining salvation, rather than good works. As one of their later ministers wrote, 'As they did not insist much either on experience or practice, the tendency of their ministry was rather lax. Their own lives, however, were such as their foes could not impeach.'

The chapel being his own property, Baring occupied a position far stronger than was usual for the minister of a Nonconformist church. Consequently when he decided to leave Exeter in March, 1819, he was able to present a successor of his own choosing. A small part of the cost of building the chapel had been borne by a Mrs. Wall, a wealthy widow of Albury in Hampshire. One of her protégés was a young man called John Mason, originally one of her servants, who had become converted to Baptist beliefs and shown a remarkable capacity as a lay preacher. When both Bevan and Baring had left the Octagon chapel in Taunton in 1817 he had been invited to succeed them. Now he was invited to take Baring's place at Exeter, and accepted. He was 29 years old. The pastoral office he accepted from the church as a whole: 'The keys of the Chapel (were) delivered to him by Mr. Baring as Trustee or Tenant of his property.'

John Mason's beliefs on his arrival in Exeter were those which had been propagated by George Baring. During the following 6 years, however, he slowly progressed towards the orthodox position on the Trinity, as the result of continued conscientious study. Although the greater part of his hearers accompanied him, inevitably there was trouble with the minority which held to their original teaching. Had Mason been entirely dependent, like any other Nonconformist minister, on the united support of his congregation, the church would have undergone a severe crisis. But the chapel itself was entirely under his control. The sequel is recorded in the church minute book:

1826. One Lord's Day the Pastor Rev. J. Mason gave notice for a Church Meeting in the evening & requested all the Members to attend. At that meeting he stated his views of the conduct & doctrinal opinions of certain discontented members & the impossibility of preserving peace in the Church while they continued members of it. He then withdrew from the Church both as its Pastor and a Member & announced his determination to form a new church the following Sabbath evening, & to receive into it all the members of the old one who were willing to unite with him, excepting the four persons already referred to. Nearly the whole of the members enrolled their names & highly approved the step which he had taken. From this period both the church and congregation began to increase.

Mason at the same time wrote to Baring, informing him of his changed opinions on the Trinity, and offering to resign the chapel into his hands again. Baring was still of the same beliefs himself, but generously confirmed Mason's possession of the chapel and the dwelling-house next door, for his lifetime. He remained minister until his death on 20th January, 1835.[1]

Following the separation of the orthodox members of Bow Meeting in 1795 and the foundation of a new Independent church in Exeter, its 68 members under the leadership of the Rev. John Giles met in the Musgrave's Alley Chapel belonging to the Wesleyan Methodists, at times when it was not used by its own congregation.[2] It was not long, however, before the new church was able to build a chapel of its own. The County Gaol was offered for sale in 1796, situated then just below the Castle, and it was bought on behalf of the Independents by Shirley Woolmer, proprietor of the *Exeter and Plymouth Gazette*. The price was £420 and on 10th June, 1796, it was conveyed and vested in Trustees.

These Trustees were:

John Giles, minister.
Nathaniel Cranch, gentleman.
William Colson, Jr. shopkeeper.
John Cox, sulphurer.
William Davis, shopkeeper.
John Tucker, watchmaker.
Thomas Sayer, soapchandler.

Samuel Davy, of Fordton, merchant.
Shirley Woolmer, printer & stationer.
Samuel Lake, serge-maker.
William Bickham, serge-maker.
William Gattey, miller.
David Hitchcock, shopkeeper.
Edward Hammerseley, machine-maker.

By the Trust-Deed the voting power was placed in the hands of full church-members and those who subscribed not less than 10s. each to the minister's stipend.

Most significant was the writing in of Calvinistic doctrine into the rules for electing ministers in future. Their experiences after the death of Abraham Tozer made the survivors of Bow Meeting resolve to prevent such things from happening again. All ministers had to subscribe to 'the following points of doctrine (videlicet) eternal election—The Divinity of Jesus Christ and particular redemption by Him, original

---

[1] Minute Books of Bartholomew St. Baptist Church, preserved in care of the Secretary of the St. Thomas' Baptist Church after 1953. Nicholson, Samuel, *Select remains of the Rev. John Mason*, etc., London, Wightman, 1836.
[2] Southernhay Congregational Church, *Centenary Yearbook*, 1895.

sin—the efficacious grace of the Holy Spirit in conversion and the final perseverance of the saints'. If at any time a duly elected minister when requested to reaffirm his belief in these articles of faith should refuse to do so, he should 'no longer officiate or preach in the said . . . meeting house or be at all considered as the preacher or pastor of the . . . congregation'.[1]

The Gaol was demolished immediately. In its place was built the customary oblong box-shaped meeting house, with a high pulpit at its short side, reached by a railed staircase. There were galleries on each of the long sides. On 22nd April, 1797, a 'Licence (was) granted to set apart a new erected Chapel in or near Castle Lane for a place of religious worship . . .' The total cost of the operation has not been preserved, but the debt incurred was not paid off until 1810.

The establishment of a new Independent church in Exeter, free from any suspicion of the Unitarian heresy, and patronized by some of the more substantial citizens, attracted some Dissenters who had previously sought refuge elsewhere. A letter of Henry Tanner (pastor of the Coombe St. Tabernacle) of 9th October, 1795, has this passage:

I suppose you might have heard of another meeting-house opened in Exeter: it began first by some orthodox dissenters, who came out from the Arians and Socinians (and very commendable); but it caused a rent both in our little church, and also in the Baptist church. I bless God, he fills up the vacant seats: but then they are the poor that hear and enjoy the gospel and feel most of its power and life.[2]

In other words the new Independent Church attracted to its communion the respectable middle-class dissenters of the city, those who were repelled by the democratic politics of Timothy Kenrick as much as by his Unitarian propaganda, for whom 'Tanner's Tabernacle' situated in one of the most crowded and insanitary regions of Exeter could never have been more than a temporary refuge.

John Giles left Exeter in 1798, having enrolled 49 new Members since the foundation of the church three years before, and he emigrated to America. His successor was R. P. Allen, and for the first ten years of his ministry he appears to have been vigorous and enterprising. Another 95 names were added to the roll of members by 1802, and the first Sunday School was set up in Exeter. Following the local example of Tiverton Congregationalists, who claim to have had a Sunday

[1] Castle Street Chapel Trust Deed, dated 10th June, 1796.
[2] Tanner, Henry, *Memoirs* . . ., 1811.

School even before the first trial of this institution by the Anglican Robert Raikes in Gloucester in 1783, Sunday Schools were quickly adopted by Nonconformists everywhere. The decision to take action at Castle St. was made at a Church Meeting on 25th May, 1800; 'That this Congregation, viewing with sorrow the ignorance and depravity of the youth of this city, consider the establishment of a School for the purpose of instructing children on the Lord's Day, an object of importance and utility.'

The School began in the following November under a permanent Master and Mistress, paid a small weekly sum for their services. Over them was a Committee, of whom three had to attend the School every week in turn, to assist the Master and Mistress in their work. Boys and girls were naturally kept separate. The number of scholars was restricted to 100, and the hours were from 9 a.m. to 10.30 a.m.; 1.30 p.m. to 2.30 p.m.; and 4.30 p.m. to 6 p.m. Teaching was based on the Catechisms of Isaac Watts and the Westminster Assembly, copies of which were supplied for use in 1801. The first Sunday School Anniversary in Exeter took place in November, 1801. The School had to use the chapel itself as a meeting ground at first, but by 1803 a house nearby was rented for the purpose. An attempt was made for some years to run a Day School, only to be given up when in 1814 a 'Lancasterian' school was opened in the city. Besides attending Sunday School at the times mentioned, the pupils were expected to attend the morning, afternoon and evening services at the chapel as well, which involved, if strictly adhered to, attendance from 9 a.m. until after 7 p.m., a formidable task by modern standards.

The Church minute books of Castle St. were destroyed in the air-raid of May, 1942, but they gave little information on the period from 1805 until 1819. R. P. Allen's health became poor, and the church began to decline with the absence of a strong leadership. He resigned in July, 1819.

At the time of Allen's departure the Castle St. Meeting had allowed its affairs to decline into chaos. At the church meeting in September, 1819, to consider the state of the society, only one surviving deacon was present, and was described as 'almost worn out with age'. There had been no legal record kept of anything concerning the Church, nor the names of members admitted, since the beginning of 1812. At once a new register of Members was called for, and two senior men were added to the Diaconate.

The church applied to Hoxton Academy for a student to be sent

M

with a view to settling in Exeter. The young man proposed to them was John Griffin, son of the minister of King St. Chapel in Portsea. He preached for the first time on 31st October, 1819, in Exeter, and remained for eight weeks. His correspondence during that time provides a useful picture of the situation of the church then. On Monday, 1st November, he wrote his cousin Joseph East: '. . . I am much pleased with the chapel: the evening congregation is capital. There is great room for much good to be done . . . There were a great number of gay young persons to hear.' And to another cousin, the Rev. J. Bristow:

> The congregation has been brought low . . . but . . . the evident spirit of attention, and the state of the sabbath-evening congregation, is sufficiently encouraging to render my visit gratifying to me . . . Here is a busy stirring population, of sufficient respectability and literature to afford a circle of intercourse, and of a disposition to hear the gospel.

To his father he wrote on 15th November, 1819:

> They told me, yesterday, they considered themselves brought to the lowest ebb, and had not known so many in the place, as last night, for many years; and the week evening congregation evidently improved . . . There is a number of active persons, in early and middle life, who are very disposed to be useful in schools and societies; and there is evidently a considerable spirit of hearing in the city, which is to be called out; for each of the other places, where there is a regular ministry, is quite filled, notwithstanding the encroachments of the new party, and they have been, by far, the least, on Castle street . . . . There are villages round . . . where there may be schools formed, and the gospel preached—there are no expences connected with the congregation—no debt on the place—there is a good grave yard round it, and two or three houses adjoining, belonging to it.[1]

The 'new party' must refer to the Antinomians such as the founders of Bartholomew St. Baptists, for the Unitarian trend was no longer new to the Exeter Dissenters.

Griffin received an invitation to the pastorate on 12th December, 1819, signed by 217 names, people who were either members or subscribers of more than 10s. each year to the Minister's fund. As the call was unanimous, this may be taken as a correct indication of the numbers actively supporting the Castle St. meeting in this year. With the addition of children and others who attended the services without actively committing themselves to membership, the figure of 500 persons connected with this society would not be too high, which

---

[1] Griffin, op. cit., pp. 380–3.

would place it at least equal in strength numerically with the parent 'Presbyterian' meeting-house in South St. Following a further stay of eight weeks in the early spring of 1820, Griffin accepted, and settled in Exeter at the end of July, a month before he reached his 24th birthday. He was not unaware of problems which might face him: one passage in a letter to a Mr. Guyer, of 5th April, 1820, reads: 'I feel . . . very much . . . the need of being a diligent student, a diligent pastor, and a prudent minister, a matter most indispensable here. There is almost every thing to do, and that in the midst of much keen-eyed watchfulness from the church folks and other congregations'. To become a Nonconformist minister in a large city was not easy for a young man of that era, when religious and social differences were so much more sharply defined than today. In the event the task proved too great a burden for a man of weak constitution. By the beginning of 1821 Griffin was ill, and frequent holidays during that year did him little good, and he finally died at Portsea on 19th January, 1822.

The Castle St. congregation was thus once more thrown back upon its own resources, but the episode had been enough to wake it from its previous lethargy, and in the 2½ years which passed before they were again able to settle with a new minister no serious decline in strength took place. Finally, in November, 1824, the Rev. John Bristow, a cousin of Griffin's, who had been considered as early as 1819, was persuaded to take on the pastorate. He remained until his retirement in 1847.[1]

[1] Southernhay *Centenary Yearbook*, p. 7.

CHAPTER XII

THE DECLINE OF GEORGE'S MEETING

ONCE the shock of Kenrick's sudden death in August, 1804, had been
absorbed by his friends in Exeter, they quickly addressed themselves to
the task of selecting his successor. On 30th September, 1804, an invitation was sent to the Rev. John Kentish, formerly a minister at Plymouth and Devonport, who had been at the New Meeting, Birmingham, since the beginning of 1803. Kentish refused by 18th October.
The Exeter subscribers then considered Charles Wellbeloved of York,
who would not move, before requesting advice from Thomas Belsham, the leading London Unitarian, and brother of Mrs. Kenrick. His
second choice fell on Lant Carpenter, a young man of 24, who had
studied at Northampton Academy and Glasgow University. He found
favour at Exeter and a unanimous invitation to the pastorate was
accepted by him on 8th January, 1805.[1]

Carpenter was an immediate success in Exeter, throwing himself into
the work with great zeal, all the more creditable to him as he never had
a strong physique. He became LL.D. of Glasgow University in 1806.[2]

Dr. Carpenter requested, in August, 1808, that steps might be taken
to make speaking in George's Chapel less difficult. He claimed that the
height of the ceiling and the position of the pulpit made preaching a
very heavy strain upon ministers. A special Committee was appointed
to consider what could be done, and it took the opinion of a London
architect, Charles Beazley. The letter recommended the lowering of the
ceiling by three feet, completely level, and the placing of the pulpit
back against the wall, instead of some ten feet out from it as it had been.
This was approved, and the work was carried out between June and
December, 1809. Dr. Carpenter and James Manning were both of the
opinion that the alterations, which had cut down the cubic space of the
building by one-twelfth, made speaking much easier, and their words
were more audible to all present. The original estimate for the work
was £134 13s. 3d., later raised to £150. But by the time all the bills
were in the expense proved to have been £201 18s. 1d.

---

[1] Throughout this section most of the material has been taken from the various Minute
Books preserved at George's Chapel. The particular sources are indicated in the text,
with dates.
[2] *D.N.B.*, Lant Carpenter.

While the alterations to the fabric were being made, no meetings could be held in the chapel, and the members worshipped in the Mint Meeting. Not only was the ceiling lowered at this time, but other extensive repairs were made to the roof of the chapel, and to the two vestries. On 7th May, 1809, the Trustees resolved: '. . . for the purpose of defraying the necessary expences of the repairs now agreed upon the rents of the seats shall be raised to double their present amount for four years. . .' And at their meeting of 24th June, when a legacy to the Exeter Assembly of £100 was reported, the trustees further decided to apply to the Assembly for this amount on loan at 5 per cent interest, which was approved when the Ministers met on 28th June.

Possibly the most significant part of Lant Carpenter's work in Exeter was his formation of a Sunday School. It was not the first in the City, for the Castle St. Congregationalists had formed one in 1800, and the Wesleyan Methodists in 1811.[1] It was at a General Meeting of Subscribers at George's Chapel on 26th January, 1812, that it was resolved 'That the establishment and support of schools for instructing the children of the poor on the Lord's Day in the rudiments of useful knowledge and particularly in the knowledge of their duty are objects deserving the attention and exertion of the Congregation.' This reso-lution casts a clear light on the attitude of mind of the majority of the members of George's Meeting at that time. Their Sunday School was at first envisaged not primarily as a means of explaining their religion to their own children and those of their acquaintances, but rather as a means of teaching the children of poor people enough to make them useful, and to appreciate the duties inseparable from their inferior position in life. The inevitable sub-committee was appointed to draw up plans and subscriptions varying from 2s. 6d. to 5s. 6d. were recorded from 46 people; the sub-committee reported back on 9th February, and already some advance is noticeable in their consciousness of the nature of the task before them. It suggested that

The great object of the Sunday School should be to communicate Re-ligious Knowledge and Principle to the Children of the Poor. Reading must of course be taught, as a necessary means to this object. Writing the Com-mittee recommend to be taught, by way of reward, and as a farther means of religious improvement, to those who are thought by the Instructors to merit this attention, for their regularity and general proficiency. If any of the Instructors think proper to give instruction in the rudiments of Arithmetic during the week, . . . the Committee conceive that this should be encouraged,

[1] Chick, Elijah, *Then and Now*, 1811 to 1912. Exeter, Drayton, 1912.

but they are of the opinion that it should not make a part of the instructions of the Lord's Day.

These principles were embodied formally in the Regulations drawn up for the Sunday School. Two regular teachers were to be appointed at a salary not exceeding £5 per annum, and Rule 11 said, 'The office of Teacher shall be to give instruction in the rudiments of reading, to secure order, and regularity of attendance, and to conduct the Children to Meeting and attend to their behaviour while there.' Two voluntary instructors were also to be appointed for each class in the school, and at this meeting were announced the names of 11 men and 17 women who were willing to take on those duties. The hours were not to be as long as in the Congregationalist Sunday School, being 'from half past eight in summer and nine in winter till the Morning Service; and from the afternoon service till half past six in summer and six in winter'. The vestry and lecture-room were originally used for the school, but to-wards the end of 1814 another room was built above the lecture-room at a cost of £154 7s. 8d. More seating was also required to allow the children to attend Sunday services, and the Trustees decided as early as March 17, 1812, to 'allow the space on each side of the Galleries next to the pulpit to the extreme end of the nearest windows being about 15 feet in length to be applied to the accommodation of the children'.

Another problem exercising the minds of the members of George's Meeting during these years was the 'regulation of the singing'. It sprang from the desire to make the best use of the revised hymnbook of 1811, and to introduce a little more order and harmony than would have been likely whilst relying solely on tuning-fork and impromptu 'raising the tune', such as was common in smaller nonconformist churches throughout the nineteenth century, and in isolated country chapels to this day. The problem was simplified by the gift of money from the defunct Mint Meeting at the end of 1812, to be used for the purchase of an organ. At a General Meeting of 17th October, 1813, it was reported that the organ had been erected, and rules were laid down for its use. 'During the time of public worship no Voluntaries or Symphonies whatever shall be introduced—No Voluntaries shall be played immediately before or after divine service, and in the usual services of the place no anthems shall be introduced.' The Committee in charge was to 'take care that the simplicity and solemnity of this part of divine service shall in no way be violated'. A voluntary choir was formed at first, but in 1823 a reorganization took place and Noah Flood [sic] 'a young man who appeared to be full competent to give instruction to the Singers' was appointed to do so, at the salary of £5 a year. The salary of the organist was not stated. Flood was given full powers, subject to final approval of the Singing Committee, to reorganize things as he saw fit. To make the regular attendance of the boys in the choir (and the organ-blower) more likely, the sum of £3 was to be distributed among them annually. As for the organist, he was instructed 'That the tune played before the singing shall be played strictly as it is to be sung, without shake, flourish or variation of any kind', and to 'keep at the organ an regular list or memorandum of all the tunes played for every six weeks in order to prevent a too frequent repetition of the same'.

On the 7th August, 1822, and again on 10th November, 1824, the Committee asked the teachers of the Sunday School to direct their children 'not to sing during divine service, their shrill voices being discordant with the choir'. This brought a prompt rejoinder from the Teachers that the children should still be allowed to 'join in singing the praises of their Creator' and should not be prevented from joining 'in so delightful a part of public worship'. The Committee agreed that all would be well if the children would sing a little more softly in future.

At the time of Lant Carpenter's resignation in 1817, the Unitarian society meeting at George's Chapel was still strong and wealthy. It is true that it no longer occupied the dominant position amongst Exeter Nonconformity that it had in 1760, and that James' Meeting had held earlier. It is true also that all the other originally Presbyterian societies in the city had now died, leaving George's Meeting as the only survivor of their proud tradition. Yet judged by any standards the cause was still strong. From 1817 onwards, however, decline again set in, gradually increasing in momentum, until by 1857 there were only 59 contributors to the Ministers' Fund left.

The decline is clearly outlined in the affairs of the Committee of Thirteen. As happened in the eighteenth century, only a steady increase in the income from property and investments prevented the decline in personal subscriptions from causing insolvency. In 1770 the average yearly income from investments and property was £104 9s. 4½d. By 1821 it had risen to £219 16s. 8d., and in 1871, following a reinvestment in more profitable stock, and letting estates to new tenants at higher rents, this income reached £383 18s. 7d. At the same time subscriptions, which were £179 10s. 9d. in 1771, were about £185 in 1821, and down to £66 9s. 6d. by 1870.

The experience of belonging to a declining society inevitably breeds strong tensions amongst its members. Above all it makes them critical of their leaders, and their ministers in particular. George's Meeting in the period from 1817 to 1862 was no exception: there occurred a succession of ministerial crises all of which coincided with further steps in the weakening of the church. Most of them concerned money. These actions took place against the background of a city with an expanding population, against industrial unrest following the death of the hitherto dominant clothing industry, and at a time when the rapid expansion of the Methodists, and comparative prosperity of other Dissenting bodies, were in sharp contrast with the declining fortunes of George's Meeting.

The vacancy caused by Carpenter's removal was filled by William Hincks, fresh from Manchester College, York. He was a Unitarian of the new school, in the same tradition as Kenrick and Carpenter. He was led to understand that he would receive a salary of at least £200 per annum, and that he would be expected to undertake, with Manning, the religious instruction of the young people of the congregation, and the children in the Sunday School and the Charity School. His did not prove a happy pastorate. As early as 31st May, 1818, a General Meeting was at pains to reject emphatically sentiments expressed in an anonymous letter received by Hincks. Almost a year later, on 21st May, 1819, Hincks himself addressed a letter to the congregation on the subject of his salary. Not only was the total amount for the first year and a half £12 6s. 10½d. short of the £200 he ought to have received, but the method of payment had been most irregular. A Committee was appointed 'to examine into the state of the funds belonging to the Ministers of the Congregation, to consider on such means as may be best calculated to increase them, and if a more desirable mode can be adopted for collecting & paying them'. The Committee reported, 'that this diminution is but small & is accounted for by deaths and other contingencies which will ever render an income dependent . . . on voluntary contributions fluctuating & uncertain'. Their proposals for increasing income involved opening the subscription lists to all who were willing to give a minimum of five shillings each year (previously it had been 10/-). The clerk was to receive subscriptions in the vestry immediately after Christmas and Midsummer each year, and the money was to be divided and paid to the ministers at once. It was also recommended that each year the collectors should report the amount of the annual subscriptions to a general meeting. At a meeting on the 24th

June, 1821, Charles Bowring, who had been appointed to examine the collector's books, made the following statistical report:

	1817.	1818.	1819.	1820.
West Qr.	£31 16s. 9d.	£34 4s. 0d.	£36 14s. 0d.	£36 11s. 6d.
East Qr.	£56 6s. 6d.	£67 3s. 3d.	£78 5s. 9d.	£78 10s. 6d.
North Qr.	£24 9s. 9d.	£20 8s. 9d.	£18 16s. 9d.	£18 7s. 0d.
South Qr.	£53 12s. 3d.	£62 17s. 0d.	£62 5s. 9d.	£60 2s. 6d.
	£166 5s. 3d.	£184 13s. 0d.	£196 2s. 3d.	£193 11s. 6d.

The centre of support for George's Meeting had thus changed radically from that in the eighteenth century. Then the East Quarter of the city had been the part contributing least to the funds: now it gave substantially more than the area round the chapel itself, the South Quarter. Charles Bowring's report also gave a list of the invested funds under the control of the Committee of Thirteen.

	Stock.	Dividends.
Old South Sea Annuities.	£236 18s. 9d.	£7 0s. 0d.
Three per cent reduced.	£812 15s. 11d.	£24 5s. 8d.
Royal Exchange.	£158 8s. 0d.	£15 14s. 10d.
Three per cent Consols.	£497 0s. 7d.	£14 16s. 2d.
Interest on £450 lent the Trustees of the meeting house.		£22 10s. 0d.
Rental of estates.		£134 15s. 0d.
Burial ground fees, after expenses were deducted, about . . .		15s. 0d.
		£219 16s. 8d.
Deduct sundry charges . .		£10 0s. 0d.
		£209 16s. 8d.

No substantial increase of subscriptions followed Hincks' complaint, although in 1819 and 1820 it was possible to pay both ministers their full stipend of £200 each.

This crisis had probably arisen through the peculiar apathy which fell on the Committee of Thirteen in the years after 1815. Between 27th September of that year, and 19th December, 1821, no meetings were recorded in the minute book. As at the latter meeting a full account was given of moneys received and paid to the ministers from 1815 to 1821 (total amount £1397 12s. 3d) it is probable that no meeting had in fact taken place. Only six members remained, and the remaining seven places were filled at this meeting, one of them being Bartholomew Parr Pope, later to figure prominently in the last crisis in which the Committee of Thirteen played a central part.

William Hincks resigned at the end of October, 1822, to accept the
pastorate of Renshaw St. Chapel, Liverpool. Behind the customary
flowery sentiments expressed on both sides can be seen the hard facts
which governed his decision. A young, capable and ambitious minister,
with a growing family, he was no longer content to work in a city
whose prosperous days seemed over, in a church which was declining
and extremely conservative in outlook, and in partnership with an aged
colleague. He referred to 'personal advantages which with my young
family it is necessary for me to attend to', a euphemism for a higher
salary.

It did not prove easy to replace Hincks. John Kenrick, Thomas
Belsham, Charles Wellbeloved, and Lant Carpenter, were all asked for
advice. Whereas a century before the Exeter Dissenters could command
almost whom they liked as their minister, now they had to search far
before being satisfied. It was not until 16th February, 1823, that an
invitation was sent to 26-year-old Henry Acton, who had been minister
at Walthamstow for 2 years only. He had studied at Dr. John Morrell's
Academy at Brighton and Hove from 1818 to 1821, and proved an able
classical scholar, for in addition to his pastoral duties in Exeter he
became second master at a proprietary school at Mount Radford. A
period of relative peace followed for George's Chapel.[1]

From 1823 there becomes evident a greater concern for the welfare of the poorer members of the society. On 28th December, 1823,
a General Meeting of subscribers resolved

that a Committee, consisting of the two Ministers, fourteen Ladies and Eight
Gentlemen be appointed for the Year ensuing; to take the management of the
present charitable Funds of this Congregation, to inquire into the State of
our poorer Members, and to devise such measures as they shall think most
proper in order to increase the said Funds. . . .

The names of this committee, the first of its kind, are worthy of
mention:

Mrs. Radford.	Mrs. W. Bowring, Jr.	Mrs. Hart.
Mrs. Powell.	Miss Parminter.	Mrs. Tricks.
Miss Drewe.	Mrs. Acton.	Miss S. Pope.
Mrs. Houghton.	Mrs. T. M. Kingdon.	Mrs. Manning.
Mrs. Hoskins.	Mrs. S. M. Cox.	
Rev. James Manning.		Mr. T. M. Kingdon.
Rev. H. Acton.		Mr. S. M. Cox.

[1] *D.N.B.*, Acton.

Mr. Samuel Pope.   Mr. J. D. Osborne.
Mr. Mackintosh.   Mr. W. Tricks.
Mr. Browne.   Mr. Hornsey.

Six of the ladies and four of the gentlemen were to resign every year, and half-yearly reports were to be made of their progress. Before this new plan was brought forward, the distribution of the Poor Fund had been in the hands of two men only, Mr. S. Pope and Mr. Wm. Tricks.

The Committee got to work promptly and reported in detail on 25th January, 1824. There were then 37 people in receipt of relief, most of whom had families to support. These had all been visited by the Ladies of the Committee, and were considered worthy of help. The Funds had previously been raised by monthly contributions from communicants, and a quarterly contribution from the congregation at large. Amounts so received had been about £36 each year, exclusive of that paid for Bread and Wine, which was £7 or £8 each year. The only constructive proposals made were that Bread and Wine should not again be charged against the Communion Fund, and that regular subscriptions to the Poor Fund should be canvassed for.

Six months later the Committee stated that only 28 people were then getting help from the Fund, as payments had been discontinued to all those not members of the congregation. Payments made for the half-year were £23 17s. 3d., with another £2 towards the clothing fund. The object of the latter was to supply extra clothing in winter, mainly blankets, to those unable to afford them themselves. Receipts in response to appeals had increased, being £41 12s 8½d. Out of the surplus of £15 odd, another £2 had been sent to the clothing fund, and coal had been ordered for distribution in the coming winter. The report continued:

... the Visitors have found cases in which the distresses of the Poor have been increased by their inability to employ themselves in any useful occupation, particularly knitting, and therefore beg to suggest to the Subscribers to the Charity School the propriety of that branch of instruction being more particularly attended to among the female children.

This referred to the Protestant Dissenters' Charity School in Paris Street, housed in the premises which had once been the headquarters of Micaijah Towgood's Academy.

This work continued on the same level for several years, though not without occasional difficulties about money. On 9th August, 1829, the

Committee reported that 'In the month of April the Ladies considered it expedient to reduce their monthly expenditure by diminishing the amount given to each poor person. . . .' The average monthly rate of expenditure was £4 in this period, and consequently no one family could have been receiving more than 3s. per month, and several probably much less. At this same meeting Dr. T. F. Barham offered his professional assistance to the poor 'whenever the Committee may think proper to avail themselves of it'.

Five years later, the report given on 27th November, 1834, showed no significant change, but an attempt was then made to define more specifically exactly who should receive help. 'All recipients shall be members of the Congregation of good character and of clean habits. . . . That all relief shall be administered according to the real necessities of the parties.'

On 25th August, 1839, the Poor Fund was found to be in debt to the amount of £26, a position which had not substantially improved a year later (27th September, 1840), when the Committee recommended that it should cease providing free medicine to the sick until its debts were paid off. The Congregation did not approve this recommendation. Doctors in the society continued to provide free medical services as far as they were able.

The Poor Fund continued at this same level, with occasional financial crises, until the ministry of Rev. Thomas Hincks, son of the former minister William Hincks, from 1845 until 1852. He reorganized the charitable institutions of the chapel into one 'Benevolent Society', in 1850, which aimed to supply funds and helpers for the Poor Fund, the Sunday School, and the Fellowship Fund (a means of aiding weak churches in the country of their own denomination.) But although this temporarily increased interest in social questions, the Benevolent Society fell to pieces during the 2 years' interregnum which followed Hincks' departure in February, 1852. A report to a General Meeting held on 9th April, 1854, revealed lack of support both in personal assistance and in money. The number of subscribers at the beginning of the venture had been 120: by this date it had fallen to 60, and the fund was in debt for £6 10s. approximately. A year later (22nd April, 1855) the Benevolent Society was dissolved, the Sunday School given more autonomy, and a Ladies' Committee given charge of the Poor Fund and an Industrial School where destitute girls were placed for 'moral, mental and industrial training under an able mistress'. The latter would have been a forerunner of the Exeter Girls' Industrial School and Servants' Home, at 42, Bartholomew Yard, designed to prepare destitute girls, or young servants who had lost their situations from incompetence, for domestic service.[1] But by April, 1856, this Industrial School was already short of funds and it was being debated whether it could be continued. Only a special appeal by the new minister, Rev. G. B. Brock, enabled it to meet its expenses for that year. By April, 1857, the Industrial School had been wound up, most of the children being accommodated at the Protestant Dissenters' Charity School in Paris Street. Finally, by 1860, the Poor Fund income had become so low that it could not meet demands made on it. Special appeals, and extra collections were made, but it is evident that by this date there just was not the wealth present in the society to enable any noticeable impact to be made on conditions outside.

By contrast with the absence of enthusiasm for Poor Relief, the Sunday Schools were kept running satisfactorily throughout this period. By 1827 the Girls School had as many as 73 pupils, and the Boys School had 56. The report presented on 22nd April, 1832, showed a decline to 61 girls and 46 boys, and a serious shortage of teachers was mentioned for almost the first time. The state of the Boys' School was particularly desperate. '10 years ago there were 8 teachers to depend on, 2 months ago there were 4, and at present only 2. . . .' The Sub-committee appointed to inquire what could be done decided to impose minor disciplinary measures to ensure good conduct by the children, and by 5th August, it was reported that 7 new teachers had volunteered for the Boys and 4 for the Girls. Two more ladies offered their services in November following. Even this did not raise the numbers to the figure recommended of 12 teachers for each school. By 27th May, 1833, the Girls' School had 11 teachers, and the Boys' 9. There were 47 girls and 53 boys receiving instruction at that time. Numbers attending again fluctuated during the next dozen years, from a highest of 65 boys and 36 girls in January, 1836, to a lowest of 20 girls and 36 boys in May, 1844. By March, 1849, the figures had risen again so that there were 66 boys, with 10 teachers, and 38 girls with 14 teachers. Following the episode of the Benevolent Society beween 1850 and 1855, the Sunday School entered on a more prosperous period. On 12th April, 1857, there were 151 scholars on the books, with an average attendance of 85. The Girls' teachers were numerous and efficient, and the boys' teachers 'more satisfactory than a short time since'. This was the high

[1] White, Wm., *History, Gazetteer and Directory of the County of Devon*, 2nd edn., 1878–9, p. 352.

noon of the Victorian Sunday School, and it would have been surprising if such an increase in activity had not taken place.

As in 1823 the succession of ministers too often was the occasion for
a crisis in the affairs of the society. James Manning died suddenly at the
beginning of September, 1831, just after he had been presented with a
silver vase by his congregation to commemorate his long service as a
Minister for 55 years. The cost of this Vase was mentioned as £112 1s.:
this from a congregation which that same year gave a mere £30 for
the relief of the poor. Now the unfortunate decision was made to pay
the two ministers different salaries. Acton as the Senior was to have all
the subscriptions and one-half of the endowments, approximately £300,
while the assistant was to have only half of the endowments, or £100.
On 15th April, 1832, it was reported that an invitation to become a
candidate had been sent to a Rev. John Cropper, M.A., of Manchester,
who did 'not object to performing infant baptism'. He accepted the
invitation.

Difficulties arose in 1836 and 1837 over a recommendation to hold
Sunday evening services during the summer months. By 1836 the
tendency in most denominations was towards making evening worship
the more important of the two Sunday services. Cropper, after a year's
trial of this arrangement, declined to take part in any more Sunday
evening services, and wished to stand by his original agreement to take
one service only each Sunday. He also complained of a general feeling
antipathetic to him in the congregation. A deputation waited on him
to sort things out, but could not help making the remark 'the ground
of complaint, whatever it might amount to, was common to himself
and colleague'. I.e. Acton had made no complaint. But on 30th April
it was resolved 'that the Evening Service appointed for the Summer
Months be discontinued'.

Cropper was not happy now in Exeter, and on 25th February, 1838,
he sent in his resignation, giving as his reason 'circumstances entirely
of a personal nature'. He was persuaded to reconsider his resignation,
but renewed it on 27th April, 'having received an invitation from a
distant church in all respects suitable to my wishes'.

It was now formally debated whether the society should still have a
second minister. The deciding factor at the General Meeting held
13th May, 1838, was a letter from Acton urging that 'in present
circumstances' he felt it necessary to continue having two ministers,
and he would not himself be able to act as sole pastor. Once again Lant
Carpenter and John Kenrick were consulted, and they were able to

recommend strongly Dr. Walter Copland Perry, who had just finished his training at Manchester College, York, under Kenrick. He was invited without trial, including a stipulation for evening services in the summer.

The small salary of £100 a year for a highly educated minister continued to create difficulties. In June 1839 Perry reported a unanimous invitation from the Octagon Chapel, Norwich, one of the most important Unitarian churches in the country. He stated very frankly that money considerations impelled him to accept it and nothing else, and that he might be able to stay at Exeter if his salary was raised. He was at once guaranteed £150 a year minimum for five years, and consequently declined the Norwich invitation: this must have represented a real sacrifice on his part. Yet this promise was not fulfilled to the letter. On 26th September, 1841, the Committee of Thirteen reported that Perry's salary had fallen to £143 11s. 2d. in the previous year, and asked for extra subscriptions. A year later his receipts were lower still—£131 8s. 1d. Perry had attempted to remedy the deficiency on his own account, by undertaking to assist the Unitarian congregation at Lympstone whenever he was free.

In August, 1843, Acton died of an apoplectic stroke. It was decided to continue with 2 ministers, but they should each receive half of the money available for salaries, and work on terms of equality. The Treasurer of the Committee of Thirteen estimated in March, 1844, that the probable income for the year would be between £350 and £360. This suggests a substantial fall if Acton and Perry had indeed been paid anything approaching the specified salaries of £300 and £150 respectively. Extra subscriptions must have been forthcoming to keep these salaries effective between 1839 and 1843: now income fell back to the normal level.

On 4th April, 1844, an invitation was accepted by Francis Bishop, of whom little personal is recorded. Then in July Dr. Perry resigned abruptly, his departure being fixed for the following Michaelmas. 'My present communication will not I imagine be wholly unexpected by any of you—to some I have too good reason to know it will be most welcome.' He referred also to a 'want of consideration on your part for my personal welfare'. The resignation was accepted without any formal expression of regret.

This vacancy took longer to fill, and it was not until 14th September, 1845, that the Rev. Thomas Hincks of Warrington was appointed as the second minister, at a salary of half the total receipts, at that time

£350. He was the son of their former minister, William Hincks. Three years later, on 2nd January, 1848, Francis Bishop resigned, to take on the job of Minister to the Poor with the 'domestic mission at Liverpool'. With his departure the society in Exeter faced the obvious fact that they were unable to support more than one minister, and no successor was appointed. This meant a substantial increase of income for Thomas Hincks. Whereas in 1847 he had received half the total income of the Ministers' Fund, which came to £167 14s. 7½d., in 1848 he had £343 0s. 4d.

Hincks did not enjoy this well-merited increased stipend for very long. In June, 1849, burst the last major crisis in which the Committee of Thirteen played a dominant part. At a meeting held on 17th December, 1848, the subscribers rejected 'certain unfounded reports' about the beliefs of Hincks 'in the resurrection of Christ and the other Supernatural facts of the Gospel History'. Unfortunately it is not recorded exactly what Hincks was accused of believing. Could he have been leaning towards Trinitarianism? Or was he, as seems more likely, applying the young science of Biblical Criticism to the New Testament as well as to the Old, and thus leading his Hearers one further step towards a modern rational and unmiraculous Unitarianism? These reports set the Committee of Thirteen to examine the Trusts under which they held the Society's investments. It was reported on 10th June, 1849, that the Committee could not 'either legally or honorably' pay the whole of such income as hitherto to their present Minister. This applied unanimously to the income from property. In addition their Treasurer, Bartholomew Parr Pope, refused to 'sign the document necessary for receiving the dividends of the funded property'. The cutting of these two sources reduced Hincks' income by something like £160. A Congregational Meeting censured Pope for setting himself up as 'the sole Judge of the nature of the doctrines to be addressed by the Ministers of George's Chapel to the Congregation. . . .'

Pope continued adamant but was removed from his post as Treasurer of the 'Thirteen', for the report given to the Annual General Meeting in March, 1850, was read by a Mr. Hill. No further account of the dispute was given, but the report for March, 1851, showed that the dividends from the invested monies were paid to Hincks in that year, though not the rents from landed property. The situation was only resolved when Hincks accepted a call to Sheffield in February, 1852, after which Pope and the other Trustees for the investments resigned and new men were appointed to replace them. There was no question of holding back any money from the next minister. The once dominant Committee of Thirteen never again attempted to dictate the policy of George's Meeting. It was almost certainly the memory of this unhappy incident which caused the society to exercise an overriding control on the Committee of Thirteen in 1863, when a General Meeting of Subscribers decided to elect a completely new body of Trustees both for the Ministers' Fund and for the Chapel itself. This was once more belatedly facing up to the facts of the situation. Since the closing down of Bow Meeting in 1794 there had been no need for a separate Committee to look after the Ministers' Fund; this could equally well have been done by the Chapel Trustees. The last minute book, which ended on 23rd February, 1914, bears the note 'Entered in Chapel Trustees Minute Bk. after the latter date.' Since 1914 one body of Trustees has in fact administered the whole of the income of the Society: and the traditional number of Thirteen no longer prevails.

A comparatively long interregnum took place before another minister arrived. The Minister's Fund was used for necessary repairs to the church building, which may partly account for the delay. Then in November, 1853, an invitation was accepted by the Rev. G. B. Brock of Swansea. He had been at Swansea for almost 17 years, and was clearly a man of considerable staying-power, who would not easily be put off by a difficult situation. We have seen how he rallied the congregation and reorganized the Sunday School and the welfare works undertaken by the church. Yet he received little encouragement from his congregation.

By 1858 serious trouble had arisen. A General Meeting of subscribers on 7th March expressed 'its regret that the Congregation and institutions of the Chapel have been for some time past in a declining and inefficient condition, and that it is highly desirable that some steps should be taken for the purpose of effecting such alterations as may lead to their improvement'. It was also 'Resolved that this Meeting considers that Mr. Brock as a Minister has not proved himself so efficient as to satisfy the wants and wishes of the Congregation.'

No one could deny the decline in prosperity, but it was unwarrantable to attack Brock in this way, and only a society thoroughly demoralized and dispirited would have done so. These resolutions proved the occasion for Brock to return a spirited defence of his ministry which gives us much invaluable information on the state of the society then. He began by saying that he had read 'with utter astonishment'

N

the two resolutions. He then appealed 'to facts which cannot be gainsayed'. He quoted from the Collector's books that there were:

In 1838	no less than	121	contributors to the Minister:			
„ 1841	„ „ „	108	„	„ „	„	
„ 1845	„ „ „	90	„	„ „	„	
„ 1848	„ „ „	82	„	„ „	„	
„ 1851	„ „ „	73	„	„ „	„	
„ 1854	„ „ „	61	„	„ „	„	
„ 1857	„ „ „	59	„	„ „	„	

He called attention to the fact that there had been a drop of only 2 in the number of subscribers during his ministry, and claimed that 'the law of decay which had marked the history of the Congregation would appear during my ministry to have been arrested although the mortality amongst the more wealthy members has been in that time very considerable'. Turning to the Sunday School, he said 'never for a series of years has it been more prosperous than at present', and à propos of the Benevolent Society, 'In nearly all but *name* it was defunct before I commenced my Ministry . . . It was established in 1850 when 121 persons were enrolled as contributors. At the end of the year 1853—the year before I came to Exeter—the number had been reduced below 30. . . . I lent the money to discharge its debts, and contributed, too, to the discharge of them.' He referred to the end of the Industrial School: 'It has passed away because it had no element of stability.'

He continued; 'I may add that since commencing my Ministry in Exeter I have attempted to bring my congregation together on week evenings by lecturing or reading to them, but I regret to say that the parties . . . who instigated the proceedings at the meeting of the 7th inst. could never on these occasions be induced to give me any countenance or encouragement.' Passing finally from defence to attack, Brock challenged the claim that the resolutions were passed with 'only one dissentient', for he had since spoken with many who were at the meeting who disagreed with them. He believed that not all present understood the purport of the resolutions. They were too plain, however, for that reasoning to hold. It is quite likely that most of the humbler members of the church would have hesitated to speak against those they considered their betters—such is the case even in 1960, and would certainly have been so in mid-Victorian England.

It is surprising that after this incident Brock did not immediately resign. He ended his defence with a hope that harmony might be restored. The subscribers decided to accept his defence and expressed

regret that the previous resolutions had been passed. A special committee was set up to 'discuss the very important questions that have
arisen.' Little progress with this was made. On the 1st October, 1858,
the committee reported a meeting with Brock in which he had objected to the idea of a second minister (how could they have paid him?)
and had said that his brother ministers had advised him to remain at
his post and not resign. He said he would consider any suggestions
offered by the congregation, but implied that he had none to make
himself. Pastor and people thus remained at odds, and it was not until
the Annual General Meeting of subscribers on the 29th of April, 1860,
that it was proposed to introduce a Missionary to work in the city,
to spread 'the distinctive doctrines of Unitarian Christianity'. The
suggestion came from Brock himself, and he offered to devote the
subscriptions to the Minister's Fund towards paying the Missionary.
The Rev. C. T. Biss was appointed. The experiment did not continue
long enough to produce results, for at last Brock's patience gave way
completely, and he sent in his resignation on 7th October, 1860. It
was a short note, accepted by an equally terse minute. To keep things
going Biss was appointed for six months from Lady Day 1861, at a
fee of £3 3s. each Sunday. A modification in suffrage occurred at a
General Meeting on the 29th September, 1861, when it was decided
that in future a payment of 5s. per annum in seat rent, or 10s. 6d. to
the Minister's Fund, should, after this had been continued for at least
2 years, entitle the subscriber to become a full member of the society
and to vote on all matters.

By the beginning of 1862 George's Meeting was little nearer a new
minister, after rejecting several possible candidates. At this point Sir
John Bowring took matters in hand. The Bowring family had been
prominent in the history of George's Meeting, and although Sir John
had been abroad on business or in diplomatic service for large portions
of his life, he remained a member of the chapel until his death. On
2nd February, 1862, the members had two names to consider, but
seemed unwilling to proceed to a decision. Then the following entry
appeared in the Minutes:

'It was considered very desirable by Sir John Bowring that the
Congregation should proceed at once to the Election of a Minister and
he therefore proposed 'That the Rev. T. W. Chignell be elected the
Minister of this Society'. This was . . . carried by a large majority.'

Bowring was a good judge of character, for Chignell remained at
Exeter until his death in 1907, and no further sign of trouble appears in

the Minutes. Chignell's letter of acceptance reveals something of his character.

'When I first entered Exeter, and . . . looked into your Chapel, and saw its size, and heard that few people attended, I pictured to myself a declining, dead community, and wished myself home again. But the first time I addressed you I felt the presence of the living open ear, which alone tempts the voice of man to speak.'

And later he wrote: 'To interest and quicken you week by week, and to bring fresh faces and voices within those noble old walls of your Meeting-House, . . . is a hope . . . I will certainly strive towards . . .' He did not succeed in this ambition, but prevented any further decline in the fortunes of George's Meeting, giving his people 45 years of peaceful leadership before his death in 1907.

Before relating outstanding questions of doctrine and politics which came to the fore during the period from 1815 to 1875, certain minor matters of church organization and administration should be noted. The duties of the Clerk to the Meeting were redefined on 27th July, 1823. The members decided that 'to the office of Clerk should be added the duties of Collecting the Ministers' Subscriptions, the Seat Rents . . . also subscriptions from the Sunday Schools.' He was also to help regulate the sittings in the galleries, and to act as secretary to all public meetings. He was to be paid £25 per annum, to be met by annual voluntary contribution from each subscriber.

For the first time in its history the congregation demanded that the chapel should be heated during the winter months. On 25th October, 1829, a committee was asked to investigate ways of heating the building, but when it reported on the 15th November next that the cheapest method would cost at least £100 to install, it was decided not to do anything about it for that winter at least. It was actually not until 11th February, 1838, that it was recommended that a scheme be accepted under which 'the Chapel shall be heated by it at a temperature of not less than 45 degrees when the external air is at 30'. On the 9th September following, heating by means of hot-water pipes was approved.

It had been common experience amongst the old Presbyterian societies that their churches became more and more congregational and democratic in polity. This process, in the case of George's Meeting, was carried a stage further on 16th February, 1845, when a General Meeting of subscribers decided to set up a 'Congregational Committee', to consist of 12 members of the Society together with the ministers. Four were to be elected each year, for a 3-year term. The Committee was to meet once a month, to keep a record of its proceedings, and to supervise the 'decent orderly and efficient conduct of the public worship in this chapel . . .' On the 23rd of the same month it was decided that retiring members of the committee should not be immediately eligible for re-election, and on 9th March, 1845, the first Congregational Committee was chosen. There was one woman amongst the 12—a Miss Manning, probably a daughter of the Rev. James Manning. The duties of the members of the Committee correspond almost exactly with those of Deacons in Congregational or Baptist churches. Legally the trustees of the chapel, and the Committee of Thirteen still retained substantial powers: but the Congregational Committee, sure in the yearly renewal of the favour of its supporters, was in a much stronger position to control the affairs of the Society. Within its first year it inquired into the state of the singing (an attempt to recruit more female voices failed), and tried to increase the number of teachers in the Sunday School. It also reorganized the Congregational Library. Users of the Library were to be asked to contribute 6d. a quarter (9 August, 1846) and 9 periodicals were recommended to be taken:

The Christian Examiner;	The Christian Reformer.
The Religious Magazine.	The Prospective Review.
The Unitarian.	The Christian Register.
Chambers' Journal.	Barkers' Christian.

The People's Journal.

Unfortunately subscriptions to these periodicals would then have cost £4 9s. each year, while the income available was only £1 2s. 6d. The solution to this discrepancy was not recorded.

As time went on the Congregational Committee took part in more vital business. During the Hincks-Pope crisis of 1849–52, it was to the Congregational Committee that Hincks appealed for help in clearing up the difficulties of his position, and the Committee occupied the position of arbitrator between the Minister and the recalcitrant members of the 'Thirteen'. Rev. G. B. Brock attempted to work through the Committee in the early years of his ministry, and its minutes contain many suggestions of his for 'stimulating and calling out the zeal and energy of all the Members of the Church for religious self-improvement and for the practice of Christian Charity and Piety'. (10th April, 1855). Yet, like other sections of the church in the 1850s, the Congregational Committee wilted through indifference and slackness. No meeting at all was recorded between 11th October, 1857, and

28th November, 1858, and as early as 31st October, 1855, the 'irregular attendance of some Members' had been commented upon. During the period between Brock's and Chignell's ministries the Committee exercised a guiding influence on affairs, and from this period onwards must be considered as the effective directing body of George's Meeting, its decisions being normally ratified by General Meetings of all subscribers.

Throughout this period of 1815–75, reference is made in various minute books to matters of doctrine and liturgy. It was the custom from the time of Lant Carpenter and William Hincks onwards for the ministers to give public lectures on Unitarian principles as well as their weekly services of worship. On 13th September, 1835, for example, the General Meeting Book recorded 'That this Congregation feeling persuaded that the popular doctrine of the Trinity is incompatible with the scriptural doctrine of the unity of God, . . . have heard with entire satisfaction the defence of this important truth lately delivered in this Chapel by their respected minister the Rev. Henry Acton.' Acton's opponent in this minor controversy had been an Anglican, the Rev. Daniel Bagot.

On the 23rd June, 1837, meetings were held to decide 'the mode in which marriages shall be celebrated in this Chapel'. This was the result of the Marriage Act of 1836, which allowed weddings to be solemnized in Dissenters' Chapels under licence and in the presence of the Registrar of the district. On 30th July it was resolved 'that the form of marriage drawn up by the Presbyterian body in London be approved of as a suitable one to be imployed in this Chapel, but that this form shall not be considered obligatory if objected to by the parties to be married'.

Between December, 1839, and March, 1840, the ministers of George's Meeting came into conflict with Henry Phillpotts, Bishop of Exeter. A child of William Tucker, a member of the Meeting, died, and was refused Christian burial by the curate of St. Thomas, the Rev. J. Wilkinson, on the grounds that the infant had been baptized by a Unitarian, Dr. Perry. The curate acted in this way on the advice of the Bishop. George's Meeting took up the matter, paid for legal opinion, including that of the Attorney-General, which condemned the Curate's action as illegal. Wilkinson made a dignified apology, which was accepted. In his remarks on the affair, Acton scathingly attacked Phillpotts: 'He has shown not only that he has little scruple in wounding the feelings of Dissenters . . . but also that he is not infallibly competent to advise his own clergy in the performance of their . . . duties.' The 'Statement of Facts relating to the Refusal, etc.', issued to explain to the public the truth of the controversy, bore the imprint of 'Latimer, Printer, Exeter', and the 'Remarks' quoted above sound more like the words of Thomas Latimer, the editor of the *Western Times* and a lifelong opponent of Phillpotts, than those of Henry Acton, although the latter's initials are printed at the end.[1]

On 15th September, 1844, was passed a resolution defining very clearly the principles on which the society was founded at that time:

... it is a free church, professing simply the Christian Religion as taught in the New Testament, rejecting the use of all further tests and creeds; and maintaining for the Church collectively, and for each individual member of it perfect freedom of opinion, on all points respecting which the sense of the New Testament is disputed among Christians.

Politically, the members of George's Meeting had, by the second quarter of the nineteenth century, abandoned their conservatism, and approved corporately of most of the radical reforms carried out between 1828 and 1846. As early as 8th May, 1825, it was decided to petition both Houses of Parliament 'in favour of the claims of our Roman Catholic brethren'. The reform or abolition of capital punishment was too much for them, however, as meetings held in April, 1830, to discuss the subject were 'adjourned sine die'. At the beginning of 1837 the Commissioners appointed to deal with the Registration of Births, Marriages and Deaths went into action, and it was resolved by a General Meeting on the 9th January 'that the Register Books be transmitted to the Commissioners by the Revd. Henry Acton. That the names and years of the Burials and Baptisms from 1760 to the present time be copied from the Register Books . . . that the necessary measures be adopted for registering the Chapel for solemnization of marriages.' And so the registers relating to Bow and James' Meetings from 1687 and for the Mint from 1720 were sent to Somerset House in 1837. If copies were made of the entries from 1760 onwards they have not been preserved at Exeter. A Register of Burials was begun in 1837 and kept until 1873, however.

On the 29th of January, 1837, a petition against tithes was sent to the House of Commons, and in 1844 the members enthusiastically greeted the Dissenters' Chapel Bill. This confirmed any congregation in the possession of its place of worship if it had occupied it for

---

[1] For Thomas Latimer and his relations with the Bishop of Exeter, see R. S. Lambert's *The Cobbett of the West*, London, Nicholson & Watson, 1939.

25 years, even if, as in the case of the Unitarians, their beliefs were no longer the same as those of the founders of the society.

Finally, a resolution sent to the Board of Education on 12th April, 1847, is worth recording, as it is an accurate foretaste of the line that all the Free Churches were to take on the subject of education later in the century: '. . . in the opinion of this meeting it is necessary to the well-being of Society no less than a Christian duty that the poor should have afforded them the benefit of education, and that such Education can only be efficiently provided by the State from the public revenue.' Later on in this long resolution the members advise a purely secular national system in consequence, leaving religious teaching to the Sunday Schools.

CHAPTER XIII

WESLEYAN METHODISTS AND BIBLE CHRISTIANS, 1800–1875

WHILE the old Dissenters were declining in numbers, the new Nonconformists—the Methodists—continued to grow. The membership of the society in Exeter, which was only about 70 in 1798, had risen to 291 in 1815. A milestone in its development was the creation of a new circuit in 1808 with Exeter as its centre, for the need to organize and minister to the country chapels led to increased activity at the centre. The old chapel in Musgrave's Alley became too small for the demands upon it, and by a stroke of fortune for the Methodists the 'Arian' chapel in the Mint came up for sale in 1810. This site was most central, and when Dr. Thomas Coke, one of the leading Methodists of his time, was consulted, he replied on 9th November, 1811, 'We are clearly of opinion that you ought instantly to buy the Unitarian Chapel.' The old meeting-house was bought early the next year for £720. Despite the fact that a subscription list, and the sale of Musgrave's Alley Chapel lease, only raised the sum of £737 13s. 6d., the Trustees decided to pull down the Mint chapel and build a much larger meeting-house, to hold about 700 persons. The first services were held there on 25th March, 1813, the President of the Methodist Conference for that year, Joseph Entwisle, preaching in the morning. Its erection severely strained the resources of the Exeter society. Financially it was crippled by the debt on the church for some fifty years. It was not until 1859 that the building was finally paid for. The cost of building was originally £3873: yet in interest, legal expenses, and other incidentals, more than £7000 in addition to this was paid out during this period. Later enlargements to the chapel (in 1868, 1884, 1895) increased the seating capacity to about 1000.[1]

The founding of a centre for Methodist work in East Devon had an invigorating effect in other ways. Already the Exeter society could claim its first missionary. As early as November, 1811, a young Methodist from the Exeter circuit went out to Sierra Leone as a missionary. This George Warren, however, fell victim to the climate and

[1] Chick, Elijah, *A History of Methodism in Exeter and the Neighbourhood from the year 1739 until 1907*. Exeter, Drayton, 1907, p. 44. Thomas, John Wesley, *Reminiscences of Methodism in Exeter*, Exeter, *Daily Western Times*, 1875, pp. 33–4.

died a year later. Thomas Bowden, hairdresser, became a Methodist in Exeter just before 1800, and later opened a school in Magdalen St., near the 'Valiant Soldier' Inn. After a short period of teaching in London, he joined a party of Methodists sent out by the Government as teachers to New South Wales. They arrived in Sydney on 28th January, 1812, the first recorded Methodist Class-Meeting in Australia occurring on 6th March following. Thomas Squance, also from the Exeter district, was one of those who accompanied Dr. Coke on the first Methodist Mission to Ceylon on 31st December, 1813. Coke died before disembarkation, but Squance and the rest of the party, six in all, worked in Ceylon for many years. John Callaway was one of the second set of missionaries to go to Ceylon, and compiled a dictionary of the Singhalese language during his ten years there from 1815 until 1825. William Oke went in 1821 to the West Indies. For a comparatively small and weak circuit this was good representation, a sign that the cause was fundamentally sound.

After the formation of a separate Exeter circuit in 1808, an extra minister was appointed to act as a home missionary. William Beal was the first of these, and succeeded in beginning new societies in both Topsham and Crediton. On 16th July, 1816, the Diocesan Registry recorded a licence granted for a 'Certain chapel standing on premises belonging to Mr. Beer in the village & Parish of Heavitree'. The denomination is not mentioned, but there was an early Methodist cause in Heavitree, and no other Nonconformist society was active there at that time. In 1810 the local preachers' plan for the Exeter circuit only included five places outside the city—Broadclyst, Topsham, Ide, Crediton, and Stoke (Canon). A preaching plan for 1828-9 showed that although the Stoke Canon meeting had disappeared, the other four continued and had been joined by small causes at Kennford, Lympstone, Morchard (Bishop), Whitstone, Whipton, Alphington, Wear, Sidford, Marshgreen and Ottery. By 1840 Upton Pyne, Exwick, Pinhoe, Thorverton and Tedburn had been added. Budleigh Salterton and Exmouth had been worked at least from 1816, and were established as a separate circuit in 1844, with Lympstone added. While Methodism was brought effectively to the countryside round Exeter, work within the city was not neglected, being most pronounced during the ministry of the Rev. Corbett Cooke, from 1832-5. By this time numbers had increased sufficiently to make even the new Mint chapel crowded, and a new beginning was made in St. Sidwell's, in May, 1835.

In 1836 another small chapel was built in Alphington, and expansion into the St. Thomas area was considered. Nothing permanent came of this last venture, and it was left to the United Methodist Free Churches to establish a society there in the later 1870s. The only other addition to buildings inside Exeter was the purchase of Christ Church, Southernhay, in 1864. This had been built in 1846, as a 'Free Church of England': a protest against the Anglo-Catholic emphasis of the Oxford Movement.[1] By 1864 the Methodist chapel in St. Sidwell's had run into debt, and the permission of Conference was obtained to sell it. No success was achieved during the 1850s, but when Southernhay Christ Church became available in 1864, it was decided immediately to transfer the work to this new position. The St. Sidwell's chapel was sold to the Primitive Methodists at a great loss, for £500. Christ Church cost over £2000, and repairs, alterations, and purchase of an organ, added another £3000. Most of this was paid off at the time, and the remainder by the end of the century. The fortunes of this church fall outside the period of this book, but the move to new surroundings did result in fresh vigour, principally noticeable in a Sunday School in Newtown, at that time a thickly populated area of the city. Again, mainly through the activities of the Southernhay members, a second Methodist society was begun in St. Sidwell's, resulting in a new Sunday School there in January, 1897, and a new church on 3rd May, 1905.

Sunday Schools were one of the main methods of Methodist expansion in Exeter in the nineteenth century. 1811 was a year of activity in educational affairs in the city, for both British (or Lancasterian) and National (Bell) School Societies were then in process of formation. The Congregationalists in Castle St. had begun a Sunday School as early as 1800: the Church of England started one in 1811, and the Unitarians followed suit in 1812. The Wesleyans began work in a small way in 1811, with half-a-dozen boys meeting each Sunday in the vestry of the Musgrave's Alley Chapel. Following the move to the Mint in 1813 the school was continued in various buildings in the town until new Day Schools were built in 1846 in Mint Lane, and the wanderings of the institution ended. From this year on there took place continued growth, and an increasing co-operation between the Nonconformist Sunday Schools after the Exeter Sunday School Union was formed in 1844. By 1863 the three Wesleyan Schools alone had at least 1100 scholars.[2]

---

[1] Morris' *Directory for Devonshire*, 1870, p. 18.
[2] Chick, Elijah, *Then and Now*, 1811 to 1912, *Historical Review of the Mint Methodist Sunday School*, 1912.

The divisions of the first half of the 19th century among the Methodists did not affect progress in Exeter until the Reform crisis of 1849. All the Methodist breakaways were occasioned by the authoritarian tradition of church government bequeathed by John Wesley. The Methodist New Connexion took away some 5000 of the estimated membership of 95,000 in 1797, when Alexander Kilham and his sympathizers wished the lay element to have more control over church policy and finance. They also demanded to have the Sacraments observed in their own churches by their own ministers: the breach with the established Church was complete. Then between 1807 and 1812 came the separation of the Primitive Methodists on the question of open-air evangelism by means of 'camp meetings'. There is no doubt that the proceedings at many of these camp meetings were irregular and highly emotional: yet the Methodist Conference was unwise to dispense with the services of evangelists of the calibre of Hugh Bourne and William Clowes. They later began work in Exeter, but Primitive Methodism never became strong in this city. The Protestant Methodists of 1826 were mainly confined to Leeds, and the Wesleyan Methodist Association of 1836, aimed at securing a reform of the Methodist constitution, had no adherents in Exeter. The Reform agitation of 1849, however, proved a major setback to Methodist fortunes in Exeter, as in the whole of the rest of the country. The dominant figure in Wesleyan Methodism from the time he was first elected President of the Conference in 1820, until after 1850, was Dr. Jabez Bunting. Although accused of desiring power, it is more likely true that his outstanding qualities as preacher and administrator inevitably marked him out for power in whatever sphere he cared to operate. He was ten times Secretary of the Conference, four times President, and throughout this period acted as 'official adviser' to the President, a post which lapsed with him. He was not averse to change as such, but the reforms to which he did agree were directed towards maintaining the authority of the movement in the hands of the Ministers. He said in 1835, 'Lay delegation is dead and buried.' Between 1844 and 1848 four anonymous 'Fly Sheets' appeared attacking the general policy of the administration, and the concentration of power in the hands of a small group of ministers led by Bunting. A pamphlet war followed in which no quarter was given. Suspicion fell on James Everett, a superannuated minister, whose views and literary style were clearly expressed in the 'Fly-Sheets'. He refused to answer the charge at the 1849 conference and was expelled, with his more zealous supporters. No action was taken against those who had gone into print with equal lack of restraint on the other side. The movement grew beyond all expectation, and it was estimated that no less than 100,000 members were lost to Methodism as a result. This was about one-third of the total membership at that time. Attempts at reconciliation failed, and in 1857 a union between these Reformers and the Wesleyan Methodist Association was arranged, the new body taking the name of the United Methodist Free Churches. This had a membership of about 40,000 only, so it is evident that most of the seceders finished with Methodism entirely. The new church was characterized by its democratic nature, with free election of both ministers and laymen to its Conference and to the chair of official meetings.[1]

In Exeter the first mention of the agitation came in the Circuit Minutes for Michaelmas, 1849, when the Rev. J. Grose denounced the movement for reform, and is said to have expelled members who did not agree with him. This continued until by 1854 the membership of the Circuit had fallen from 803 to 526, local preachers had declined from 36 to 15, and preaching places from 20 to 14. The effect was more pronounced to the east of Exeter. After 1855 the Wesleyan Methodists had not one preaching place to the east of the city: in the triangle formed by Woodbury, Heavitree and Bradninch not one Methodist chapel of any branch existed at the end of the nineteenth century. It was probably the Reform Movement which wrecked the prospects of the St. Sidwell's Wesleyan chapel, hitherto fairly prosperous.

Owing to loss of members the Exeter Circuit fell into debt. 1854 proved the worst year: after this things slowly improved. In 1856 a peacemaker arrived in the Rev. William Williams, who 'found the Circuit all to pieces, he left it happy and united'. Not only were the immediate effects of the 1849 crisis repaired, but the old outstanding debt on the Mint chapel was cleared by 1860. 'How this was done seemed a surprise to everybody; and is so to me to this day.' Much of this reconstruction was done with the help of William Brock, prominent Methodist businessman of the city, who died in 1864.

The 'Reformers' who left the Mint church in 1849 and the years following, at first met in a room in St. Sidwell's, then from 1851 in the old Musgrave's Alley chapel behind High St. In 1857 a site for a chapel was purchased at Northernhay Gate, Queen St., and the first services in the new building were held on Sunday, 28th March, 1858. The chapel was finally paid for by 1884. It had a mildly prosperous existence until

[1] Harrison, A. W., and others, *The Methodist Church, its origins, divisions, and reunion,* 1932.

the union of the United Methodist Free Churches with the Bible Christians and Methodist New Connexion in 1907.

The Primitive Methodists made little impression on the Exeter scene. A first attempt to gain a foothold occurred in 1831, but proved unsuccessful. In 1853 a Thomas Drew was sent to Exeter and Exmouth, gaining more success at the latter place. Work was also started at Lympstone, Budleigh, Woodbury, Topsham and Broadclyst, and by 1863 there were four ministers working in the circuit. In Exeter the Primitive Methodists took over the old Musgrave's Alley chapel in 1858, after it had been vacated by the United Methodist Free Churches, and they used this as their base until 1864. In that year they bought old St. Sidwell's Wesleyan chapel, which they continued to use until 1881. In 1872 an attempt was made to work in the West quarter of the city, where a small chapel was opened in Coombe St. between the White Hart Inn Yard and the entrance to James' St.[1] It seems that by 1881 the attempt of Primitive Methodism to establish itself in Exeter was at an end.

The Bible Christians were a native product of the county of Devon, and remained singularly free from the divisions which beset the main stream of Methodism. The denomination arose at Shebbear, in North Devon, from the meeting of William O'Bryan, recently expelled from the Wesleyan fold because he would not submit to its discipline, and John and Mary Thorne, owners of Lake Farm, Shebbear, in the year 1815. The countryside in North Devon at that time was the preserve of the nineteenth-century 'hunting Parsons', and the chance was there for an earnest evangelist to relight the flame of faith. The ground had been prepared at Shebbear by an evangelical curate, Daniel Evans, between 1813 and 1815. On 9th October, 1815, 22 persons at Lake Farm formed the first Bible Christian society, all of whom had been previously attendants at the parish church. James Thorne, son of John, proved to be the statesman of the new denomination throughout his long life (1795–1872). The movement spread rapidly in its first fifteen years, though mainly confined to rural areas. By 1817 it had 920 members, including 66 preachers, and by 1823 there were 5,050 members. Women were admitted freely to the ministry, and proved to be some of the most effective agents of the new society. To mention only three of them, Mary Ann Werrey was sent to the Scilly Islands in 1821, Catherine Reed to London in 1821, and Mary Toms to the Isle of

---

[1] White's *History, Gazetteer and Directory of the County of Devon*, 1878–9. Exeter Street Directory section, under Coombe St.

Wight in 1823. It was in 1819 that O'Bryan first tried, unsuccessfully, to obtain a room for preaching in Exeter, and again in January, 1821, Henry Freeman met with violent opposition when trying to preach in the streets in Exeter. But in September of that year a foothold was gained. On 4th September a licence was granted for 'A Building situate in Preston Street in the City of Exeter in the possession of William O'Bryan.' In 1823 another of their outstanding early preachers, William Mason, a champion wrestler in the days before his conversion, was brought before the Exeter magistrates on the charge of holding an open-air meeting in Paul Street. No witnesses could be found to testify against him, but Mason began to make his defence nevertheless. The chairman of the bench 'interrupted him and said he did not want a sermon there. William had not had such a congregation for some time before, and did not know when he might again, so it was well to make hay while the sun shined'. The magistrates warned him that they would not allow preaching in the streets, but he later told O'Bryan, 'I promised nothing. So I went my way.' [1] This is typical of the Bible Christian's attitude to life: a cheerful determination to preach at all times the truths of Christianity, whatever the consequences. Unlike many extreme Protestant sects the Bible Christians seldom became narrow in outlook or obnoxiously pious. They always remained a part of the life going on round about them: they did not believe in an other-worldly separation from things which might contaminate. Their best-known Cornish evangelist, Billy Bray, made of his religion a thing of joy, and one of his favourite tales was of the time he had danced along the Truro road with the result that his little girl's new frock was danced out of his basket and lost.

William Mason was again in Exeter in 1825, with the address of J. Hoar, Baker, North St., and in February, 1826 (the 8th), he took out a preaching licence for this place, 'A Room on the 2nd floor in the house of Jacob Hoare, Baker'. He was at this time acting as Superintendent of the Exeter district, and was joined by Mary Hewett, another itinerant preacher who later became his wife.

In 1828–9 occurred the only serious dispute in Bible Christian history, when William O'Bryan, who had claimed increasingly dictatorial powers over the denomination, broke away. At the Conference of 1828 for the first time he was not elected President (this

[1] Deacon, Lois, *So I went My Way*. William Mason and his Wife, Mary, 1790–1873, London, Epworth Press, 1951. Most of the information about William Mason is taken from this work. See p. 63 especially.

honour went to Mason) and in 1829 came a complete break. The Bible Christians were not the sort of people who could be ordered about, and in James Thorne, the Secretary of the denomination, they had an alternative leader of great ability. Few followed O'Bryan, and when he went to the United States in 1835 a reunion took place.

In Exeter, the room previously occupied was taken over in 1832 by 'another religious society', and there was difficulty in obtaining another. In the years immediately before 1851 they were using the old Musgrave's Alley Chapel, whence they moved on 9th March in that year to Providence Chapel in Northernhay St. This had been built in 1839 on behalf of the Plymouth Brethren by Sir Alexander Campbell, and its size and central position made it an admirable headquarters for the Bible Christians in the county town. The cost was £1500, a large sum for a denomination composed predominantly of country farmers and farmworkers. The new chapel was the venue of its Conference of 1853, the first time this yearly gathering had been able to come to Exeter. The society in Exeter was still very small in 1851, only about 20 members taking part in the procession from Musgrave's Alley to the new chapel when it was opened for their use. Inside, the pews were arranged on a circular plan, with a central well facing the pulpit, and for the first few years the whole of the congregation could be accommodated in this central portion, which was surrounded with curtains to remove the sight of empty pews. The congregation grew steadily, and in the last quarter of the century the whole of the building was used for services.[1]

The picture of Exeter Methodism in the nineteenth century is one of steady growth, apart from the major setback between 1849 and 1854, yet with no spectacular successes such as occurred in some other parts of England. From the time of John Wesley onwards Methodism found it difficult to establish itself in the city, even though the story was quite different in the rural areas of Devon and Cornwall. For a city with strong Dissenting traditions this is at first sight surprising. Yet the old Protestant Dissenters had not based their Nonconformity on emotion so much as on the more prosaic grounds of conscience attended with sound commercial advantages. The Methodist insistence on a thoroughgoing emotional conversion of one's whole being was alien to the middle-class merchants who had formed the backbone of old-style Dissent in Exeter. Furthermore, for success in an important city a

---

[1] Bourne, F. W., *The Bible Christians, their origin and history*, 1815–1900, London Bible Christian Book Room, 1905. Used extensively for the general history of the denomination. Chick, op. cit., pp. 150–1.

well-educated ministry was essential. Apart from the Wesleyan Methodists this was not provided. The Bible Christians only produced their first graduate minister in 1887, with the ordination of the Rev. H. W. Horwill, a former boy at Shebbear College who had by then obtained an M.A. at Oxford. In the country districts and among the poorest classes in the towns this was not a disadvantage: but in a Cathedral city it made progress slow and uncertain. All the Dissenting societies suffered from this disadvantage to some extent, but the Methodists and the Baptists most of all.

CHAPTER XIV

THE PROGRESS OF ORTHODOX DISSENT,
1824–1875

It was still the custom in the first half of the nineteenth century for ministers of all denominations to stay much longer in their pastorates than happens nowadays. From 1824 until 1875 the Exeter Congregationalists worked under the leadership of only two men. The church progressed from its state of stagnation in 1819, which had been only temporarily stirred up by the brief interlude of John Griffin in 1820–1, to the mid seventies when, in a new building, the church shared with the Mint the privilege of being the most important of the Nonconformist societies in the city and district. The members chose wisely when they invited John Bristow to be their minister, in November 1824. He immediately called for a revision of the roll of members. Not only were lapsed members removed from the roll, but greater caution was taken when admitting new members. This was no more than a revival of the normal rule. Membership of a 'gathered' community was something more than a mere joining of a society: it was to mean a complete change of life, and a dedication of the member to the service of God through his fellow-men. Discipline of this nature is necessary for the smooth running of most religious communities: yet when over-emphasized it tends to lead to a pious, self-satisfied, at times hypo-critical attitude among those who submit to it. This is what the twentieth century dislikes about Victorian religious life: discipline is no longer fashionable.[1]

The only other minister of the Castle St. church in this period was the Rev. David Hewitt. Bristow resigned in 1847, remaining in Exeter until his death in 1852. Hewitt stayed from 1850 until his death on 18th December, 1875. There was no trace of controversy during his 25 years service, and he must have had administrative abilities above the average to cope with the problems of rebuilding and reorganization which took place.

A growing society needs constant increases in its accommodation. At first confined to the single small chapel off Castle Lane, in which both the services of worship and the Sunday School were conducted,

[1] *Southernhay Congregational Church Centenary Book*, 1795–1895. Much of the information before 1870 is taken from this.

the church in Bristow's ministry built a small schoolroom by the side of the chapel. The licence was recorded in the Diocesan Registry on 28th October, 1833: 'Building lately erected on the South side of the Avenue leading from Castle Lane to Castle Street Chapel situate in the parish of St. Lawrence.' The new school only consisted of one floor, boys' and girls' sections being divided by a movable partition. By 1852 it was found necessary to build an additional storey, but continued increase in the numbers of pupils soon made this again inadequate.

Castle St. Chapel itself was in need of repairs by 1839, and had to be completely renovated, at a cost of about £800. The whole expense was met by April 15th, 1840, donations ranging from £120 down to 5s., a generous piece of giving for a small society.

By 1865 the chapel was again in need of repair and enlargement. The decision was made not to repair but to build a completely new chapel on a fresh site. A Church Meeting of 24th July, 1865, authorized the Building Committee to purchase suitable ground. One site was bought on Southernhay East for the price of £1400, but this did not prove to be that on which the new church was finally built. A more suitable position at the entrance to Dix's Field, Southernhay, became for sale in 1868, consisting of the land on which the 'Old Baths' stood, and two dwelling houses. A meeting held on 13th April, 1868, decided to take this, which was done, but it proved rather more difficult to sell the first site than had been expected, and it was only disposed of, at a 50 per cent loss, in 1871. The revised plans were approved, and the foundation stone laid on the 24th June, 1868. With £1400 locked up in the first site, financing the building proved difficult, but the congregation decided not to cut down the scale of the enterprise, and pressed on to make their new church as beautiful as possible.

For the first time a Nonconformist meeting-house in Exeter had been built differing from the plain oblong-box structures of earlier days. It proved a successful attempt at a revival of the Early English Decorated style of Gothic architecture. The height of the building gave light and space for a congregation of 1000, and the graceful spire became a landmark in the city: the only remaining part of the chapel after its destruction by air raids in 1942, and now incorporated in the post-war rebuilding. The total cost of the 1870 chapel was about £9000. Immediately afterwards the old chapel in Castle St. was adapted for the Sunday School, and at last enough class rooms could be provided. In 1875 a final addition to the church's accommodation was made by the erection of a Lecture Hall adjoining the new church.

Statistics of membership are only available at rare intervals, for the original minute books relating to the Castle Street days were destroyed in the 1942 air raids. From the 68 founding members in 1795 the church had grown to the 217 members and friends who signed the invitation to John Griffin at the end of 1819. This should not be taken as representing many more than 100–120 full members of the church, however. At the time of John Bristow's retirement in 1847 the state of the church was said to be:

Church Members	.	.	.	140
Usual Congregation	.	.	.	about 500
Chapel Accommodation	.	.	.	800
Average stipend of minister	.	.	.	about £200

When the move to Southernhay took place in 1870 it was found necessary for legal purposes to constitute the church afresh. The total number of members enrolled at this date came to 232.[1] As has already been made clear, membership in a 'gathered' church, of the type that Congregationalist and Baptist churches always are, involves a definite commitment: the numbers of those affected by the work of the church would have been at least four times the actual membership. The numbers of those in the Sunday Schools, for instance, grew spectacularly after 1850. In 1849 there were 183 children on the registers, but this had doubled to 361 when the additional School buildings were opened on 16th May, 1853, and in 1875 after the conversion of the old Castle St. Chapel for Sunday School purposes this had risen to 579, boys, girls and infants.

The Calvinistic nature of the Trust Deed of Castle St. church in 1795 was toned down in 1870 when the Southernhay Church came into being. Yet the beliefs of the society were still laid down with clarity in the Schedule attached to the Trust Deed. It had seven parts.

I. The Divine Inspiration of the Holy Scriptures of the Old and New Testaments and their supreme authority as the rule of faith and practice.

II. The Unity of the Godhead and the essential deity of the Father, of the Son and of the Holy Ghost.

III. The fall and depravity of man and the absolute necessity of the grace and power of the Holy Spirit for his regeneration and sanctification.

IV. The Incarnation of the Son of God in the person of the Lord Jesus Christ. The Universal sufficiency of the atonement by his death upon the Cross and the free justification by faith alone in Him.

V. The election unto holiness and eternal life according to the gracious

[1] Southernhay Congregational Church, Minute Book, 1870–1900.

purpose of God of a multitude that no man can number, which in no way interferes with the moral freedom of man and his duty to seek his own salvation and that of others.

VI. The immutable authority of the moral law of God as the rule of human conduct.

VII. The immortality of the soul, the resurrection of the dead, and the final judgement when the wicked shall go away into everlasting punishment, but the righteous into life eternal.[1]

This was keeping the best of Calvinism while removing the sting from the belief in Election: there is no practical difference between the 'election unto holiness and eternal life . . . of a multitude that no man can number' and Wesley's preaching of grace free to all who will accept it. No minister could hold office in the church unless he accepted this Schedule in full, and each member was required to adhere to it as well.

Church government remained in the hands of the monthly Church Meeting of members. The number of lay officers (Deacons) was originally three, to be elected annually. By the time the move to Southernhay took place in 1870 there were seven deacons, elected for three years, and by 1895 this had been increased to nine.

Owing to the loss of the pre-1870 records, the leading personnel of the Castle St. church are no longer known to us. The five acting deacons at the time of the removal in 1870 were Edward W. Gates, William Nichols, William Jerred, Thomas Easterling, and Alfred H. Heathcote. The two vacant places were not filled until the 27th March, 1872, when those elected were Joseph Hayman and John Bevans. The original trustees for Southernhay were:

James Nichols, gentleman;
Alfred Evans, merchant;
Robert Armstrong, draper;
Segar Bastard, merchant;
William Brown, draper;
William Robert Bradbeer, brush manufacturer;
William Carter, grocer;
William John Couch, accountant;
Thomas Easterling, accountant;
Edward Wilson Gates, draper;
Joseph Hayman, cabinet-maker;
Henry Hodge, stationer;
Alfred Heathcote, dyer;

[1] Southernhay Congregational Church, Minute Book, 1870–1900.

Edwin Lancey, ironmonger;
John Plimsant Nichols, furniture dealer;
John Courtis Webber, ironmonger;
John William Petherick, solicitor;
Thomas Hutchings Pinder, woollen draper;
William Nichols, gentleman.

The list of occupations shows drastic changes from those prominent in Exeter Dissent one hundred years before. The textile industry in Devon had almost died out in face of competition from Lancashire and Yorkshire, and only one of these trustees has any connection with the industry, as a dyer. Drapers are well to the fore, illustrating Exeter's growing importance as a shopping centre; retail trade rather than manufactures had become the basis of Exeter's life.

With the society in a state of growth, the Congregationalists do not appear to have been seriously embarrassed financially throughout this period. The few difficulties arose only when renovations and new building became necessary, as in 1840 and 1868–70.

Two incidents throw additional light on the way such societies organized their work in the first half of the nineteenth century. Before 1829 the singing was led in Castle St. chapel by the bass viol, and in 1825 Bristow had to complain at Church Meeting that its player had found fault with him for having closed the services without any singing at all. An organ was added to the chapel in 1829.

In 1836 a 'Society of Young Men' applied for the use of the school-room one evening each week 'for the purpose of reading essays and discussing them, on subjects tending to spiritual and moral improvement'. It was obviously considered to have political bias, and conditions were imposed which the young men refused to accept. By 1850 the atmosphere was more tolerant, and an application then by the 'Mutual Improvement Society' gained permission to use the school-rooms, and in 1853 the senior classroom. In 1854 the young men were also allowed to use the small library attached to the church. Their leader was John Plimsant Nichols, later one of the trustees for the new Southernhay church.

From 1829 to 1845, the Exeter Congregationalists had the benefit of a ministerial training college in the city. The Western Academy had been founded in 1752 by a number of Congregational ministers meeting privately in Exeter. With the Universities closed to Dissenters there was great difficulty in maintaining a supply of candidates for the ministry well educated and yet free from the Arian tendency of so many of the old Nonconformist Academies in the 18th century. With the help of the Congregational Fund Board in London, four men were placed under the tutorship of the Rev. John Lavington (son of the Exeter minister who had taken such a prominent part in the controversy of 1717–19) at Ottery St. Mary, where he was the minister of the Presbyterian church. It became the custom for the Academy to be held in the town where the tutor was minister, and consequently from 1764 until 1780 it was at Bridport under the Rev. James Rooker, then at Taunton under Rev. Thomas Reader from 1780 to 1794. After being at Axminster under Rev. Samuel Small from 1794 until 1828, it came to Exeter. 18 students passed through the Academy at Ottery, 20 at Bridport, 19 at Taunton, and 53 at Axminster. Numbers had fallen low by 1828, and the Congregational Fund withdrew its support. The local committee governing the institution decided that the scope of the Academy should be widened and modernized. The curriculum was broadened and the tutorial staff increased: and, more important, its migratory nature was to end. In this form the Academy moved to Exeter in 1829, under the headship of the Rev. George Payne, LL.D., previously head of an Academy at Blackburn. At first two houses in Alphington Terrace were used, and in 1832 Marlfield House was purchased for £2600. The name of Western College was adopted from this time. Assistants to the Principal were Daniel Currie, Jonathan Glyde, J. W. Pope, O. W. Dobbin, and Samuel Newth, all academically of good standard. In 1837 the Congregational Fund resumed its old relationship with the College. Dr. Payne, the Principal, had a reputation as a theologian and philosopher which gave the College a publicity and importance which reached beyond the western counties. By 1845 the premises in Exeter had become unsuitable, and it was decided to move to Plymouth, partly on financial grounds. Here the College stayed until 1901 when its final move took place, this time to Bristol, where it is now a recognized part of the University of Bristol. 34 students passed through the College while it was stationed in Exeter.[1]

Although most of the expansion took place in the last quarter of the nineteenth century, at no time were the Castle St. and Southernhay Congregationalists unaware of their duty to evangelize the countryside round them. By the end of the century branch churches had been established at 10 places:

West Hill, 1814.
Marsh Green, 1837.

[1] Sims, Arnold W., *The Western College, Bristol*, 1952.

Whimple, 1860.
Ide, 1864.
Heavitree, 1867.
Pinhoe, 1886.
Aylesbeare, 1893.
Friernhay, 1899.
Woodbury Road, 1900.
Clyst St. Mary (Foundation not known:
    in being in 1900).

Most, if not all, of these were not founded by a definite decision of the Church itself, but by the action of individual members who lived in these areas, or who were particularly interested in the people who lived there.

The Whitefieldite Calvinist Tabernacle in Coombe Street was reformed on the 2nd October, 1807, a year after the death of its first minister, Henry Tanner. The new leader was James Trego, 'Minister of the Gospel in the Connection of the late Countess of Huntingdon'. There were then three deacons—John Salter, William Vicary, and Francis Nicks—and 42 members. A further 8 people were admitted before the end of that year. The new Church Book begun then has a Declaration of 'Faith and Practise' written in the earliest leaves, together with the Rules for the conduct of the church's affairs and admission of members. The declaration of faith committed them uncompromisingly to the Inspiration of the Scriptures; the Trinity; Original Sin; that Christ was a 'substitute in their room and stead, whereby he made all that satisfaction for their sins which the Law and Justice of God could require'; that redemption is only for the Elect of God; that redemption is by Christ's action alone, and 'without the consideration of any work of righteousness done by them'; Eternal life for the Elect; the last Judgment; and that there are two sacraments only—Baptism and the Lord's Supper. The Declaration added, 'This Church . . . may properly be stiled an Independent Church maintaining the power within itself of admitting refusing or discharging members according to its own rules.'

The Church Book covers the period from 1807 to January, 1847, but the entries are very irregular. The Register of Members was only continued as far as 1826, and entries thus far were in the hands of the ministers concerned. The last entry in Trego's handwriting was dated 1812. The next group of entries began on 30th June, 1815, and a meeting held on 3rd September was presided over by a new Pastor, John Barton, previously at Sheffield. Barton removed to Wincanton in 1819.

The next entries in the Membership list are in the handwriting of R. H. Carne (who will be dealt with more fully later). According to the Answers to the Primary Visitation Queries of Bishop Carey in 1821 there were two ministers officiating at the Tabernacle, 'Messrs. Carne and Edwards'. Only one meeting is recorded under their joint signatures, on 3rd May, 1822, when 'it was agreed unanimously that no Minister shall ever be proposed, as the permanent Pastor of this Church, except he be an Independent, that is to say, a Paedobaptist. Also agreed, that any Baptists, who wish to join this Church, shall be admitted to Membership, provided they are duly approved of by the Members'. There had always been a friendly association between the Tabernacle and the Baptists in South St. This move made it possible for members to be transferred without great difficulty from one cause to the other. A later resolution, of 4th April, 1823, restricted attendance at the Lord's Supper to members only.

No entries appear in Carne's writing after April, 1822, although a few names are given in another hand (Thomas Edwards'?) later this year. Then there is a gap until 1826, when a new list of members appears, containing 55 names. This is in John Barton's hand. After a gap of two years the Tabernacle had invited him to return. His resumption of duties could not have been without trouble, for he wrote a memorandum on 30th December, 1832, stating that he had resumed his charge on 8th March, 1829, and had continued 'Without any annoyance or any one Person forbidding the same, till the Present Day ... and so Continue, by the help of God, Proclaiming Salvation for Elect Sinners by Jesus Christ.' Whatever the troubles that had arisen between 1826 and 1829 they had severely reduced the strength of the church. A list by Barton dated 4th January, 1834, included 13 names only.

Another gap in the Church Book occurred between February, 1834, and December, 1837, and Barton passed from the scene in this period. A Church Meeting of 2nd February, 1838, reconstituted the Church and reaffirmed the 1807 Declaration of Faith with one deletion. A paragraph in the original Declaration had specified Infant Baptism: this was now discarded. The inference is that the membership, or a large proportion of it, had come to believe in Adult Believer's Baptism. 35 names were included on the Church Roll at this date, a considerable increase. As will later be shown South St. Baptist church declined in numbers at this same period: some of their members probably joined the Tabernacle. No further permanent pastor was appointed.

At last this following sorry note is found under the date of 19th December, 1846:

'The Baptist friends meeting in this Church engaged to supply the Tabernacle to the 25 of March 1847. But on the 19th of the above date, finding the(y) could not make it a Strick [sic] Baptist Church, the(y) broke throu there engagement and left the Church and formed themselfs in Strick communion at Zoar Chappel.

Zoar Particular Baptist Church in Longbrook St. had been founded in 1841.

The final entry in the Tabernacle Church Book was dated 1st January, 1847;

The following names remained as Members when the above Division took place:
>   Henery Fisher. (Died July 20, '50.)
>   John Sercombe.
>   Jane Southwood. (Died.)
>   Sarrah Gale. (Died Octr. 1849).

This was the end of the Tabernacle as a living religious society, although its name appeared in various Exeter Directories down to the end of the century.

By 1831, Besley's Directory of Exeter mentions a High Street Chapel, Musgrave's Alley, under a Rev. R. H. Carne. This is the former Wesleyan Chapel, and this is the minister who was mentioned as being at the Tabernacle in Bishop Carey's Visitation records of 1821. Robert Harkness Carne (1784–1844) was born at St. Austell, and was an Oxford graduate. He served as curate at Crediton, Drewsteignton and Torbryan, but in 1820 Bishop Pelham refused to renew his licence, as he was believed to hold doctrines inconsistent with those of the Church of England. His beliefs were Calvinist, though he never followed the Antinomian tendencies of George Baring and his friends, even writing a tract against them in 1818. He came to Exeter, and after a short spell at the Tabernacle in 1822, he started another Independent cause in the High St. chapel. He spent his last years at St. Helier, Jersey.[1] The High St. chapel under Carne was run on the lines advocated by the Countess of Huntingdon's Connexion, of which it is now necessary to give an account.

[1] D.N.B., Carne.

Selina Hastings, Countess of Huntingdon, was one of the outstand-ing figures of the Evangelical Movement. She was greatly impressed by George Whitefield, whom she made her personal chaplain in 1748. A woman of considerable organizing ability, she assumed an unofficial leadership over Whitefield's followers, and with the aid of her wealth built chapels and engaged ministers to preach in them, finally founding a small College at Trevecca, South Wales, for the training of Calvinist preachers. Her beliefs, and those of Whitefield and his followers, were almost identical with those of the Church of England, and the forms of worship used in her chapels were not markedly different, though there was a greater emphasis on extemporary prayer. Even in her own life-time, official dislike of the pious enthusiasm of her preachers compelled her in most cases to take advantage of the Toleration Act, and to register her chapels as Dissenting Meeting Houses. Her successor, Lady Anne Erskine, continued this policy, although the Training College was transferred to Cheshunt, in Hertfordshire, in 1792, the year of Lady Huntingdon's death.[1] In the course of time the individual chapels assumed a great degree of autonomy, becoming very close in polity to the Congregationalist churches, and they are now (1961) listed in the Yearbook of the Congregational Union.

In 1835 the High St. Chapel was replaced by a small building seating about 300 in Grosvenor Place, in St. Sidwell's Parish. It was described as 'a small neat building, with a turret and bell . . . the cost . . . about £1200'.[2] The minister was Nicholas Hellings, trained at Hackney College in London, and he remained until 1860, when this cause merged with that of the Free Church of England.

In keeping with its long Protestant tradition, the West of England took the lead in organizing a practical opposition to the Catholicizing tendencies of the Oxford Movement in the 1840s.[3] The action which immediately caused the birth of the denomination which came to be known as the Free Church of England was the persecution by Bishop Phillpotts of the Rev. James Shore, who had been curate of the chapel-at-ease at Bridgetown in the parish of Berry Pomeroy since 1832. This chapel had been built by the Duke of Somerset, the patron of the parish, and prolonged controversy had taken place relative to its con-secration and endowment. The Duke decided, finally, agreeable to the

[1] *Life and Times of Selina, Countess of Huntingdon*, 2 vols. An anonymous work.

[2] *Evangelical Magazine*, 1837. Also White's *Devonshire Directory*, 1850.

[3] Vaughan, F., *A history of the Free Church of England, otherwise called the Reformed Episcopal Church*, 1936.

wishes of his people at Bridgetown, to register the chapel as a conventicle under the Act of 1689, and in this way the first Free Church of England was born. Bishop Phillpotts summoned Shore before the Court of Arches to explain why he, a fully ordained Anglican, was officiating in a Nonconformist chapel. Appeals to the Court of Queen's Bench and to the House of Lords, carried out by Shore's friends, all failed by 1846, and in 1849 Phillpotts, still pursuing his vendetta against the unfortunate curate, had him imprisoned for preaching in the Countess of Huntingdon's chapel at Spa Fields, London. He remained in prison for three months, until his friends raised the money to pay the fine and the Bishop's costs.[1]

There had in the whole of this unpleasant case been no connection with the contemporary agitation against the ritualist innovations (or revivals) associated with the Oxford Movement. Yet the example provided by the setting up of a Free Church of England in Totnes in 1844 was followed very quickly at Exeter and Ilfracombe. In 1844–5 and again in 1848, riots broke out in Exeter over the use of the surplice in public services. Bishop Phillpotts was not very much in sympathy with ritualism, but he was a High Church Tory of the old fashioned type, who welcomed the increased emphasis on the authority and dignity of the priesthood, and he decided to take his stand on the actual wording of the Prayer Book. This in his opinion authorized the use of the surplice, while it did not require the Puritan black preaching gown, and on the 19th November, 1844, he issued an order requiring his clergy to wear surplices in the pulpit in the interests of uniformity of practice 'whenever the sermon is part of the ministration'. The agitation against this centred on St. Sidwell's Church, where the Mayor himself had to turn out to quell the disturbances. This Mayor, Edward Woolmer, who had family connections with the Nonconformists, presided over a protest meeting at the Guildhall, and wrote officially to the Bishop asking him what steps he proposed to take to preserve order among his clergy. The Bishop withdrew his order on 23rd December, and after fresh disturbances in January, 1845, the agitation gradually died down.[2]

The Protestant Party was not deceived by this apparent victory, and it is from this year that the Exeter Free Church of England dates its formation. By April, 1845, support was enough to begin to build a large church in Southernhay, next to the Royal Devon and Exeter

[1] Lambert, R. S., *The Cobbett of the West*, 1939, pp. 132–6.
[2] Shapter, T., 'The Surplice-riots in Exeter'. A manuscript account in Cathedral Library in Shapter's own hand.

Hospital. This was opened on 5th April, 1846, and according to the *Exeter Flying Post* of that date James Shore preached at its initial services. The cost was £5000 and the building seated up to 1000.[1] It was described in 1850 as

The Free Church, or Christ Church, in Southernhay, the property of a gentleman, and is not within the pale of the Established Church, though its services are conducted in a similar manner. . . . It is in the Roman style, with a turret and bell. The interior has three aisles, and three galleries, and will seat 1000 persons. The whole has a chaste appearance, and the east window is enriched with painted glass. The Rev. A. L. Mitchell is the minister.[2]

Before the erection of Christ Church the seceders had worshipped in rooms on Tuckett's Hill, and a Rev. E. R. Cowie was minister. He remained only until 1848. Andrew Lumsden Mitchell remained in charge of the church from 1848 throughout the time it remained in Southernhay. On 30th January, 1855, the church committee held a meeting for seat holders at which Rev. Thomas Dodd (minister at that time of the Countess of Huntingdon's Chapel at Worcester) explained the doctrines and constitution of the Connexion he belonged to, and the meeting approved the identification of Christ Church with the Countess of Huntingdon's Connexion.

While the anti-Tractarian feeling was at its height the Free Church remained prosperous, and the church was full. The fear of Anglo-Catholicism remained strong until the middle 1850s, reinforced by the conversions of leading Tractarians to Roman Catholicism which took place after Newman had led the way in 1845. The 'Papal Aggression' scare of 1850, when the Roman Catholics were once more organized into dioceses in Britain, with Bishops and Archbishops, added fuel to the flames. At least two other Free Churches were set up at this time as a protest against ritualism in South Devon, at Babbacombe in 1852, and at Bovey Tracey in 1857: these eventually joined the Congregationalists.

By 1860 feelings had cooled noticeably, and the numbers attending the Southernhay Free Church dwindled until the building became too large for them. Another factor was that Christ Church had been the personal property of the first incumbent, and had later been sold to a member of the Congregation. He died in 1860 and the other members could not afford to purchase the church. The decision was made to combine with the Grosvenor Place chapel, and this took effect at the

[1] *Exeter Flying Post*, 2nd April, 1846.
[2] White's *Devonshire Directory*, 1850.

end of 1860. The Register of Baptisms kept by the Free Church from 1848 onwards shows that Mitchell's last entry was made on 28th October, 1860. The number of baptisms for the five years 1849 to 1853 was 112, an average of more than 22 each year: even in prolific mid-Victorian days that indicates a following of several hundreds. By the 1860s these figures had fallen considerably. On the removal to Grosvenor Place the chapel there was reconstituted as St. James' Free Church of England. The first baptism of the new minister, Richard Samuel Henderson Spilsbury Short, was entered on 10th February, 1861. Both Hellings and Mitchell retired in 1860, which must have facilitated the union of the two causes. It was not until 1863 that the constitution of the new Free Church of England, as a national religious body, was worked out, and registered in the High Court of Chancery (31st August, 1863). From this time onwards the Free Church of England was legally in being 'as a separate branch of the Church of God: with a Presbyterian ministry; with a recognition and provision for Episcopacy; and pledged to the Doctrines of the Church of England as set forth in the 39 Articles of Religion, and to the principles and practices associated with the Evangelical tenets of the Established Church'. Although it did not set much store on the Apostolic Succession, a link with the historic episcopate of the Church was provided by the consecration as Bishop of Benjamin Price by Bishop Edward Cridge of the Reformed Episcopal Church of America, on 15th August, 1876.

In Exeter little remains to record except the succession of ministers at Christ Church, Grosvenor Place, for the cause very soon reverted to its original name. 10th April, 1865, was the date of the last baptism performed by R. S. H. S. Short. The dates of the first and last baptisms performed by other ministers in the nineteenth century, taken from the Register, are:

J. S. Skinner.	1866, May 9th, to 1867, June 26th.
John Spencer Hill.	1867, Dec. 15th, to 1872, Nov. 6th.
James Wonnacott.	1873, Aug. 17, to 1878, Aug. 25th.
Walter H. Sisterson.	1878, Oct. 6th, to 1881, Aug. 17th.
George Slater.	1882, Feb. 1st, to 1914, Oct. 4th.

Between the end of 1860 and 1864, when the building was sold to the Wesleyan Methodists, Christ Church in Southernhay was worked by a group of Presbyterians. Where they came from, where they went afterwards, is a mystery. That they were orthodox Calvinists is witnessed by an entry in the *Flying Post* for the 2nd March, 1864: Charles

Haddon Spurgeon had visited Exeter the day before and preached to crowded audiences at Bartholomew St. Baptist chapel in the morning, and in the evening 'at the Presbyterian Chapel, Southernhay'. Spurgeon was a man of extreme Protestant views and would certainly not have appeared in any chapel used to expound opinions which he regarded as unsound.

In contrast with the more or less steady progress of the Exeter Independents, the Baptist churches in the city had a checkered career in this period. The parent society in South St. went into decline after 1829, and did not revive until the 1870s.[1] Many of the ministers had short pastorates, insufficient for them to achieve very much, and only one, George Gould (1846–9), subsequently distinguished himself. He became President of the Baptist Union in 1879, after a successful ministry at Norwich.

The Assistant Pastor, E. H. Brewer, became full minister in March, 1829. Immediately the rules of the church were restated in full, and they contained a significant addition.

Resolved that . . . no person shall be permitted to sit down at the Lord's Table with us but those who have been baptized in the manner that the Ordinance is plainly set forth in the New Testament, viz. Baptized Believers by immersion (except those who have been accustomed so to do up to this date).

By this the South St. Baptist church became a Strict or Closed Communion Church. This was followed by other restrictive alterations in the practice of the church. On 8th April, 1830, it was decided that 'All Instrumental Music shall be done away in our Worship and we will endeavour to follow the advice of the Apostle "by singing and making melody in our hearts to the Lord" '. In May, June and July, 1830, Church meetings were stormy, and so it was resolved on 5th July: 'That as our Monthly Church meetings have afforded so many opportunities for strife and contention that from this evening they are done away with, and Prayer meetings be held instead . . .'

Throughout Brewer's ministry individual members are recorded as asking 'dismission to Mr. Kilpin's church in St. Sidwell's' (the Refuge Chapel). This suggests that they found the narrowness of doctrine preached in South St. uncongenial. The number of members in May, 1833, was 101, showing that Brewer had just held the total steady (it had been 99 in 1829). Finally in December, 1833, Brewer resigned.

[1] South St. Baptist Church Minute Book, 1812–68.

None of the customary letters of regret were inserted in the Church Minute Book. In March, 1834, 5 who had previously withdrawn were readmitted to membership, and on 25th May, 1834, '23 persons formerly members of the Refuge Chapel in St. Sidwell's' were admitted to South St. Kilpin's death had meant the end of this cause.

It was consequently at a moment of encouragement that Peter Anstie, formerly minister at Chard, became the new pastor in September, 1834. He was only offered a salary of £80 for the first year, a slight increase on Brewer's £71 in 1829. Immediately the rule relating to communicants was altered.

Oct. 26, 1834. 'Resolved, that . . . we are willing in love most heartily to receive as communicants with us at the Lord's Table any person whom we believe to have been baptised with the Holy Ghost. . . .

Other relaxations in strictness occurred under Anstie. On 19th April, 1835, it was decided that the practice of requiring persons to relate their experiences at the time of conversion when they were baptized should be discontinued. It is the custom nowadays for such candidates for baptism and membership to be examined by the Church officers before final acceptance. This does not rule out the making of a declaration at the time of public baptism, should the candidate desire to make one, which often happens.

The first year and a half of Anstie's ministry was prosperous. The annual letter to the Devon Association of Baptist churches on June 7th, 1835, claimed that 62 members had been added in the year and only 4 lost, though the grand total was not given. Yet from February, 1836, until November, 1841, there comes a complete break in the Church records, and conditions were very different when they resume. At the end of 1841 Anstie first exchanged pulpits with William Welsh of Brixham, and then resigned. Welsh was invited to take his place in Exeter, and accepted. In his acceptance, Welsh referred to the 'present depressed condition' of the church, and when the usual letter to the Association was compiled in May, 1842, the membership was 116, which must have represented a fall of some 30 to 40 people from 1835. It was in 1841 that the Zoar Particular Baptist Chapel in Longbrook St. was built, and it is probable that this was founded as a secession from South St. by those who believed in a Closed Communion Church, and disagreed with Anstie's more liberal policy. A few others joined the Tabernacle in Coombe St.

Under Welsh's pious guidance the Church went in harmony for a few years. Discipline was maintained, for several people were excluded for immoral conduct at this time. On 1st August, 1844, the minister 'made several remarks on the evil prevailing of members of the Church being united in marriage to unbelievers . . .', and on 1st January, 1845, 'Sarah Frost excluded for marrying an unconverted & irreligious man.'

Finally, on 29th June, 1845 Welsh resigned, giving no specific reason. The resignation was accepted without comment.

In January, 1846, George Gould, from Dublin, was invited to the church, at a salary of £120 for the first year, somewhat higher than had been possible before. He accepted, but warned the members 'That you are not to expect your Pastor . . . to do everything which may be necessary in the way of active exertion for the revival of the Church.' He also candidly stated that whilst prepared to take £120 at first 'I should by no means be content with it hereafter. Nor should I like the Church to rely upon the endowment which it possesses, inasmuch as I think such a Fund should be used for the extension of the Gospel in districts where it is at present unheard'.

Gould meant what he said. On 29th April, 1846, 'At the pastor's request every member was importuned prayerfully to consider . . . in what . . . christian labour he would engage, whether as visitor of the sick, teacher in the Sunday School, distributor of tracts, or in any other manner.' Such a survey of resources under the names of 'Every Member Canvass' or 'Christian Stewardship' is now in the mid-20th century part of the programme of all denominations.

At the same time the membership was revised, those being no longer resident in Exeter being dismissed altogether. As a result the annual letter to the Association in June 1846 reported that only 91 members were left, 34 having been dismissed, or had resigned.

Gould's undoubted abilities failed to win support in Exeter. Membership did not increase (it was only 90 in June, 1848) nor did attempts to add to the church's income gain any success. On 2nd September, 1847, 'it was unanimously resolved that for the future every member of this Church shall be required, unless prevented by extreme poverty, to contribute towards the income of the Pastor and the general expenses of the Chapel, & in case of refusal shall be regarded as resigning their membership . . .' In this way and in others attempts were made to get extra subscriptions for the minister's salary, but all in vain. Finally in April, 1849, 'Rev. George Gould gave notice of his intention to resign the pastorate, in consequence of the Church not raising an income sufficient for his support.'

P

The short pastorate of Christopher Middlemas Wightman, which followed from 1850 to 1852, was one of continued rapid decline. It ended with the decision to give the minister three months' notice. Disputes between members and deacons occurred and on 29th April, 1852, it was decided that 'The practice of choosing Deacons annually be discontinued on account of the unpleasantness it produces'. By June, 1853, the church made an appeal for help to the Devon Association. At that time, it was said, the Church consisted of only 50 members, 14 males and 36 females. 'Many of the members were aged & infirm—that not more than 2 or 3 in the Church were in a position to render counsel or other wise assist in the affairs of the Society—that the average attendance of members on the ordinances of religion did not exceed 25.' The endowment of the Chapel was given in this appeal. It was then:

	Gross rent.	Nett.
House in Belmont Place.	£28	£19
House in Mount Radford.	£18	£12 10s.
Houses in front of chapel.	£35 10s.	£19
Taunton Property.	£51	£23
	£132 10s.	£73 10s.

The seat rents amounted to about £12 each year and the quarterly collections to about £3.

Years of doctrinal controversy and divisions on church order and discipline had caused the loss of the middle-class element which had been the backbone of the church.

Following a recommendation by the Committee of the Devon Baptist Association, Stewart Williamson, of Appledore, became minister at South St. in October, 1853. He received a welcome response at first, the congregation increasing fourfold in his first few months. He stayed until 1861, and worked conscientiously for the good of the church. Yet he was throughout fighting against a succession of misfortunes that even a prosperous church would have found it difficult to survive. At the time Williamson came there were only 47 members. The following spring his two chief deacons were excluded for 'unfaithful' conduct, and the accounts were found to be in a chaotic state when handed over to their successors.

No sooner had this trouble been sorted out than the City Surveyor reported that the houses in front of the Chapel were unfit for habitation. It was decided that the property was not worth the cost of restoring, and so the houses were pulled down and the materials sold by auction. Although this represented a loss of revenue it was a blessing in disguise, as now for the first time the chapel was in view from the street, and the citizens of Exeter would daily be reminded of its presence there.

The letter to the Association in June 1855 reported this and continued 'we are happy to inform you that the contributions for the current year—exclusive of the various endowments—will amount to upwards of £140'. The membership had increased to 70.

But the most crippling blow was yet to fall. From 1856 to 1859 the Chapel was involved in a complicated lawsuit. It will be remembered that the chapel had to be 'kept free of all incumbrances for ever'. Yet when it had been rebuilt in 1822–3 part of the cost had been met by the loan of £500 by the three deacons, Messrs. Culverwell, Moxey and Westlake. The first two were completely repaid, but not Westlake. When he died the interest on the debt (£156 13s. 4d.) was paid to his wife, and on her death to her niece, Miss Elizabeth Darke. In 1856 she refused to accept interest from the Church Treasurer and claimed repayment of the whole debt. No negotiations made her change her mind, and a suit in Chancery followed. The judgment went against Miss Darke, but the Baptist Church had to pay the costs of defending itself, and was forced to meet a Lawyer's bill of £196 4s. Five of the Trustees lent the money at once, and the local solicitor cut £20 from his bill. Stewart Williamson himself lent nearly £37. The repayments were not easy and remained a heavy burden on the members for some years.

Williamson resigned at the end of 1861. The membership roll was revised at his request before he left, and exactly 80 names were recorded. Considering the difficulties faced by Church and Pastor throughout the 1850s this was a creditable improvement.

In April, 1862, the Church tried the experiment of calling a student fresh from Bristol Baptist College, Samuel Mann. His pastorate of 6 years was uneventful: steady progress began then which bore fruit later. A broadening of the basis of the church took place, witnessed by such resolutions as these:

That the Lord's Table shall be freely open to all Christians, & those who may desire statedly to commune with us may on application to the Minister or deacons, be received as regular Communicants of the Church.

That the privileges of Church membership be extended to all Christians who may desire to join us, but that only the baptized members shall take part in, or vote for, the election of the Minister and Officers of the Church.

When Mann resigned in April, 1868, the membership was 106, which meant that the church had fought its way back to the position of 40 years before. The letter to the June meeting of the Association that year at Torquay reported that under Mann's ministry 'All the organizations of the Church have been put in order—& we feel the general aspect of things to be one of encouragement and promise. In the past year our service of song has been considerably improved by the erection of an Organ.'

For their next minister, the South St. church aimed high. On the 13th September, 1868, it was decided to invite Frederic Bosworth, M.A., who had formerly been Hebrew Tutor at Bristol Baptist College, and was at that time minister at Weston-super-Mare. The letter of invitation was a psychological masterpiece, making no attempt to conceal the weakness of the Exeter cause, and using that weakness itself as the main ground for this appeal to a man of undoubted ability and experience. It was the type of invitation to attract a truly dedicated man, and it succeeded. A sign of the increased prosperity of the Church was that a salary of £200 was offered.

Bosworth was 55 years old when he came to Exeter, and with his considerable experience he brought fresh vigour to each of the organizations of the Church. He took particular interest in Sunday School work, being one of the examiners for the competitive examinations of the Exeter Sunday School Union. His preaching was of a high standard, and it was under him that in 1875 the South St. Baptist Village Preachers' Society was formed, to assure that the small country churches round about were regularly served each Sunday. By the time of Bosworth's death, in 1881, the membership had reached 274, and the church had attained the prosperity which has remained with it ever since.

The Bartholomew St. Baptist church, whose members had numbered 90 in September, 1823, gradually increased in size until Mason's death on 20th January, 1835. For the five years before this his stipend had averaged £142 per annum. His death caused a major crisis, for the possession of the chapel reverted to George Baring. The church was able to purchase the property for £1000, 'although £3000 was the sum at first required'. Appeals were sent out, but the total subscriptions came only to £593 19s., and a mortgage of £500 was arranged with the widow of John Mason, at 5 per cent interest, a debt which was not cleared for ten years.

From this time the Church was in command of its own property, and entered upon the most stormy half-century known to any of the

Exeter Nonconformist societies. It is as though the dominating position occupied by both Baring and Mason, through their possession of the chapel premises, had deprived the church members of the training in self-government which they would otherwise have received. John Offord of Devonport became the third minister in 1836, but 'between Lady Day & Midsr. 1840 resigned his charge and joined a religious society designated the Plymouth Brethren'. On 8th June, 1840, it was reported that several members had joined the Plymouth Brethren, so Offord took others with him, leaving the Bartholomew St. church sadly disheartened. On 6th July, 1840, after several meetings of indecision, the Rev. C. T. Keen of Pershore was invited to the pastorate. Less than half the members were present, and the voting was 78 for, 7 against, but Keen accepted despite the absence of unanimity. He agreed to the salary offered of £120 (Offord had averaged £113) but looked forward to some increase later.

This increase did not come, and the church had difficulty in fulfilling its promise. In November, 1841, a letter was addressed to the Church as a whole by the three chief deacons, Edwd. Buxton, Joseph Roleston and W. Davies, two of whom had been deacons since the foundation of the church. '. . . the number of members has greatly diminished, and the amount of income is now so reduced as to be quite insufficient to supply the necessity of our Pastor and his family.' The tone of the letter suggested the fault lay with Keen, and he resigned with effect from 25th March, 1842.

On 29th September, 1842, it was reported that, having decided to re-enrol all members, by that date 100 people had done this, and promised to help in raising money for the minister's stipend. In December, the pastorate was accepted by the Rev. J. Bigwood, of Modbury. Only £80 was offered to him and 22 members were neutral when the vote was taken whether Bigwood should be invited or not. The new minister proved a good worker. By means of Tea Meetings, Collecting Cards, and begging in other towns, Bigwood organized a campaign to pay off the Chapel debt, an aim which was achieved by 26th February, 1845, after only two years work. Immediately he got the members to agree to repair the church thoroughly, which cost another £270. By 23rd January, 1848, this debt had also been paid. During the period when the chapel was under repair the members had been meeting with the South St. church, with the ministers officiating alternately.

Following his strenuous efforts, Bigwood was justified in expecting that the members of the church would next make an attempt to increase his small salary. The Treasurer's report of February, 1848, showed 'a payment of £100 as usual to the Pastor, which elicited a declaration that he could not support himself on that sum'. On 22nd March Bigwood was asked to wait for six months for consideration of an increased stipend. On 1st November, 1848, however, the Finance Committee reported that the 'Nett income appears to be £118 4s. 11d. and that this be submitted to the Pastor's consideration . . .' It is not surprising that this exhibition of ingratitude was followed on 12th November by Bigwood's resignation. That something could have been done was shown when the next pastor was promised £120.

The new minister was George Cole, elected on 14th May, 1849. The voting showed that there were 126 members at that time. Cole came from Church St., Blackfriars, London. A marked increase of membership occurred in the 5½ years he was at Exeter. Increases of 53 in 1850, and 44 in 1851, with smaller figures in other years, were reported to the annual meetings of the Western Baptist Association. In July, 1854, even after a revision of the membership lists had caused the deletion of 83 names, the total left of active members was still 205. This could have been due to several causes. It may have been the work of Cole himself; it may be due to the secessions from South St., which took place in these years; and it may have been the result of the division among the Methodists in 1849, which caused many to forsake Methodism altogether.

Despite this unprecedented membership figure George Cole resigned on 28th January, 1855, 'assigning as a reason the apparent want of success'. His letters show him to have been a hypersensitive man, probably disheartened unduly by the striking off of the 83 lapsed members in the previous July.

The next minister of the Church, elected on 29th April, 1855, was a man of strong character. This was Elias Hetton Tuckett, previously at Kingsbridge. Only half of the membership were at the meeting when he was chosen, 116 voting for, and 8 remaining neutral. He was offered £120 each year, the same as his predecessor. Small increases of membership continued to be reported, the total rising to 235 in 1860, and 256 in 1862, the highest figure ever reached.

Tuckett led the society in harmony for several years, until in March 1862 controversy again broke out. William Davies, son of one of the founding members, and himself a deacon and member for 36 years, resigned. He had had sole charge of the distribution of the funds

available for relief of the Poor, and complaints had arisen of his conduct. A church meeting wished Davies to reconsider his resignation,
but Tuckett refused to sign the request, which was therefore not made.
Davies supplied a light relief by complaining bitterly that 'when he
... preached on a Wednesday evening in the Pastor's absence the
people would not hear him—they would look in & seeing Mr. Davies
in the desk would go out again'. It was finally decided on 26th March,
1862, that 'the distribution of the poors money collected at the Lord's
Supper be vested equally in the hands of the deacons'. The incident led
to a small secession for the Annual Report presented on 1st June, 1862,
said that there were 256 members, of which 'about 30 were expected to
withdraw through the removal of Mr. Davies'. At this time there were
346 children in the Sunday School, with 32 teachers.

Further discipline was imposed in the following January (1863)
when it was resolved: 'Members of this Church absenting themselves
from the Lord's Table for three successive months shall be visited... and
if no satisfactory reason be assigned for such absence their names shall
be reported at the next Church Meeting and they shall be considered as
no longer members.' This was not unusual: most of the Congregationalist and Baptist societies of that time had such rules, and did not
hesitate to apply them.

The 1862 difficulty was merely the forerunner of a more violent
storm. Although it did more damage to the well-being of the church
than any other incident in its 19th century history, the cause itself was
trivial enough. At a Church Meeting on 23rd March, 1864, the election
of an extra deacon was proposed. Tuckett objected on the grounds that
no one was suitable for the office. 'What is the use? They are all
immersed in business.' One deacon resigned on the spot in protest, and
from this point affairs went rapidly to the worse. An entry in Tuckett's
handwriting (his last in the minute book) relating to 27th April reads:
'Circumstances arose at this Church Meeting of far too painful a nature
to allow the Pastor to transcribe them—and it is sufficient to record that
the Pastor's word being rudely contravened by some present and by the
Deacons, the Pastor then and there resigned his charge.'

The Secretary of the Western Baptist Association, the Rev. E. Webb
of Tiverton, attempted to mediate between the two parties. But on
4th May, Tuckett sent a peremptory take it or leave it note to a Church
Meeting, demanding the immediate expulsion of five members, one of
whom was a Deacon and three of whom were Sunday School Teachers.
This could not be accepted.

On the following Sunday Tuckett preached to almost 70 of the members of the church in a room in Mint Lane, where they formed themselves into a separate society, under the name of the Priory Church, through their propinquity to the remains of St. Nicholas' Priory. Later that year, when the old Musgrave's Alley Chapel became vacant through the move of the Primitive Methodists to St. Sidwells, the Priory Baptists moved there. This secession church maintained a separate existence until the end of 1871 when Tuckett retired from active life. Instances were recorded in the minute book of the parent church of members being transferred from one society to the other during these seven and a half years. Finally, on 1st May, 1872, at a Bartholomew St. Church Meeting it was 'Proposed . . . that the following brethren and sisters (26 names given) lately members of the Baptist Church worshipping at Musgrave Alley, High St., Exeter, and now dissolved, be received with hearty welcome as members of this Church.' Others followed individually at later dates.

This 1864 secession left the Bartholomew St. church in a much weakened position. With membership reduced by one-third it was not able to aim high for a new leader. It invited John Field, a student from Spurgeon's College in London, on 19th October, 1864. They offered him £100 a year. He appears to have been a good worker, for the bulk of the Minutes of Church Meetings in his pastorate is filled with cases of candidates for membership. Yet these could not all have completed their courses of instruction; the membership continued to decline in numbers. There was a deficiency in the accounts in February, 1866, of £156 17s. 2d., and finally on 31st March, 1869, 'the Pastor then addressed the members present on the very low state to which we are reduced, and said he felt it to be impossible to go on preaching to such empty pews....' On 7th April Field was persuaded to stay, after a proposal to bring about 'the union of the Baptist churches in this City under one Pastor' was not seconded. Little progress was made during the next year despite the innovation of weekly offerings in church instead of the old occasional collections. As has been noted in the case of the Presbyterian churches, the normal method of financing the work was by seat rents and regular subscriptions towards the Minister's salary. Collections at each service supplemented by special money-raising efforts such as Bazaars, Gift Days and the like, are of comparatively recent adoption.

John Field resigned again on 4th September, 1870, without protest. Dr. Charles Frederick Cooper was appointed to succeed him on

12th December, but he was only promised £80 a year salary, an indication to what straits the church had been reduced. From his handling of the crises he had to face he was a man of experience, and successfully rode a storm potentially of worse proportions than that of 1864. At the close of his first year in Exeter, when he had had time to examine the prospects, he brought forward a scheme for the amalgamation of the Baptist churches of the city under one minister. There were no less than four Baptist causes compared with the one of the Independents; South St., Bartholomew St., Priory, and Zoar Chapel in Longbrook Terrace. Committees met but negotiations failed through the prejudices of the members concerned. South St. was a member of the Baptist Union whereas Bartholomew St. was not; South St. had an 'open' membership (i.e. membership was not restricted only to those who had undergone Believers' Baptism) while Bartholomew St. was a 'closed' membership church. Cooper's efforts did secure the return of the Priory Church members to Bartholomew St. in May 1872, but efforts at a wider union failed.

It is probable that Cooper's advocacy of Baptist union in Exeter was viewed with disfavour by the more reactionary of his officers, for at a Church Meeting on 3rd January, 1872, he read a letter he had received from three of the Deacons.

In every way we have been disappointed (in your ministry) and . . . the close of the year finds us more in debt than the commencement. And being convinced that another year under your ministration would lower us even more both numerically and financially, and being unable to continue our guarantee for any amount . . . we think you will agree . . . that . . . it will be well for you to withdraw from the pastorate . . .

Cooper countered this blunt and discourteous broadside with another letter signed by 78 friends, 45 being members of the church, disagreeing entirely with the Deacons' action. It became evident that the Deacons had acted without the knowledge of the membership, and their letter was vigorously repudiated by the Church Meeting. One Deacon retracted, the other two were expelled.

Some slight increase in support was forthcoming in the next two years, until Cooper resigned on 29th April, 1874. He was then able to state that 'when I came here there were 78 members . . . there are now 127'. Most of these, however, had come from the reunion of the Priory Church. In his farewell message Cooper returned to his desire to see a Baptist union in the city;

I find there never was a time when even two Baptist chapels in this city were well attended, and, as the same difficulties are in the way, I feel . . . that the same state of things will continue, and . . . I feel it my duty to resign my pastorate, leaving you free to negotiate once more to endeavour to amalgamate the Baptist churches of Exeter should you think it advisable to do so . . .

They did not.

One of the necessary periodic revisions of the church membership roll took place on 10 June, 1874, which left exactly 100 members. On 9th September of that year the church was fortunate in obtaining as its new minister the Rev. E. S. Neale. He was a man of experience, and left a church in Sunderland, giving up a certain £150 a year there for the doubtful receipts of the freewill offerings at Exeter. He remained until his death in March, 1882, and successfully set about the painful task of rebuilding the society. He had to face crises, especially in 1878–9, not essentially dissimilar to those already described, but was able to overcome his difficulties with patience and sincerity of faith.[1]

While the stormy history of Bartholomew St. Baptist church was exceptional in Exeter Nonconformity (and similar crises recurred at intervals well into the twentieth century) it should be borne in mind that the middle years of the nineteenth century were times of religious ferment both in Exeter and in the country as a whole. We have seen what a violent reaction there was from the Ritualism associated with the Oxford Movement in the Church of England: there was the lamentable Methodist division of 1849: there were controversies taking place on smaller or greater points at issue in both South St. and Bartholomew St. Baptist churches: and George's Meeting, the oldest Nonconformist cause of all, underwent a series of troubles between 1848 and 1860. Only the Independents escaped trouble—a tribute to the sound leadership and charity of their two ministers, John Bristow and David Hewitt.

The fourth Baptist society in Exeter was the Zoar Chapel. This was situated at the junction of Longbrook Terrace with Longbrook Street. White's *History, Gazetteer, and Directory of Devonshire* for 1850 described it as 'a small building, erected in 1841'. Its members were Particular Baptists, of the type known as 'Strict', for they would only admit to their Communion services those who had undergone Believers' Baptism. It is most probable that its original members were seceders from the South St. church in the period 1836–41, of which we have no record.

[1] Bartholomew St. Baptist Church Minute Books, 1817–1900. In custody of the Secretary of the St. Thomas (Cowick St.) Baptist Church.

No records of the Zoar Chapel have been preserved. Some transfers of membership from 'the church in Longbrook St.' are mentioned in the Bartholomew St. Church Book in the 1840s: none of any movement in the reverse direction. Some of the Baptist members of the Coombe St. Tabernacle joined Zoar Chapel in December, 1846. Slater's Devonshire Directory of 1852 gives the name of the minister then as Simeon Emery, and Morris's Directory for 1870 gives the name of the pastor then as Rev. John Hunt Lynn. That the church was never very large may be taken without dispute: it disappeared sometime in the late 1870s, as in the 1883 Kelly's Directory for Devonshire the building at the corner of the Longbrook Terrace appears as a Brethren Meeting.

The Brethren form the most extreme of the small Protestant groups found in Exeter in the nineteenth century.[1] This movement arose, as had all other Protestant societies, from a desire to return to the state of affairs which existed in the primitive Christian Church. Allied to this were an ascetic desire to remain aloof from all worldly things which might contaminate, Baptism by immersion, the commemoration of the Lord's Supper every Lord's Day, and a literal belief in the words of every book of the Bible. The movement sprang to life in Dublin in the winter of 1827, under John Nelson Darby, formerly a curate in the Irish Church. A little later B. W. Newton met Darby when the latter visited Oxford, and formed a society on similar lines in Plymouth, from which the generally known name of Plymouth Brethren has been derived. Both these men insisted not only on a return to the simplicity of organization which they saw in the primitive church, but also upon a complete aloofness from the affairs of the world, and literalism in Scripture interpretation. This latter became the dominant principle of the Brethren, and as the Bible may in all sincerity be interpreted quite differently by Biblical students, the subsequent history of the Brethren was punctuated by bitter disputes on the interpretation of vital passages. Literalism led the Brethren to insistence on the doctrine of the imminent Second Coming of Christ, and preparation for this advent the paramount interest in every believer's life. The Brethren gained many adherents almost at once from evangelicals in both Church of England and Nonconformity. They failed, because they broke away from orthodoxy only to set up an even narrower orthodoxy of their own: an exclusiveness which prevented the movement from gathering an impetus which might otherwise have proved irresistible. Any slight

[1] Clark, H. W., *History of English Nonconformity*, 1913. Vol. 2, pp. 338–43. Noel, N., *History of the Brethren*. Denver, Col., 1936. 2 vols.

chance of Brethrenism becoming a truly national movement was wrecked in 1845 when a bitter quarrel took place between Darby and Newton on the 'Great Tribulation', a persecution supposed to occur just before the Second Advent of Christ. Each side excommunicated the other, and the separation of the Brethren into 'Exclusive' and 'Open' sections began, Darby leading the Exclusive Brethren and Newton the remainder.

Although individual adherents of the Brethren may have appeared in Exeter earlier, it was in 1839 that their first meeting-place was established. This was Providence Chapel in Northernhay Street, built by Sir Alexander Campbell, an associate of Newton at Plymouth. It was modelled upon the Great Ebrington Street meeting place of the Brethren in Plymouth, with seats arranged in rather more than a semi-circle facing a central long table, at which the speakers stood. Everything was absolutely plain, without ornament, and the whole services were arranged so as not to give undue prominence to any one member of the society. Like the old Independents and Baptists they firmly believed in the Priesthood of all Believers, and have always rejected the idea of a ministry set apart for special authority over them. Naturally those with special gifts for teaching and exposition of the Bible would take the lead in the Brethren's activities, but not by virtue of ordination.

The Brethren in Exeter at first attracted considerable support, especially from the extremer Nonconformists already in the city. We have seen how a Minister of Bartholomew St. Baptist church joined them in 1840 and was followed by several of the members of that church. The quarrel between Darby and Newton in 1845 must have wrecked the Exeter society, however, for in 1851 the chapel had to be sold to the Bible Christians, who took possession on 9th March, 1851. At the time of the national Census of Religious Observance which took place on Sunday, 30th March, following, the Brethren had another meeting place capable of holding 200 people, and reported attendances there of 150 in the morning and 120 in the evening. Morris's *Directory of Devonshire* for 1870 places them in Friernhay St., White's *Gazetteer* for 1878–9 gives them two rooms, one in Friernhay St. and the other at Market Hall.

Finally the later fortunes of the Society of Friends must be related. The Quakers had shared in the general decay of religious fervour of the early and middle years of the eighteenth century. Their ranks had become largely hereditary, thanks to their insistence upon marriage as far as possible within their own membership, and to their distinctively plain modes of dress and behaviour. The Exeter society became torpid and allowed its Meeting House in Magdalen St. to fall into decay. In 1832 it was sold, and by a strenuous effort a new place of worship was built at The Friars, costing £3000. Why the Society built a chapel so much larger than they had been accustomed to worship in is not known. It may have expected an increase of membership, or may have hoped that an imposing building would in itself convince the outside world of its piety and prosperity. A list of the members of the East Devon Monthly Meeting, dated 1826, showed 210 names, which was the maximum which then had to be allowed for: weekly Preparative Meetings would have been very much smaller, restricted to those resident in Exeter. In any case a meeting-house seating 700 had attendances of only 54 in the morning and 37 in the evening of Sunday, 30th March, 1851, and it proved far too expensive for the resources of the Society. In 1868 it was sold to the Salvation Army at a low price, and it still remains the Exeter Temple of the Salvationists.

From 1868 until 1875 the Friends met in hired rooms adjoining Radnor Villas, Bouverie Place, off Wonford Road. Then F. W. Dymond purchased the original site in Magdalen St. and gave it to the Society. On it, at a cost of £1626 10s. 8d. a new meeting-house was built, first used on 17th December, 1876. From then until the present day the Quakers have continued to witness quietly there.[1]

[1] Dymond, R., *Early records of Friends in Devonshire*, n.d. Thomasson, W. J. M., 'The Friends of East Devon and their Meetings, 1654–1928'. Typescript copies in Exeter City and University Libraries.

CHAPTER XV

CONCLUSION: THE SITUATION IN MID-CENTURY. THE CENSUS OF RELIGIOUS WORSHIP, 1851

IT is fitting that this survey of Exeter Nonconformity should be concluded by a summary of the religious situation in mid-Victorian times. Accurate statistical evidence is available in the form of an official census of attendances at public worship on Sunday, 30th March, 1851. When the Census of Great Britain for 1851[1] was planned it was considered desirable to take the opportunity to collect information upon both the religious and educational institutions of the country. It was made quite clear that churches and religious societies were not by law compelled to answer the inquiry. But the response was 'nearly as complete as could be wished for; and . . . now, for the first time, there is given to the country a full picture of the state of its religion as exhibited by its religious institutions'. The picture given may be taken as true of the situation throughout the third quarter of the nineteenth century. What evidence there is suggests that church attendances increased gradually from 1850 until 1910.

Two kinds of Census Forms were issued, one for the Established Church, and one for all the others. The particulars differed only on minor points. The Anglican churches were asked for the dates and circumstances of their consecrations and licensing, who built them, and at what cost. In the other form, the precise religious denomination of each chapel was asked, and whether it was used exclusively for public worship. But the most important questions were the same in both cases: how many people were actually in the congregation for Morning, Afternoon and Evening Services on 30th March, 1851. If for any reason the numbers actually present on that day were abnormal, then the person making the return was requested to fill in another section with the average number of attendants during the twelve months preceding the date of the Census. On the forms separate places were printed for numbers in the General Congregation and for Sunday Scholars: in fact many of the returns did not distinguish between these, merely giving

---

[1] House of Commons Papers, 1852/3, LXXXIX. Census of Great Britain, 1851. Religious Worship, England and Wales. Report and Tables.

the total numbers attending, and in the statistical part of the Census report total numbers of the Congregations only are given.

In Devon as a whole out of a total of 1297 places of worship, 549 belonged to the Church of England. The Wesleyan Methodists came next with 219, followed by the Bible Christians with 146 and the Independents with 142. Baptists of all kinds had 112, the Plymouth Brethren 36 and the Society of Friends 8. The Unitarian descendants of the once dominant Presbyterians only had 12 meeting-houses left, ten of which had been built before 1801. 38 of the Independent chapels had been built before 1801, and may be considered to be either causes which were originally Independent, or, more frequently, once Presbyterian societies which had remained orthodox. All except 9 of the Wesleyan Methodist chapels had been built since 1801, a remarkable growth of activity, even when it is remembered that, except in the bigger towns, these were usually much smaller structures than the parish churches or the old Dissenting Meeting-houses. The tendency in Nonconformist causes to make the evening service the more important of the day is noticeable. Whereas the morning congregations of the Church of England were 103,301 out of a total of 164,263, in the evening there were only 30,170 out of 101,624. Independents had 16,993 persons attending morning services, but 18,025 in the evening. The figures for the Wesleyan Methodists were 16,829 and 22,884; Particular Baptists (the most important of the Baptist divisions) 9877 and 9553; for the Bible Christians 5153 and 8792; and for the Unitarians 1181 and 756.

The tables for Exeter follow in full:

Exeter: Population 32,823.

Denomination.	Number of Buildings.	Sittings.	A.M.	P.M.	Evening.
Church of England.	25	10840	7852	5438	4655
Independents.	2	1072	557	133	507
Baptists.	3	1030	960	290	1050
Society of Friends.	1	700	54	—	37
Unitarians.	1	800	364	—	250
Wesleyan Methodists.	2	1380	920	150	980
Bible Christians.	1	800	130	165	220
Wesleyan Reformers.	1	345	300	60	345
Brethren.	1	200	150	—	120
Undefined.	2	1000	700	200	800
Roman Catholics.	1	200	250	—	—
Jews.	1	90	48	12	28
TOTALS:	41	18457	12285	6448	8992

Comparing first of all the total Nonconformist figures with those for the Church of England, it is seen that the Nonconformists provided sittings for 7327 compared with the 10,840 of the Anglicans, and 14 places of worship to 25. This suggests that the average size of the chapels was larger than that of the Anglican churches, despite the fact that these included the Cathedral itself. This ceases to be surprising when one remembers the very small size of the ancient parish churches of the city, such as St. Stephen's, and St. Pancras'. The most prosperous of the Nonconformists taken singly were the Baptists, with their 3 chapels in South St., Bartholomew St., and Longbrook Terrace (Zoar Chapel), and their combined congregations of 960 in the morning and 1050 in the evening. But this Census was taken just two years after the disastrous Methodist split of 1849, and to form a better picture of the place of Methodism in Exeter the figures of the Wesleyans and the Wesleyan Reformers should be combined. This would restore them to their rightful place as the most numerous body of Dissenters, with three chapels (the Mint, St. Sidwell's, and the Musgrave's Alley Chapel) attended by 1220 in the morning and 1325 in the evening. The two Independent chapels mentioned would be the one in Castle Street, and the Grosvenor Place congregation under the ministry of Nicholas Hellings. The two 'Undefined' causes were Christ Church in Southern-hay (Free Church of England), and the Calvinist Tabernacle in Coombe St. There was one other undefined meeting which failed to make any returns of attendances: most likely it was connected with some branch of the Brethren who disliked identifying themselves with any sect whatever. George's Chapel still retained a sizeable congregation, despite its continued decline, and was half full on the morning of the Census Sunday with 364 people for the estimated 800 sittings.

It is not easy to estimate the proportion of the population of the city which may be considered to have been Nonconformist in 1851. Detailed attendance figures for morning, afternoon and evening services on this Sunday are available, it is true, and they may be considered a fair enough indication of the relative strength of the denominations concerned. Yet there is no way of telling the numbers of people who attended more than one service on that day, and the totals of attendances at all three services give a much inflated estimate of the number of people concerned. This problem was discussed in the Report prefacing the Census Tables, with the conclusion that the number of individuals attending church each Sunday was about two-thirds of the total number of attendances. Much the same result was

obtained if the number of persons attending the best frequented service
in each church was taken, and one-third added to that. The latter
method would give the following table:

Independents	743
Baptists	1400
Society of Friends	72
Unitarians	485
Wesleyan Methodists	1307
Wesleyan Reformers	460
Bible Christians	293
Brethren	200
Undefined	1067
	6027

With the total population of Exeter at this Census being 32,823, just
under one-fifth of the population was thus in the habit of attending
Nonconformist places of worship. Even if the rather large numbers
which are listed as of undefined denomination—the larger proportion
of which would have belonged to the Free Church of England—are
omitted from our calculations, it is still true that one-sixth of the
population worshipped regularly in modes not recommended by the
Anglican Prayer Book.

If the same method of calculation is applied to discover the proportion of the population attending any place of worship on that Census
Sunday, the figure of 16,380 people out of 32,823 is arrived at. Only
half of the people of Exeter attended church at all. Of the 16,380 the
Nonconformists accounted for 36½ per cent, or rather more than
one-third.

Nonconformity in Exeter was therefore in a strong position in mid-
nineteenth century. There had been some decline from the high level
of 1715 when Dissenters may have numbered as many as one-third of
the total population of the city: yet it certainly represents a large rise
from 1800, when Nonconformist fortunes were at a low ebb. Although
no further Census of this nature was taken, it is probable that the
percentage of churchgoers increased as the reign of Queen Victoria
grew older, for it was not until the twentieth century, and especially
after 1918, that church attendance declined spectacularly to the low
level of today. At the same time it must be remembered also that
although Dissent was still strong in Exeter in 1851, it had not developed
here to as great an extent as in the industrialized parts of the country.
The returns for the whole of England and Wales showed that numbers

Q

attending Anglican and Nonconformist services were almost equal, while in Exeter we have seen that Nonconformists accounted for only 36½ per cent of church attendances. Whereas in the period from 1687 to 1750 Exeter had been one of the most important strongholds of Dissent outside of London, it now, despite a definite revival since 1800, occupied a much less prominent position.

APPENDIX A

Pamphlets issued during the course of the Trinitarian dispute which have a bearing on the situation at Exeter.

The most important are those marked *

1. Innocent Vindicated, The. September, 1718. (Showed the unreasonableness of condemning persons at the rate which was common at this time.)
2. Mr. Trosse's Catechism. 1718. (Severely censured departures from orthodoxy.)
3. Hallett, Joseph, II: A pamphlet explaining his position in the September, 1718 Assembly.
4. A Caution against Deceivers with respect to the Subordination of the Son of God. November, 1718.
5. Hallett, Joseph, II: A Letter in answer to the Caution against Deceivers. November, 1718.
6. An Answer to Mr. Trosse's Catechism. London, December, 1718.
7. A Letter to a Dissenter in Exon. December, 1718.
8. Moore, John (of Tiverton): A Calm Defence of the Deity of Jesus Christ. With remarks on a Letter to a Dissenter at Exeter. London, J. Clark, 1719.
* 9. Peirce, James: The Case of the Ministers ejected at Exon. Exeter edn. at end of March, London edn. on 7th April, 1719.
*10. An Account of the Reasons why many Citizens of Exon have withdrawn from the Ministry of Mr. Joseph Hallet and Mr. James Peirce. Being an Answer to Mr. Peirce's State of the Case. Published by order of the Committee. London, J. Clark, 1719. Exeter edn. before 11th April.

    (This includes as a postscript 'A Letter to a Minister in London' by Josiah Eveleigh, which began a separate but parallel controversy between Eveleigh and Peirce. See below, Nos. 15-18.)
*11. Peirce, James: A Defence of the Case of the Ministers ejected at Exon. Exon, Andrew Brice, 1719. (In London on 30th April.)
*12. A Defence of the Account of the Reasons why many Citizens of Exon have withdrawn, etc. In Answer to Mr. Peirce's Defence of the Case, etc. Published by direction of the Committee. London, J. Clark, 1719.
*13. Peirce, James: A Justification of the Case of the Ministers ejected at Exon and of the Defence of it, being a reply to the Defence of the Account, etc. London, J. Clark, 1719.
*14. A Plain and Faithful Narrative of the differences among the Dissenters at Exeter relating to the Doctrine of the Ever Blessed Trinity, so far as gave concern to some London Ministers. (London, Clark & Cruttenden, June, 1719.)

15. Peirce, James. Animadversions upon a pamphlet entitled, A True Relation of Some Proceedings at Salters-Hall, to which is added, A Letter to Mr. Josiah Eveleigh. London, J. Clark, 1719.

16. Eveleigh, Josiah: A sober reply to Mr. Peirce's angry and scornful letter. London, E. Matthews, 1719.

17. Eveleigh, Josiah: A Vindication of Mr. Trosse from the Charge of Uncharitableness: proving . . . that the Doctrine of the Trinity and true Deity of Jesus Christ, is Fundamental. Etc. London, E. Matthews, 1719.

18. Peirce, James. A Second Letter to Mr. Eveleigh, in answer to his Sober Reply, etc., to which is added, A Confutation of a Slanderous Report. Exon, Brice. 1719.

*19. Arius Detected & Confuted: or, a short and familiar direction for plain Christians . . . how to understand the Language of the Disciples of Arius, etc. London, J. Clark, 1719. (Issued on the eve of the May Assembly.)

*20. A True Account of what was transacted in the Assembly of the United Ministers of Devon & Cornwall met at Exon, 5th and 6th May, 1719. Publish'd by order of the Assembly. London, J. Clark, 1719.

*21. Peirce, James: Remarks on the Proceedings of the late Assembly at Exon. 1719.

22. Peirce, James: Plain Christianity Defended: being an answer to a pamphlet lately printed at Exon, intitled, Arius Detected and Confuted, etc. Parts I and II. London, J. Noon, 1719.

23. Jacomb, George: A particular account of the proceedings of the late Assembly at Exon. 1719.

*24. A Defence of the Proceedings at the late Assembly at Exon, being a Reply to Mr. Peirce's Remarks on those Proceedings. London, J. Clark, 1719. (Probably John Enty).

*25. Peirce, James: The Western Inquisition, or a Relation of the Controversy which has been lately among the Dissenters in the West of England. London, 1720. (Actually appeared on 28th October, 1719).

26. Peirce, James: An Answer to Mr. Enty's Defence of the Proceedings, etc. 27th November, 1719.

27. Peirce, James: Propositions relating to the Controversy. 1720.

28. Enty, John: Truth and Liberty consistent. 1720 (October 25).

29. Peirce, James: A Reply (to Enty's Truth and Liberty Consistent). 1721.

30. Peirce, James: The Security of truth without the asistance of persecution and scurrility. 1721.

*31. Enty, John, ed. An Answer to Mr. Peirce's Western Inquisition, etc. London, J. Clark, 1721.

*32. Peirce, James: Inquisition-Honesty display'd: or, The Western Inquisition defended against the pretended Answer to it. London, J. Noon, 1722.

33. Hallett, Joseph, III: A Sermon preached in Exeter, April 3, upon the occasion of the Death of the late Reverend and learned Mr. James Peirce, who died March the 30, 1726, in the 53rd year of his age. London, 1726. (There was a 2nd edn. of this.)

34. (Hallett, Joseph, III): The Reconciler, or, an Essay to shew, that Christians are much more agreed in their notions concerning the Holy Trinity than has been commonly represented, with a Reply to Mr. Ball's answer to some common objections. London, J. Noon, 1727.

35. Stogdon, Hubert. Poems and letters, ed. N. Billingsley, 1729.

36. Enty, John: A Defense of a late Pamphlet entitled, A Preservative, etc., in answer to an Abusive Letter of Mr. Joseph Hallet, Jun. London & Exon, for Aaron Tozer, 1730.

APPENDIX B

Records preserved at George's Meeting.

1. The Committee (of Thirteen) to Administer the Minister's Fund, first appointed in 1687.
   a. One Book containing Minutes for 1724–61 and the Accounts for 1708–61. Also includes list of the original Committee of 1687 and their successors.
   b. Minutes and Accounts for 1762–1821, in one book.
   c. Minutes and Accounts for 1863 (5th September) to 1914 (23rd February).
2. James' Meeting. Account Book for 1687–1760. Gives the list of original contributors to the fund for its building, and accounts relating to repairs and alterations throughout its life.
3. George's Meeting.
   a. Minutes of Trustees' Meetings, 1760–1817, and accounts for same period.
   b. Minutes and accounts for 1818–80.
   c. Minutes and accounts for 1881–8.
4. Minutes of General Meetings of all Subscribers. Up to 1795 these included the members of Bow Meeting as well as George's, and after 1810 the remnant of the Mint Meeting joined.
   a. 1791–1813.
   b. 1815–34.
   c. 1835 to the present day.
5. Exeter Unitarian Fellowship Fund Society. Minutes, 1817-34.
6. One Book which begins by recording the proceedings of meetings of members of the 'Devon and Cornwall Unitarian Association residing in Exeter', continues as 'The Book Committee', then gives a rudimentary catalogue of books in its possession, and ends up as a record of book-loans made. Covers 1814–20, app.
7. George's Meeting Sunday School: Minutes of General and Committee Meetings, 1827–45.
8. George's Meeting. Committee for Regulating the Singing, etc., 1822–7. Several pages have been torn from the beginning and end. The label on front says 'Committee 1788 to 1827' which indicates what may be missing.
9. George's Meeting. Congregational Committee, Minutes for 1845–76.
10. George's Meeting. Committees appointed to 'make inquiries for a minister' at various times. Begins when James Manning died in 1831 and ended in 1862.

11. Poor Fund Accounts. One Book which was used at different periods, as follows:

1741–4. Gives lists of the Poor belonging to James', Bow and Little Meeting-houses, and the amounts given to them each quarter.

1801–36. The same information for George's Meeting.

1741–1800. Monies collected from the Meetings.

12. Poor Fund Committee. Minutes from December, 1823, until 1857. Includes accounts.

13. Dissenters' Burial Ground. Reports and Accounts, 1782–1832.

14. Register of Deaths, 1821–80.

15. Accounts Book which appears to record subscriptions to the Minister's Fund in detail from 1761 to 1772.

APPENDIX C

Records preserved by the Exeter Assembly, and normally kept by the trustees at the National Provincial Bank, Exeter.

1. Minute Book A, 1655–9. This volume also contains, gummed between the leaves which follow the minutes:
    a. Parchment Certificate of Mr. Joseph Hallett's Ordination, 28th October, 1652.
    b. List of the Ordinations and Deaths of the Ministers in Devon and Cornwall. Two copies of this, both probably written between 1755 and 1765.
    c. An account of the trial of Joseph Hallett I and John Palmer before the Mayor at the Guildhall on 2nd June, 1673.
    d. A list of students at Taunton Academy under Grove, 1715–38, and under Amory (1738–59).
    e. Four more lists of students.
        i. Under Joseph Hallett II at Exeter, 1700–19.
        ii. Under Mr. Moore at Tiverton, in the 1720s.
        iii. Under Towgood, Merivale, Turner and Hogg at Exeter, 1760–1770.
        iv. At Shepton Mallet under Matthew Towgood.
    f. 'An account of Ministers settled in Devonshire from 1662 to the present time, with their number of hearers in 1715 and 1794'. In the handwriting of James Manning, minister of George's Meeting, Exeter. The 1715 figures were taken from Evans' List: those for 1794, which are few, were Manning's own.
2. Minute Book B, unbound. Contains Minutes for 1721/2, and 1744–53, ending with the meeting in which the decision not to impose a Trinitarian Test on future candidates was made.
3. Minute Book D (for C refer to Addendum below), for 1733–43. Unbound.
4. Minute Book E, 1763–92.
5. Minute Book F, 1792–1862.
6. Minute Book G, 1862–1923.
7. Parchment Licence to Preach of Joseph Hallett III, in 1713.
8. Certificate that Joseph Hallett III had taken the necessary statutory oaths under the Toleration Act, 14/7/1713.
9. Certificate of ordination of Stephen Towgood, dated Axminster, 4th July, 1716.
10. MS. Sermon preached before September Assembly, 1752, by G. H. Waters.
11. Letter dated 25th August, 1767, from William Prior in London to Micaijah Towgood in Exeter about a bequest of books for the Academy from a Dr. Hodges.

12. Burgess Act in favour of the Revd. Doctor Rice Harris, 1769, at Banff. (Seems to have no relation to rest of documents.)
13. MS. sermon by Joseph Bretland, at May Assembly, 1786.
14. Printed circular requesting Devon and Cornwall Ministers to support the Assembly, 7th May, 1795.
15. Bound volume of sermons, including one by James Manning in 1818, which gives a short history of the Assembly.
16. Murch, Jerom: History of the Presbyterian and General Baptist Churches in the West of England, London, 1835.
17. Prime, Priestley: A Record of the United Brethren of Devon and Cornwall, presented . . . at . . . Exeter, June, 1899. Printed by H. Rawson & Co., Manchester. 44pp.
18. MS. short history of George's Meeting, Colyton, by W. B. Matthews, 1911.
19. Letter from Jeffery Worthington of Cullompton to Rev. W. E. O'Connor, giving information about closed chapels at Honiton, Lympstone, Gulliford and Topsham. Dated October 17th, 1911.

Addendum: Minute Book C, which covers the period 1722–8, and a small volume known as 'Gilling's Transactions', which contains in the miniature handwriting of Isaac Gilling, minister at Newton Abbott, the minutes of proceedings of Assemblies from 1691–1717, are both in Dr. Williams' Library, 14, Gordon Square, London, W.C.1. The Minutes of the Exeter Assembly are therefore complete up to the present day, with the exception of the years 1717–21, 1728–33; and 1753–63. All those from 1691 to 1753 have been microfilmed and copies are available at Dr. Williams' Library; the City Library, Castle St., Exeter; and the Roborough Library, University of Exeter. 'Gilling's Transactions' are to be published in 1962 by the Devon and Cornwall Record Society, edited by the present writer.

Q*

INDEX